VIKING
CANADA

Other Books by Joanne Thomas Yaccato

Balancing Act: A Canadian Woman's Financial Success Guide

Raising Your Business:
A Canadian Woman's Guide to Entrepreneurship
(with Paula Jubinville)

THE 80% MINORITY

reaching
the real
world of
THE 80% MINORITY
women

JOANNE THOMAS YACCATO
with Judy Jaeger

consumers

VIKING
CANADA

VIKING CANADA
Published by the Penguin Group
Penguin Books, a division of Pearson Canada, 10 Alcorn Avenue, Toronto, Ontario,
Canada M4V 3B2
Penguin Books Ltd, 80 Strand, London WC2R 0RL, England
Penguin Putnam Inc., 375 Hudson Street, New York, New York 10014, U.S.A.
Penguin Books Australia Ltd, 250 Camberwell Road, Camberwell, Victoria 3124, Australia
Penguin Books India (P) Ltd, 11, Community Centre, Panchsheel Park,
New Delhi—110 017, India
Penguin Books (NZ) Ltd, cnr Rosedale and Airborne Roads, Albany, Auckland 1310,
New Zealand
Penguin Books (South Africa) (Pty) Ltd, 24 Sturdee Avenue, Rosebank 2196, South Africa

Penguin Books Ltd, Registered Offices: 80 Strand, London WC2R 0RL, England

First published 2003

10 9 8 7 6 5 4 3 2 1

Manufactured in Canada.

National Library of Canada Cataloguing in Publication

Thomas Yaccato, Joanne, 1957–
    The 80% minority : reaching the real world of women consumers / Joanne Thomas Yaccato
and Judy Yaeger.

Includes bibliographical references and index.
ISBN 0-670-04357-5

    1. Women consumers. 2. Marketing. I. Yaeger, Judy II. Title.

HC79.C6T48 2003   658.8'04   C2003-901157-7

Visit the Penguin Books website at **www.penguin.ca**

To all Canadian women and girls,
especially my mother, Dianne, and my daughter, Kate

Contents

Acknowledgments   XIII

Introduction—The 80% minority: Not a contradiction in terms   1

1   Grasping the concept of gender intelligence   11

2   Two different worlds   55

3   Communication: Relevance through gender intelligence   111

4   Multidimensional marketing for multidimensional women   149

5   Wear your soul on your sleeve   175

6   More than the sum of its parts   207

Endnotes   225

Index   229

Detailed Contents

Acknowledgments XIII

Introduction—The 80% minority: Not a contradiction in terms 1

1 Grasping the concept of gender intelligence 11
      Women Consumers Not Taken Seriously 12
      How Bad Is It Really? 15
      Not So Long Ago . . . 26
      The Genesis of Gender Intelligent Marketing 28
      Acquiring Gender Intelligence 32
      Our Four Principles 46
      Discovering Women: Air Canada 46

2 Two different worlds 55
      Vive La Différence: Women and Men 55
      Market Research—Best Friend or Worst Enemy? 75
      Product Development—Yes, Virginia, There Is a Difference 88
      Pricing—Fair Is Fair 100

3 Communication: Relevance through gender intelligence 111
      Is Recruiting Women the Answer? 113
      Communicating Through a Gender Lens 115
      Language: Creating a Gender Intelligent Sales Experience 119
      Learning Different Rituals for Different Cultures 123
      Using Gender Intelligent Information Channels 132
      Creating Gender Intelligent Information Online 140

4 Multidimensional marketing for multidimensional women 149

   The Truth about Time 154

   Women Are Busy. And This Is News? 157

   Advertising and Marketing "Busy"—A Double-Edged
      Sword 158

   Reap the Rewards from Multidimensional Marketing 172

   Remember What Women Value 174

5 Wear your soul on your sleeve 175

   The Marketing Consequences of Soul Searching 177

   But What Kind of Soul? 187

   How to Create a Gender Intelligent Inside 204

6 More than the sum of its parts 207

   Learning to Look Through a Gender Intelligent Lens 209

   Starting Out with a Gender Intelligent Perspective 215

   Where Does All This Get Us? 223

   Endnotes 225

   Index 229

Acknowledgments

It slays me how, in every book that I've written, I end up acknowledging the unflagging support of my family, the women I work with, the subject matter experts, and last but in no way least, my banker. This one is no different.

This is my assistant Rosa Morra's third book with me (fifth, if you count revised editions) and, amazingly, she still continues to work with me. I think she's nuts, but would be dead without her.

Thank you, Judy Jaeger, for jumping in so wholeheartedly, especially having never done this before. Your left-brain insight into the manuscript and research material and calm, methodical approach (to life) was a fabulous complement to my right-brained, "jump on and ride off in eight directions" approach.

Barbara Frensel worked on many of the case studies and her natural curiosity made her one of the finest interviewers I've ever come across. After months of teeth gnashing and angst, we had all but given up hope of ever finding a decent title for this book. Thanks to one of Barbara's passionate rants in which she blurted out "corporate Canada treats women like they were some kind of 80% minority," a title was finally conceived.

I discovered that when it comes to marketing, everyone is an expert. However, the following people have distinguished themselves, not just because of the quality of their vision, perspective, and debate, but because they were my strongest moral supporters: Mary Koven, Debbie Gordon, Liz Torlee, Elspeth Lynn, Lorraine Tao, and Allan Kazmer.

Bobby Gaunt, Marilyn McCrea, Michael Beckerman, Betty Wood, Graeme Harris, Brian Harrod, Benjamin Vendramin, Sabine Schleese, Wendy Montergomery, Donna Clark, and Jim Kenzie also contributed their valuable time and insights. Ian Thompson and Linda Todd of Maritz: Thompson Lightstone were incredibly generous with their research expertise and resources, as was Statistics Canada. Simply too numerous to name but of equal value were the hundreds of women who shared their fascinating consumer experiences with us through letters, telephone calls, and coffee-shop chats. Though it may be my voice telling the story, it is their voices you hear. It is precisely because of this added dimension of kitchen-table research that we were able to write such a "rich" book. Thanks, too, to the companies that us let in, spent time with us, and responded to our many, many questions. Unfortunately due to space limitations, some companies didn't make the cut, but they contributed to the overall tapestry nonetheless.

Imagine telling your banker that you want to take two years to write a book. Not only did John Cormier not slam the door in my face, but the odd time when I called him in a panic, he would invariably reply, "You do your job and let me do mine. Now get off the phone and get back to writing." Mr. Cormier, you are gold, an unusual descriptor for a banker.

Thank you, Michael and Dorothea Schmidt, for sharing your glorious farm and giving me the mental and physical space to get this damn thing started.

Judy, Barbara, and I thank our friends for enduring our preoccupied brains and our families for enduring absences at one too many family events.

And, finally, to my own husband, Michael, and daughter, Kate; to Judy's husband, Wolfgang, son, Peter, daughter-in-law, Cathy, and grandchildren, Amy and Allison; and to Barbara's husband, Ian, and son, Cole, I say this: This is an important book that was not only made possible, but palatable, by your support and love. Thank you all for sharing the woman in your lives.

Introduction

The 80% minority: Not a contradiction in terms

The light thud of the newspaper landing on the floor outside my hotel room door was music to my ears. I threw back the covers, having already been awake for several hours, thanks to the time change. It's the fall of 2002 and I was in Vancouver, having just crossed the country for the umpteenth time to speak at a conference of a group of financial services execs on meeting the needs of Canadian women consumers. I was feeling groggy and not just a little grumpy when I flipped to the stock pages. My mood got considerably worse, and not for the reasons you might think . . .

Staring up at me in the middle of all those tiny, depressing numbers was a prominent black and white ad for a new luxury hotel that had recently opened in Montreal. The copy read,

"*Right Away, Sir*" *is pretty much our answer to everything.*

I blinked. "Sir?"

I looked around. I'm in a luxury hotel in a major Canadian city, in a business class room, having gotten there on a business class flight. "Fascinating," I said aloud. "This ad just rendered exactly half the business travelling public invisible. This will make great fodder for my speech." I ripped it out with a flourish.

As life would have it, there are legions of these types of issues that I see daily in my professional life. But because of a particularly busy month, when I got home this one fell by the wayside, albeit just for a moment. A couple of weeks later I was in my kitchen, coffee in hand, settling down with the paper. I flipped to the stock pages (being a sucker for punishment) and staring up at me is that same ad, only this time it reads:

"Right Away" is pretty much our answer to everything.

Clearly, someone had gotten to them before I did. I picked up the phone.

Though curious as to why "Sir" disappeared, I started the conversation with the hotel's general manager by pointing out that North American women control 80% of the consumer dollars spent. This includes, I told him, half the business travellers who stay in hotels. Referring to the first ad, I asked why was his hotel interested in doing business with only half the travelling public? It turns out that the hotel didn't pick up on the inappropriateness of the "Sir" remark until the phone started ringing. In fact, he went on to say, he wasn't sure what had disturbed him more, the fact that this "Sir business" had flown under the hotel and ad agency's radar or the agency's reaction when it was finally brought to their attention. It was adamant that the hotel was over-reacting and maintained there was nothing wrong with the ad. The general manager said it wasn't until the hotel owners called the agency that it gave in and came up with a neutered version of the original.

This story isn't a particularly unusual one, I told him. Canadian women, though the dominant consumer force in this country, often find themselves metaphorically with their noses pressed against the glass.

It would appear our conversation had an impact. A week or so later, I was brought out of my chair, complete with a whoop. This time the ad said:

We're bringing the phrase "Yes, Madam" back in style.

This prompted two reactions from me. First, I was amused by how quickly the hotel attempted to redress its unbalanced worldview by trying to create the impression that using "Sir" and "Madam" were an intentional part of the whole ad campaign. My second reaction? They completely and utterly blew it. In an effort to prove the hotel wasn't really ignoring women, which it was, it ignored men. And here's the real irony: We all know, consciously or unconsciously, it was men the hotel really wanted to reach in the first place.

Now, one might be forgiven for pondering the genesis of this book title. "Since when," you might ask, "is a group that controls 80% of what gets purchased a minority?"

As this story attests, when it is women.

I've struggled for years with sports equipment and clothing that doesn't fit. I'm uncomfortable in airline seats and seem to be invisible to most airline staff. As an entrepreneur, I don't get access to maternity benefits. Many salespeople seem interested in talking only to my husband, even when I'm doing the buying. I'm surrounded by images of either middle-aged or buffed white guys and if women are present, they're paper-thin with big pouty lips. In the rare case when I do see a woman who looks a little like me, she's usually charmingly exasperated with her children, who have written all over the walls or watered her prize-winning plants with cranberry juice. Or she's dancing with a mop. And yet I'm part of the most powerful and desired consumer demographic in the country.

Women's consumer influence is wide and far-reaching, yet there remains an alarming disconnect between women and the companies they buy from. In the summer of 2002, The Thomas Yaccato Group and Thompson Lightstone & Company conducted a study called "Reaching Canada's 80% Minority" to get to the heart of the consumer experience for Canadians. We surveyed 2,000 women and men across the country to ask them how well they thought corporate Canada was doing in meeting their needs as consumers. What we learned wasn't pretty.

Here are a few compelling insights. We found that women and men ranked pretty close in wanting to deal with companies that market to them authentically and provide for an ongoing business relationship that starts before any kind of sale is made. Both women and men felt companies are doing a less than stellar job in this regard and felt that both genders are unrealistically represented in advertising. However, women were much more likely than men to say this visual representation was important to their purchasing decision.

Almost two-thirds of those surveyed said a company's understanding of women's different needs would be reflected in the way that company presents its products and services. They could tell if a company understood their needs by the way a salesperson talked to them, and they said they wouldn't buy anything from a company that didn't demonstrate this understanding.

Makes sense so far. But we found out other things that made us scratch our heads.

More than half of the women surveyed reported feeling discriminated against or treated differently because of their gender. Only a fifth of the male respondents agreed with this statement.

The majority of women said they are the primary influence in household consumer purchases, but half of them felt that most companies didn't recognize that fact. The same number of women said that companies took men much more seriously than women.

Slightly more men (53%) than women (50%) surveyed said that reaching and understanding the woman consumer should be a company's top priority. (The detailed results of the study are available from The Thomas Yaccato Group and Thompson Lightstone.[1])

These findings are surprising considering study after study and story after story show women wield considerable consumer clout, making and influencing an average of 80% of all consumer decisions made. We know that the number of wealthy women around the world is growing faster than men, and that women control most of the consumer spending. We know that single women are buying more homes than single men and that in families women do most of the househunting, along with making most of the decisions about what household goods to buy, where to go on holiday, which cable and telephone services to choose, and what Internet service provider to go with—not to mention which vehicle is best for the family. We know that women buy most of the over-the-counter drugs and herbal remedies and vitamins, and they buy half the computers and sports equipment sold.[2] Yet research also shows that women consumers continue not to be taken as seriously as men purely on the basis of their gender. Interestingly, our research showed that men's consumer experience needed to improve as well, but for entirely different reasons. "The 80% minority" may sound like a contradiction in terms, but it is a reality: 80% of the decision-making consumers are treated as a marginalized minority by most marketing efforts.

This is flat-out consumer discrimination. When this kind of behaviour is exhibited towards an individual because of race or disability, often there is a public outcry and considerable resources are allocated to remedy it. Yet millions of women deal with this form of consumer discrimination every day, with barely a ripple. Of course, the experience of all women is not the same, but we can unequivocally say this: If mainstream white women consumers have bad consumer experiences, the experiences of women of colour, women with disabilities, women who live at or below the poverty line, new immigrants, single mothers, seniors, and Aboriginal women are likely to be worse. We heard stories from women of colour who could never be certain if their experience was due to their gender or their colour but knew theirs was an inferior experience. We know that people with disabilities have less access to jobs, transportation, and education and thus economic independence and consumer power, and that women of our mothers' and grandmothers' generations are marginalized by lack of access to technology and economics.

By no means are we suggesting that every woman's experience is the same, but we can say with certainty that overall, regardless of race, creed, marital status, and ability, women's consumer experience radically needs improvement.

Research is also a problem. We found that many studies excluded gender completely and among those that did include it, few offered segmentation of results by gender. Plus, we noticed a strange phenomenon in those studies that did, in fact, look at gender. For some reason, people have the propensity to discuss male and female traits in terms of opposites rather than as two parallel universes that converge and diverge at different points, which is more accurate. Being different doesn't necessarily mean diametrically opposite. Gender differences operate on a very wide continuum, not in cut-and-dried female and male categories. Good gender-based market research is not about classifying everyone into pigeonholes—it should illustrate different trends or tendencies. Quality gender-based research reports information such as "in quantitative numbers, more women than men seek financial help from an advisor" or "research shows that women are more likely to emphasize social issues when asked about the key problems facing Canadians and men are more likely to focus on the economy and budgetary issues." It doesn't claim that the wide range of behaviour of men and women is exclusive to either gender—other factors, such as culture, age, occupation, and even geographic influences, must be considered, too. Every one of us can point to exceptions to just about any claim or research finding made about the sexes.

But what good research says is that for every one exception, there are five people that support the general contention of the finding. There are assertions throughout this book that "men do X and women do Y"—the exceptions to the rule are already accounted for. What you read may not reflect your own experience, but according to the research, it's the experience of five of your neighbours. And though the sexes are often described separately, it's not to say one is better or worse than the other. Different is simply that—different.

Another thing you'll notice in this book is that although I've made a living educating companies about women (at The Thomas Yaccato Group, we call ourselves "corporate Canada's gender lens"), most of the time I'm speaking from the perspective of the consumer. I see things through a different lens from most ad agencies and marketing departments. So this book is not just about how to market. It's about reaching not only the company's marketers and ad agencies, but speaking to everyone within that company—everyone who is face to face or voice to voice with the customer as well as human resources and product development people. They all have one thing in common: meeting the needs of the consumer.

So many times when writing this book I would read what I had just written and wonder why I had to spell out what seems so obvious. Then my experiences as a consumer and working with corporate Canada would come flooding back, and the research results would stare me in the face. The thousands of stories from women that I've collected over the years would ring in my ears. Stories about women who get told by car salesmen that they're not strong enough to handle that "stallion" of a sports car. Stories about women paying twice as much for a haircut or dry cleaning than men pay for the same services. Stories about women who run successful businesses and law firms and medical practices but still receive mail from their financial institutions addressed to their husbands, or are refused credit, or are just plain ignored. Sure, we may have come a long way, but Canadian women are demanding companies go much, much further.

But let's get one thing straight right off the bat. I may represent a particular kind of person—a strong feminist married to another strong feminist, mother of a seven-year-old daughter who has no clue about Disney's toy *du jour* because, instead of watching television, she plays violin and piano and frolics in the mud, a woman who tries to take good care of her body and soul by eating well and exercising regularly but considers chocolate a more important food group than vegetables—but I don't represent the same worldview as all women.

I do, however, have an unbridled passion for how women are portrayed in advertising, and I do represent a growing group of women consumers and concerned marketers who are championing the skills and mindset required to market authentically, responsibly, and creatively. Which is why this book is filled with stories about companies that are doing just this, and why we turned for advice to a range of advertising experts—Mary Koven, Debbie Gordon, Liz Torlee, Elspeth Lynn, Lorraine Tao, Benjamin Vendramin, Brian Harrod, Marilyn McCrea, and Allan Kazmer, all giants in the advertising and branding worlds who have all held senior positions from creative directors to presidents of the biggest advertising agencies in the country. All this plus the cumulative expertise of human resources maven Judy Jaeger, renaissance retailer Barbara Frensel, women's market pioneer Bobbie Gaunt, master market researchers Ian Lightstone and Linda Todd from Thompson Lightstone, and the merry band at The Thomas Yaccato Group.

With more than 400 years of collective experience among us, our team manages to make sense out of all this information. After all, women's consumer DNA contains the information that companies need to construct and operate successful strategies to establish meaningful and long-term relationships with them. Because those relationships differ depending on the product and the company, what works and what doesn't work can vary dramatically. But we've got a quartet of powerful principles that will improve the chances of getting it right with women consumers. Even though these principles may be practised in your business today, and even though there seem to be lots of examples in this book, one of the most valuable points we've got to make is that almost no one views common sense marketing through a gender intelligent lens. Which is precisely why women feel like a minority.

The Fundamentals of Gender Intelligence

There are four fundamentals for successfully meeting the needs of Canadian women. Applied authentically, they'll get you to the heart of what women want in a consumer experience—a fulfilling business relationship—and will produce increased customer satisfaction, increased market share, and a huge referral base.

> Be intelligent about gender differences.
> Get through with intelligent communication.
> Recognize that women live multidimensional lives.
> Live your corporate soul.

These four concepts share several common characteristics: They foster successful business relationships through improved customer experiences and internal employee practices. They help companies recognize important gender-based differences and develop equitable strategies. They facilitate understanding what women consumers want. And they combine to create a comprehensive company-wide strategy with a singular view to increase revenue responsibly.

Fostering a meaningful business relationship doesn't mean the same thing as it did a short 10 years ago. It was pretty simple then—good listening skills, a friendly smile, a product that didn't break 10 minutes after you got it, value for the price, good customer service, and maybe even sending out newsletters and birthday cards. Today, the definition of the relationship between company and customer has gone beyond anything previously imagined. More than half of the women in our study said that their relationship with a company's products and services starts long before they buy and continues long after they have bought.

The challenge today for consumers is that companies have gone into "hyper branding" mode in an attempt to create the ultimate relationship/lifestyle/image experience. They promise to transform who you are merely by buying their clothes, cars, or shampoo. The reality is that authentic relationships that translate into long-term bottom-line results are not created between a computer screen or phone and a person, or by promises that a product will make you a better person. Now more than ever, companies need to go back to basics and remember what a relationship actually means—an emotional connection between two people.

And here's some good news. It doesn't matter if your company is trying to forge relationships with women by becoming more inclusive or by getting a whole new message out. The advice offered here covers both. Each chapter of this book explores usable, realistic strategies based on each of these four principles. As women progress through their life cycles, their needs and attitudes change, but these principles don't. They are as relevant to a 13-year-old teen as they are to her 45-year-old weary mother and her 75-year-old sprightly grandmother.

The companies in this book represent all shapes and sizes for a diversity of approaches and a variety of situations. We sought out companies that have had some measure of success in the women's market, whether by accident or by design, by gut instinct or by complex market research. They run the gamut from small entrepreneurial shops to large-scale corporations. They illustrate the rewards of picking the low-hanging fruit—low-cost, easy-to-implement solutions—straight through to massive internal and external corporate overhauls. What did they do to garner increased market share? How are they making their brands authentic and enduring to Canadian women? How do they manage to stay on women's radar?

Most of the space in this book is dedicated to the finer points of better marketing specifically in the world of women; however, by no means do these principles apply exclusively for women. It nets out to this: What can you do to better reach women consumers and, as a natural consequence, reach all consumers better?

Successful companies understand that you can meet the needs of women consumers without alienating men. Frankly, the minute you introduce gender into the mix, you can run into headwinds that can slow you down. That's why it's critical to get it right. But understanding women consumers can lead to interesting results with every other customer target group—men, the gay and lesbian market, the Aboriginal and Asian markets, the youth market, pretty much any other market segment you can think of.

My goal is to deliver equal parts awareness, illustrations, and useful information. If you understand women's consumer DNA and implement strategies that ring with authenticity, you will improve all of your marketing efforts. If you make it women-friendly, you make it everybody-friendly.

1

Grasping the concept of gender intelligence

Remember the story about the race between the tortoise and hare? The tortoise methodically moves along, never distracted from what must be done, always forward and with a single purpose. The hare—slick, fast, and noisy—jumps about frenetically trying to get the tortoise's attention, running off in 18 directions at once. The tortoise pays little attention to the hare's speed and schemes, considering the hare's attempts to catch his attention largely irrelevant in the overall scheme of things. The tortoise simply continues forward and eventually wins the race.

Stop 100 Canadian women on the street today and 99 will say that women are the tortoise and corporate Canada is the hare. Women continue to shrug off much of the marketing noise emanating from all sizes and shapes of companies trying to catch their attention, deeming much of what they see, hear, and experience as irrelevant. Instead, they vote with their pocketbooks, and share their disgust with friends.

Like the tortoise, women are moving past corporate Canada, shaking their heads at what they see, leaving the offenders behind in the dust. They share their stories of bad service, insulting advertising, and lame marketing, and take matters into their own hands. Four out of five small businesses started in this country are started by young women.[1] Many of these entrepreneurs aim to capitalize on the opportunities presented by the chronic unmet needs of Canadian women consumers. In fact, many of these small businesses are in the marketing, communications, and branding fields. Consequently, women are casting their votes on the state of marketing with their feet, their brains, and their wallets.

Frankly, this "women's market revolution" is largely contained within the realm of women consumers and is still very much the "minor" leagues within the business world. With some exceptions, which we happily highlight in this book, there is ample evidence to show that where companies think they are in terms of reaching women consumers is quite far from where women *know* they are. A number of companies are showing real promise, but a wide gulf remains between those who get it and those who don't. At one end of the spectrum are serious contenders who know how to market to women consumers and serve their needs. Close behind them are those that have acknowledged the power of women consumers and have begun to learn. In the middle—dominated by the benign, the innocuous, the silly, the superficial, and the stereotypical—are companies too numerous to count. At the other end of the spectrum are those that border on or fall into the outright offensive category. But right across the board, one thing resonates. Canadian women aren't happy.

Women Consumers Not Taken Seriously

Our study and instincts told us the mood was bad, but nothing prepared us for the degree of what actually happened. We had struck something huge—a kind of collective, often unspoken, extremely annoyed, feminine consumer psyche. Along with our consumer survey, we put the word out that we were looking for anecdotal consumer experiences. We specified that we were looking for stories where women encountered either really bad or very good service based on what they perceived to be gender. In short order, we were overwhelmed with responses, especially with stories about women's disastrous experiences with car companies and banks. We're still waiting for a good one.

Any company (and there are many) that has had the courage to conduct women-only focus groups has likely seen the wrath of women consumers up close or felt the backlash. We did a series of women-only focus groups for one company with the president and the marketing people observing behind glass. I still can't decide what was more fun: watching the women offer funny, sharp, often brutal insights and observations, or watching the stunned expressions of the executives.

Often when I tell a prospective client that many women consumers feel they aren't taken seriously, the mumbled response is something about how miserable it is for men as well. This may be so, but it misses the point. Men don't say that substandard consumer experience has anything to do with their gender. Rather, it has to do with poor service, product design, or a salesperson's product knowledge.

Miserable is miserable, no matter what way you cut it. But men's customer service issues can usually be fixed with common, conventional tools like off-the-shelf sales training and more rigorous quality control. For women it's more complex.

As an example, most financial companies have a policy of the highest income earner as principal holder of the account, loan, or mortgage. But as advertising expert Mary Koven points out, "My sister and I own a house together, and the correspondence comes addressed to both of us. We don't make the same amount of money, and one doesn't seemed to be required to take a secondary role in the correspondence." At one of our workshops for a group of credit unions, a marketing manager commented that all the paperwork for her accounts came in her husband's name, yet he wasn't the one who worked there. If a man and woman are in a partnership and the correspondence defaults to the man, the woman feels diminished in that financial arrangement. This kind of policy is just one example that contributes to the sense of not being taken seriously.

Consider the following story about how the customer service experience differs between men and women from one of the country's highest ranking civil servants.

"My story is about the two biggest purchases that my wife and I made together, our house and our minivan. In both cases, the decisions were mine, based on my own research. It was even my money that was used for the down payment. We financed the mortgage through the bank where I had been banking all my life. My wife's money was at another bank. The house and mortgage were in both our names as co-owners. A few months after signing the papers, we received an unsolicited credit card from my bank—in my wife's name only! I called the bank to complain that there was no accompanying card in my name and was told that since the woman's name is the first one listed on the mortgage by default, they had sent it to her. If men are ever going to get any kind of economic parity, policies like these need some gender-based analysis.

"We leased a minivan from a local dealer, after I'd figured out what we needed and done all the research. I decided what we bought. Again, we are both co-lessees on the financing agreement and we both signed all of the paperwork. A month after we signed the lease, we received a message from a man at the dealership inviting my wife to a complimentary automotive workshop. At the end of the message, he said that my wife could also bring her husband along if she wished. He didn't even mention my name, as though I didn't even exist. I didn't bother to complain this time, because it would probably just fit into the misguided perceptions of the men who work in car dealerships and would accomplish little."

Sound a bit odd? The truth is this story came from a woman, and I've reversed her experience with that of her husband's. It sounds considerably more plausible now, doesn't it? Rarely do you hear men commiserate with each other about how they were rendered invisible in a sales transaction when their wife was present or how they ceased to exist after the deal was done, even if they were equal partners in the transaction. We heard versions of this same story from hundreds of other women.

This story, by the way, has an interesting postscript that illustrates a deep, pervasive problem on a societal level. This particular woman gave us permission to use her story only if it was rendered anonymous. She explained that her husband would have difficulty with this story becoming public, as it would undermine his role as head of the family and make him look bad in the eyes of his relatives, friends, and colleagues. He deferred all major financial and consumer decisions to her, yet neither of them wanted this to be known. "When I say this out loud," she said, "it sounds pretty weird even to my own ears, but I'm asking you to respect my situation."

What is so compelling is that our study reached the same sobering conclusions as did recent consumer studies from Air Canada, RONA, the Center for Women's Business Research, Zaget, Deloitte and Touche, and the Canadian Automotive Association. Women consumers feel that they aren't being taken as seriously as men. Herein lies the stunning paradox— Canada's major consumer power feels like a minority player.

How Bad Is It Really?

"Each of these stories reflects only one woman's experience," you're saying. "How bad can it really be?" One might be forgiven for thinking that industries with a primary audience of women (food, clothing, cosmetics, fitness, and health, for example) get it right. And who would disagree that the insurance business, automotive, travel, and liquor industries have had a challenged history with women? You'd only be half right. Our research explored the extent to which Canadian women's needs were being met in 22 industry sectors. Very few really get it right. Take a look at the numbers in this chart—and keep in mind that since women wield the primary influence for purchases in Canada, any industry satisfaction rating below 80% should be considered a loud wake-up call.

Clearly, women's bad consumer experiences are not isolated incidents. Only one industry received a close to positive majority vote from women— 76% of women said they were satisfied with the supermarket and grocery store industry. The results of our study were extremely disappointing—all industries other than food and the supermarket and grocery store industries fell well below the 80% satisfaction level, with most coming in under 60%.

INDUSTRY SATISFACTION AMONG WOMEN*

Supermarkets and grocery stores	76%
Food companies	63%
Pharmaceutical and drug companies	61%
Restaurant and food service companies	60%
Book publishers	57%
Cosmetics companies	56%
Hotels	54%
Newspapers and magazines	53%
Movies and videos	52%
Home electronics	51%
Banks	50%
Clothing manufacturers	48%
Telephone companies	46%
Hospitals	45%
Alcoholic beverage companies	40%
Car manufacturers	37%
Computer companies	36%
Exercise/fitness clubs	36%
Insurance companies	36%
Airline companies	33%
Car dealers	27%
Oil companies	23%

N = 1,020

---

*Based on a five-point "agreement" scale.

Source: The Thomas Yaccato Group/Maritz: Thompson Lightstone

There are innumerable reasons why so many companies rate below average. This is a complex issue, but let's tackle two major factors: advertising and product development.

TRUTH IN ADVERTISING

We continually hear that advertising must appeal to the lowest common denominator, and there is plenty of evidence to this point. Yet women have indicated that they will purchase or stop purchasing products on the basis of how they are portrayed in marketing materials. The Television Bureau of Canada suggests that some marketers and advertisers may simply miss the boat in their efforts to appeal to women—it found that three out of five women feel that advertising does not connect with them, and an estimated 70% of advertising campaigns directed at women are ignored.[2]

Our study confirmed that this area of contention appears to affect women more than men. You don't often hear men complain about the biased and stereotypical assumptions made by salespeople, advertisers, and marketers about their societal role.

Case in point: Dave and Ellie are watching TV. A commercial comes on showing manly men doing manly things. Dave turns to Ellie and exclaims, "I've had it with these ads with corporate guys in suits talking about ways to amass a gazillion dollar portfolio and guys in hard hats humping huge logs into enormous trucks. I'm so tired of being portrayed as powerful, successful, and brilliant. I've had it with always being shown as strong and together. I feel so . . . exploited!"

At least men aren't having a nervous breakdown over "ring around the collar" or dancing blissfully around the house with a mop. There may be a growing advertising trend to dumb down men, and billboards and magazines seem awash with washboard abs, muscular chests, and chiselled chins, but these constitute a relatively recent phenomenon. And the men we interviewed rarely took exception to this advertising approach. They understood it to be low-brow humour. But men don't have a long history of being the object of the gaze, unlike women, so it's easier to take it in stride—especially when, for the most part, they still wield much of society's power.

That said, advertising has started to become smarter and more respectful, though there is no shortage of evidence that women continue to be dragged around by their hair. Frankly, in my opinion, only a mass lobotomy can explain the following true stories.

In 2001, Ford, a supporter of the women's market, illustrated the roominess of trunk space in one of its vehicles in an ad with a woman who kidnaps a grocery boy by throwing him in the trunk of her car. (Didn't they think people would get angry?)

In 2002, in an ad for Betty Crocker's microwavable lunch, a kid proclaims, "Us kids know our mothers are too busy to cook." Excuse me? Like I need more guilt? Where's dad, and doesn't he know how to use the microwave?

Every year for the last four years, more than 1,000 women, men, and youth across the country cast their votes for MediaWatch's satirical review of the worst media portrayals of women. Here are some of the "winners":

> The "Pinch an Inch" Award to Vichy for using clothes pegs on a woman's thighs to highlight the need to remove "dimples." That Vichy subjected the thinnest of thighs to this painful "test" belies the statistics and growing public awareness about the relationship between media images and eating disorders among Canadian women.

> The "Multiculturalism Run Amok" Award to Browns Shoes for stereotyping a black woman as a spear-wielding ice-age savage, out to skewer a shoe. Perhaps Browns hasn't noticed that African-Canadians have struggled for more than 150 years for freedom from negative stereotypes.

> The "Keep It to Yourself" Award to Kahlúa Black Russian for its portrayal of a giant Cossack sticking out his tongue to catch skimpily clad women reclining on snowflakes. This ad gives new meaning to the term "edible woman."

> The "Been There, Done That" Award goes to Calvin Klein for tiresomely re-working the image of a thin, naked woman lying in what purports to be an alluring manner. This time, the lucky waif gets to lie on some damp earth . . . how romantic.

At times it looks like Homer Simpson is running the show.

A study on sex differentiation in magazine advertisements analyzed 2,000 ads appearing in *Vogue, Ladies Home Journal, Playboy,* and *Time* between 1960 and 1979 according to age, activity, occupation, and product use.[3] The study found considerable stereotyping, and little change in the extent of stereotyping over time. Comparing portrayals in ads with data on consumer behaviour, the authors conclude that ads portray more sex differentiation than is actually present in men's and women's real-life roles. Another study examined the female roles portrayed in radio commercials for various products.[4] It found the female presence in radio commercials to be almost nonexistent—women featured in only 7% of the commercials studied. Those few ads that used women typically placed them in consumer or worker roles; women were underrepresented in the area of banking and in professional areas such as medicine and law. Another study analyzed 253 television commercials and found that they non-verbally described women as lacking authority and possessing less power than men.[5] Yet another study looked at the effects of the sex and the attractiveness of the salesperson in direct mail advertisements and found that ads featuring a highly attractive female were likely to lead to purchase of the product advertised.[6] Another study investigated the effect of role portrayal (housewife versus professional) in magazine ads on people's perceptions of managerial attributes; respondents who looked at the ads with professional roles evaluated women as having more managerial attributes than those who looked at the ads with housewife roles.[7]

WHAT CANADIAN ADVERTISERS SAY ABOUT WOMEN AND ADVERTISING

We asked Canada's top advertising experts to give us their views on the "state of the nation" of women and advertising. We learned that women's "pissed-off consumer psyche" is actually shared by a somewhat "pissed-off advertiser's psyche."

Two of Canada's most respected advertising veterans are Allan Kazmer and Brian Harrod. Between them, they have not only won the respect of their peers, but have also won just about every advertising award in Canada and around the world. Drop their names to a room full of ad types and watch everyone fall to their knees in genuflection. The passion and respect of these two men for a consumer's intelligence drove their agency philosophies.

We asked them whether advertising has become better at portraying and reflecting women's reality. They responded emphatically and in unison: "Absolutely not."

Harrod says, "It feels like two steps forward and three steps back. The ratio of bad advertising or images to good is about 50 to 1." Kazmer concurs. "The business hasn't changed all that much in the last 50 years," he says. "It's not some kind of conspiracy. It's just general levels of ignorance. It comes down to how people are raised. To educate that many men on what women really want is a long process."

Kazmer says, "I was surrounded by strong women growing up, in the company of my mother and two sisters. And frankly, any of the kudos I've received in advertising that appealed to women were because I had to go home at the end of the day—I married a strong woman, and I knew if I was going to create something that resonated with women, I had to pass it by my wife first. We'd be watching TV and a commercial would come on and I'd ask Karen, 'How'd you like that?' She'd invariably reply, 'I didn't notice it. There's so much that's awful, I simply mute it out.' I'm sure millions of women do the same."

"Sadly, we are not liberating women," Kazmer continues. "We're now beginning to enslave men with the same attitudes we used with women. I'm deeply offended by the current sophomoric advertising trend of dumbing down men." He tells his evenly gender-split classes at the Ontario College of Art and Design that their target audience is probably smarter than they are. "I tell them never talk down. Talk up."

Fellow creative director Bruce Harrod agrees. "It's important to look through cultural and gender lenses, so recruitment is also vital. You have to have women in top decision-making roles in the agency. If half the world is made up of women, then the agency should reflect the same. Currently, they are few and far between."

Chris Staples, partner at one of Canada's premier agencies, Rethink, says the industry simply must get more women writing advertising. "That's why there are so many bad ads," he concludes. "If you look at Canada's major advertising agencies, there are probably fewer than five women creative directors." When I asked him about Rethink's record on this front, he replied, "Appalling. But we have gay men and that counts for something. You know the stereotype—gay men have a much more developed feminine side than straight men." And to what does Staples attribute his own success? I asked. "I'm gay," he says, bluntly. (I had just taken a sip of water, when he said this, and it came right out my nose. Apparently I'm not used to hearing such refreshing candour.)

All the agency people we spoke to lamented about one constant. You can come up with brilliant, cutting-edge stuff, but unless you have a client who is prepared to take a chance, it won't go anywhere. Staples uses Kellogg's as an example. The person in charge at the time of the groundbreaking "Look Good on Your Own Terms" campaign (more on this in Chapter Six) has left the company, and they've reverted to the same old stuff about diet. Staples says, "Kellogg's has gone back to the playbook written in 1984."

Jean Kilbourne is creator of the immensely popular "Killing Us Softly" film series and the author of "Can't Buy My Love." She has been studying the image of women in advertising since the late 1960s. In her view, the image of women in advertising has gotten much worse in many ways. Kilbourne says pervasive thinness and agism are rampant across all media, including advertising, movies, sitcoms, and magazines. Most of the time, women of different racial and ethnic groups are considered beautiful only insofar as they look Caucasian. The media's portrayal of African-Canadian, Asian, or Native Canadian women is sometimes glamourized but usually stereotypical. "These images normalize all kinds of unhealthy attitudes and behaviour and often end up doing real damage to women's self-esteem. They also undermine the possibility of successful intimate relationships between women and men."

Kilbourne suggests that companies and their agencies use a wide range of models that includes older, ethnic, and plus-sized women. "However, advertisers that do this are sometimes met with resistance due to cultural conditioning. We've all learned to think there's only one way for a woman to be beautiful. The Catch-22 is that it is difficult for us to change our attitudes until we are exposed to a wider range of images. For example, we are conditioned to 'read' women's faces with wrinkles as old, exhausted, and unattractive, whereas men with wrinkles and grey hair are still considered attractive and desirable. If we began to see more unretouched images of older women in the media, we would develop a broader and more diverse definition of what constitutes 'attractive.' The good news is that we can turn this conditioning around, and that would make a profound difference in women's lives."

This is why media literacy in classrooms and on the homefront is so important. You can swallow this cultural conditioning lock, stock, and Visa or you can chew it up and spit it out if you don't like the taste.

Speaking of media literacy, Debbie Gordon is the Managing Director of Mediacs, which takes media literacy into school classrooms. She started conducting Mediacs workshops in 1998 when she was still a vice-president at Bozell Worldwide Advertising, after her five-year-old daughter one day described how Mr. Clean would come out of the bottle and solve the problem of getting into those nasty kitchen corners. That convinced her that the marketing industry had a responsibility and a role to play in developing media-savvy kids.

Having worked on child- and adult-directed brands with clients such as Hershey, Heinz, Kraft, Alberto Culver, YTV, Much Music, and Global, Gordon understands the strategic thinking that goes into creating the thousands of advertising messages that eventually find their way into children's lives. Just as important, she is the parent of two children who watch their share of TV.

"I wish I could say that the advertising industry has left tired old stereotypes in the dust," says Gordon. "But for too many companies, hauling out those tried and true images of women doing 'women's work' represents the path of least resistance. It's an easy sell, it clears all those inane creative test hurdles, and it builds on tired, lazy thinking." But that comment doesn't do justice to the depth of her disgust. "Why is it always women who are the role models for cleanliness?" she asks. "Is it not part of the male genome to clean up salmonella on the countertop and clean toilets? Why is it that 80% of the voice-overs that accompany these stereotypical selling scenarios are the soothing, empathetic timbre of a man?"

Gordon reels off a list of ads that misrepresent reality and reinforce gender inequality—an ad with a woman coming home from work to find her husband proudly putting a bowl of steaming soup on the table, apparently unable to cook a full meal ("Since when was meal prep a woman's domain?"); ads for processed cheese and crackers with kids saying "Awesome, Mom!" as if our children will love us more if we buy this stuff ("Children deconstructing this ad consistently recognize it insults their mothers' intelligence—they just say it's dumb"). "Shouldn't the advertising and marketing industries, which are the key drivers of popular culture and attitudinal shifts, have a role to play in changing these prehistoric images?" she asks. "Too often this type of advertising falls back on hackneyed stereotypes and is the byproduct of a multinational system where brand managers can only prove their worth and justify made-in-Canada advertising by using the research that has displaced collective wisdom as a crutch. Research can help us understand all the idiosyncrasies that make up our consumer. But we filter, filter, filter creative to the point where the unique and influential ideas are screened out and those ideas that offend the least and play it safe survive the process."

Enough said.

WHERE ARE THE WOMEN IN PRODUCT DEVELOPMENT?

There is still considerable evidence that a female lens is nonexistent or seriously lacking in much of the product development that goes on. I read recently that the Hooters restaurant chain was considering taking over a struggling discount airline in the U.S. The article said: "'Women in beach outfits may help a U.S. airline bounce back from bankruptcy,' a judge suggested." And won't the women be first in line?

Another one that got me, though at first pass it may seem minor, really speaks to this unidimensional lens evident everywhere. Volvo is probably the least macho car brand on the planet, with a well-deserved reputation for products that women love. Myself included. I had just picked up my brand-spanking new 2003 model. I'm driving home with my husband (who's a self-professed car nut) when I happened to look down. I blinked twice in order to be sure I had seen what I saw. Smack in the middle of the steering wheel was the male symbol with the name "Volvo" proudly nestled in the middle. You know the one, the circle with the little arrow pointing off to the right at the top. I started to howl. My husband, who is quite used to my eruptions, looked at me in anticipation of yet another stunning insight. I pointed to it and he was floored. "I wonder how many people in the organization actually saw this and didn't pick up on it before it ended up here," he said. This was an opinion shared by the 49 women and 42 men (by the time of writing) to whom I have since shown the logo. All said they saw "man." When I contacted Volvo, they told me that it is the scientific symbol for iron. While inhabitants of Volvoland may recognize it to mean "iron," in the real world it's the universal symbol for "male." There is no doubt that Volvo have women on their radar—they apparently tested this logo with women in Europe. But this is a classic example of what can happen if you treat "gender" homogeneously. The worldview of North American women is clearly not the same as European women. If this can happen at a gender-intelligent company like Volvo, trust me, it can happen anywhere.

Noni MacDonald, Dean of Medicine at Dalhousie University, says, "Airline seats in business class are clearly meant for those over 5'4", which most men are. My feet can't touch ground and the headrest pushes the top of my head down into my chin." We turned to a senior engineer at DeHavilland for an explanation, and he told us about the 95-percentile rule—designs are based on the needs of 95% of the people using the product. He acknowledged that the design of aircraft seats is rooted in a 50-year-old reality that hasn't adjusted to women being close to half of the people in business class on airplanes.

This one-dimensional view of the world is more commonplace than most realize. MacDonald continues: "I am often not able to reach pedals in many cars, which makes them unsafe to drive. When I buy a car, the main criterion is whether I can drive it. It's always amusing to watch the salesperson emphasize colour, gas mileage, quality of the seats, etc., but when I ask if anything can be done to reduce the distance to the pedals, there is just a shoulder shrug. They always seem surprised that I won't buy it. They always try to sell it to my husband, who is 5'10", even though we both have to be able to drive the vehicle."

A few years ago, The Thomas Yaccato Group was hired to work with an investment firm to help it connect better with women. The vice-president of marketing, a brilliant woman, had done considerable research on women investors and was intent on creating a viable strategy that would be valuable to women and also sellable to one of the toughest audiences out there—investment advisors. At our first strategy session, she smiled as she said, "When I told my boss my plan was not only to increase the investment advisors' business, but also to reflect the actual needs of women, he turned to me and said, 'Just take what we do for men and put it on pink paper.'"

Financial services clearly need to expand their product worldview. It's still not standard practice for banks and car leasing companies to look through a woman's lens when creating products. For example, women entrepreneurs face different cash flow concerns than men. Payment deferral options make sense on loan products for women entrepreneurs on maternity leave, because entrepreneurs who own more than 40% of the shares of their companies don't qualify for the federal government's Employment Insurance Program (because they have the power to lay themselves off). But maternity benefits are EI. As a result, Canadian women entrepreneurs don't have the same access to government-sponsored maternity benefits as the rest of employed Canadian women.

Ignoring gender differences in product development can in fact have disastrous consequences for women. George Iny, president of the Automobile Protection Agency, describes what was, in effect, systemic discrimination against women in the original design of automobile airbags. He explains, "Airbags in many early- to mid-1990s models pose a significantly higher risk of injury to shorter people," he says. "Despite some deaths and injuries to young kids in the front seat, the overall risk to young occupants is lower." Children don't drive, after all, and there are car seats for the very young, who are more likely to be seated safely in the rear to begin with. Consequently, Iny says, "women bear a disproportionate portion of the risk." Until 1994, Canada relied on the U.S. specifications for airbags instead of setting its own standards to acknowledge the fact that unlike most American drivers, Canadians buckle up. "The U.S. is now correcting a problem that is more than 10 years old," says Iny, "and that could have largely been avoided in Canada."

In 1998, Canadian car manufacturers agreed to inform owners of pre-1998 vehicles of the safety hazards and left it for the dealers to disconnect the airbags, although they didn't follow through to make sure dealers would actually do it—an act Iny calls "willful blindness." Significant numbers of pre-1998 vehicles are still on the road, driven mostly by women. Far more women than men drive intermediate, compact, or subcompact cars, so they are much more likely to fall into the category most affected. And while the number of deaths attributed to airbags in Canada may be small—"perhaps four or five in the last ten years," according to one car manufacturer—avoidable injuries, usually facial bruises and the occasional broken bones in the face or wrist (sometimes quite serious) number in the thousands.

The future holds more promise. Airbag design has improved significantly. Transport Canada has recently developed safety protocols that include testing with female crash-test dummies. But why didn't this happen in the first place?

Some marketers don't understand the idea that there is any need or benefit to marketing differently to women. Some even resist it. One of the first tenets of the "marketing to women" world trotted out was that persuasive communications should be driven by the prospect, not the product. I humbly disagree. At first pass, it seems it should be true. Gender-specific cars aren't the answer. However, cars with adjustable gas pedals, dimming interior lights, airbags that won't kill people under 5'2"—these appeal to women, without leaving men out. This isn't only about how to sell cars; it's about making sure the car fits a wide constituency of drivers, including women. The same applies to any product that has a physical component to its development. Gendered products, if done intelligently, are not just money in the bank, but give a respectful nod to a mere half of the population.

There is a dearth of women's perspective in advertising and product development. Part of the reason is because there has been a dearth of women in companies' processes. Let's go back and visit the turbulent 1960s to get a full picture on how we got where we are.

Not so long ago . . .

In the 1960s and into the 1970s, the hospitality industry, notably hotels, decided to capitalize on the growing population of women business travellers. One might have assumed they would actually ask women what they wanted in a travel experience. Had they done so, they would have heard suggestions like improve overall security, provide irons and ironing boards in the rooms, and put more counter space and full-length mirrors in the rooms. Instead, they appeared to turn inward and came up with a stunning campaign to appeal to women: turn the rooms into pink palaces, with pink curtains, bed spreads, walls, and toilets. Needless to say, to anyone with eyesight anyway, this campaign completely bombed. This would be what gender intelligence is not.

It's been quite a journey to today's world order. You wouldn't see this happen today (although that hotel in Montreal does give one pause), but the 1960s are not really that long ago. It's also not so long ago that 80% of the workforce was white able-bodied males. Today most of the new entrants to the workforce are women, visible minorities, Aboriginal peoples, and people with disabilities. In fact, close to half of the overall workforce is made up of women.[8] It's not rocket science to figure out that this new workforce reality is also a marketplace reality.

Starting in the 1960s and well into the 1980s, the buzz everywhere was "home and workplace equality," thanks to women's growing resistance to being pigeonholed into roles as housewives, nurses, teachers, and secretaries. Among those voices demanding change, we began to hear opposition to the dated way women's role as consumers had been presented, especially in the realms of media and advertising. Women were demanding to be taken as seriously as men on all fronts—at home, in the workplace, as well as in the consumer marketplace.

However, we were soon to see inherent flaws in society's interpretation of the term "equality," especially in the realm of consumer equality. The dictionary describes equality in terms of quantity, magnitude, value, or intensity—having equal rank or power with others. Which got interpreted as sameness. Because corporate Canada's business model was based on a male paradigm, the principle of sameness became about treating women consumers the same as the default—as though they were men. It's not too difficult to see how equality principles in service, product development, and marketing put women at a decided disadvantage. What happened was many people, especially recruiters and marketers, thought that equality meant women wanted to be treated the same as men, so nothing changed appreciably within the corporate male-based culture. However, in a marketing context, to respond to women's growing presence in the marketplace, the unisex concept was introduced everywhere—in hair salons, clothing, and sports equipment, to name but a few.

In reality, male-designated products or services were simply being repackaged or relabelled. When companies did differentiate consumer needs according to gender, they essentially made their products smaller and painted them pink. Anyone remember the Dodge La Femme, Chrysler's answer to women's car-buying dreams back in the 1950s? It set the standard of what not to do. It came in pink, with a matching raincoat, rain boots, keystone-shaped purse in a gold-coloured box, calfskin makeup compact, lipstick holder, comb, vanity mirror, cigarette holder, and matching lighter. All failed to help sell the car, which quickly sank out of sight. Even though there may have existed a gender-based "colour" or "smaller version" differentiation, unisex meant that it was acceptable to create, market, and sell the same product for both women and men, unless of course we're talking about selling laundry soap or manufacturing bras. This principle of treating everyone the same continues to flourish in industries that have historically sold primarily to men—cars, financial services, travel, liquor, and so on.

There is no question that women, marketers, and product developers have made quantum leaps over the last few decades, but it takes generations for ingrained historical realities and biases to fade into the woodwork. Marketing based on the male model is still alarmingly evident today, and not surprisingly, women continue to struggle with how they aren't taken as seriously as men.

The Genesis of Gender Intelligent Marketing

Equality may be about sameness, but equity—fairness—acknowledges differences. Marketing that draws on an authentic definition of equity reaches out to meet the consumer needs of our diverse population. Be cautious, however, because equity means different things at different times.

When ad agencies talk about equity, they mean developing brand equity. This is the value of the image of the company that takes years to develop, building value by establishing an emotional connection between people and the product or service over time. Think: How do consumers respect the name and how much will they pay for it? What is the product, message, and image you are trying to create and sell "out there"?

Developing brand equity is mandatory so consumers can cut through all the marketing noise. But how does gender factor into this? Women have always been society's shoppers, which has made them savvy consumers, wary of any branding that doesn't ring true. They wield enormous consumer influence. And given the current trend of global consumer cynicism about companies that appear more concerned with image (advertising) than with substance (company ethics, human resource policies, the environment, quality products, customer service), today it is simply imperative to recognize women's consumer needs. Gender intelligent brand equity means providing a sales experience free from biased and insulting approaches, with pricing that isn't jacked up merely because the consumer happens to be a woman (more about this later). Inclusive brand equity understands that women want information and options based on the realities of their daily lives. Authentic brand equity doesn't assume that women are conservative investors or need their partners to help them make decisions. It understands that because of biological and sociological realities, women may consider different issues than men do when planning their finances or purchasing a car, house, or computer.

Another form of equity commonly used in business refers to human resources—workplace equity. This is about making sure there is a balance of gender, race, Aboriginal peoples, sexual orientation, age, people with disabilities throughout an organization. The idea here is to be sure that a diversity of worldviews and experiences is represented throughout to meet the needs of employees. This internal branding process asks what kind of message or cultural change is being created and sold "in here"—inside the company.

A third meaning is used by accountants and companies to refer to the actual dollar value built up in a business. In this case, equity is the difference between what the company owns (its assets) and what it owes (its liabilities), and relates to its net worth.

It occurs to me that, when done properly, integrating brand equity and workplace equity can create a powerful fusion for building business equity or net worth. Said another way, a gender-inclusive brand equity or external message generated from a gender-balanced and intelligent workplace produces amazing results in terms of customer satisfaction and market share. The idea is to harmonize and streamline everything into an inclusive, integrated package. This, folks, is what we call gender intelligent marketing.

Gender intelligent marketing doesn't just target a marketing and advertising campaign to a specific demographic—what is usually called market segmentation. It has a deep and profound insight into the values, moods, life stages, cultural and gender-based attributes of its market, meaningful not only to the marketing department but to the entire company. In all cases where gender intelligence is evident, it's because it is considered a business imperative that directly and positively affects the company bottom line, and the CEO and senior management team not only support the concept but also allocate resources so gender intelligence is integrated into everything the organization does: strategy development, public relations, human resources, sales, marketing, training, product development, and delivery channels. This is an absolutely essential part of the gender intelligence equation, because women are relatively new participants in decision-making within corporate Canada and have yet to be integrated significantly into all parts of companies. If you do this piece right, whatever initiatives you introduce will rise above the competition and transcend any individual champion of the "women's market" internally. And it will ensure that women's consumer needs aren't discarded in a market downturn, because it's not simply the flavour of the month.

What Can Gender Intelligence Do for a Company? Let's put all the benefits of gender intelligence in one list, so you can see just how much impact it can have.

> Gender intelligence recognizes that women and men are different and that women are different from one another, but it also recognizes universal characteristics.

> Gender intelligence can create market segmentation that resonates with women, without relying on the separate archetypes of "woman as business owner," "woman as mother," "woman as sexy," "woman as athlete," and so on. They can all be the same woman.

> Gender intelligence makes any gender "difference" or "characteristic" accurate rather than stereotypical. It helps marketers and advertisers avoid disastrous generalizations.

> Gender intelligence contributes to an inclusive marketing and advertising experience and will go a considerable distance towards protecting your advertising investment.

> Gender intelligence makes it possible to create and interpret market research data correctly.

> Gender intelligence ensures gender-specific or -inclusive product development that's authentic and that happens only where it makes sense. It eliminates the possibility of making products and services for women that have no business being gender-specific.
> Gender intelligence helps provide an unbiased sales experience.
> Gender intelligence is the first step to creating corporate soul—the process of translating authentic gender differences into a company's external systems: sales, marketing, advertising, public relations, and product development processes, as well as its internal systems.

SEPARATE OR INCLUSIVE? THAT IS THE QUESTION

A huge element of the gender intelligence equation is answering the question of whether you need to target or create a separate program to reach women. You can get to your answer by asking more questions:

> Does your industry/company have an unchallenged "history" with women?
> Is your industry perceived as taking women seriously?
> Are women and men represented adequately in decision-making capacities throughout the entire organization, including sales and marketing and product development?
> Does your company treat everyone equitably, recognizing diversity?
> Can you say your sales force or other customer contact points are free from unconscious gender-based stereotypes and biases about women consumers?
> Does your sales force reflect the market you are attempting to serve?

You can see from these questions that the key is a mindset rather than a fixed set of instructions. For example, if you answer yes to all of these questions, simply being inclusive will work beautifully for you. Mountain Equipment Co-op, for example, sells to everyone but also totally understands the consumer DNA of Canadian women, with lines of appropriate gender-specific gear, ample change rooms, plenty of sales staff in the right places, and profound corporate soul. Do companies like Procter & Gamble and Nestlé need a special "women's strategy"? Absolutely not—their market is women. But these kind of companies still need to be sure that their market research, products, pricing, and advertising are authentic and relevant. In other words, gender intelligent.

However, if the answer to any of those questions was negative, you need to look very carefully at how you are doing business. Your organization needs to find creative ways to break through women's existing expectations of gender-biased, poor-quality service from your industry or company. But this can only be done if you actually take steps to get rid of the problems. In other words, you can work towards being gender inclusive, but you'll need to issue some kind of declaration to the world at large that it isn't business as usual.

Acquiring Gender Intelligence

You might think companies would know immediately if they have gender intelligence. They don't. Many may think they do, but most don't. Some actually have it in spades, but don't even know it. This isn't surprising considering the complexity of the issue. You're dealing with socialization, biology, social, cultural, and religious norms, and so on. Meeting the needs of women consumers properly is not just about marketing.

The strategy for increasing the number of women customers may be the same for two different companies, but the tactics will be different. What you do with this kind of realization depends on what you sell, what your corporate culture is, and what your history has been with women. You have a choice of any or all of four ways to go about acquiring gender intelligence.

> You could blow the system apart and start over, which I call the "green field approach."
> You could align the necessary personal and corporate values by acquiring or finding someone internally who recognizes the value of gender intelligence.
> You could balance x and y chromosomes in all your company's decision-making capacities and make sure you use both worldviews.
> You could walk before you run—figure out how to pick the low-hanging fruit and then begin to build a more comprehensive strategy.

Let's look at some very different companies and how they acquired their gender intelligence. They actually employed a little bit of each of the four methods. As you'll see, these are by no means mutually exclusive categories, but the stories do illustrate the strength and success of each approach. When it gets really exciting is when all four come together.

TAKE THE GREEN FIELD APPROACH

An exciting trend has emerged: Companies are casting aside the existing model and starting over. This is the "green field approach"—creating an empty space where it is easier to build something new rather than to fix a broken system. The effectiveness of this approach is apparent in industries that have historically sold predominantly to men with little understanding of real gender differences, and have needed to deal with "unlearning" and "untraining" a male-based system.

Green Fields of Saturn. The best way to explain the green field approach is to tell the story of General Motors' Saturn. When I contacted brand manager Doug Airey, I talked about Saturn's reputation for being one of the best at targeting women consumers.

"Saturn doesn't target women," he said.

"Yes, you do," I replied.

"No, we don't."

"But every woman on the planet thinks Saturn is about her," I said.

"But we've never targeted women specifically," he answered.

Eleven years ago, GM saw an opportunity to change the traditional sales experience associated with buying a new car. It started fresh with new dealerships, new salespeople, new management, new business structure, new models, new everything. They asked focus groups what they wanted done, rather than what they wanted fixed. As Airey said, "It was easier to start over than go in and change. We wanted a kinder, gentler way to buy cars. Our target was customers who wanted a better experience. We are not selling cars, we are selling the whole experience."

What happened was a car-buying experience so different from what women were used to that they thought it was designed for them. Saturn's

"No hassle/no haggle/no pressure pricing" policy eliminated the dreaded "backroom visit." The manufacturer's suggested retail price for new models was the same everywhere, the only variation being finance rates and used car value. Retailers actually gave out price lists and posted prices in their showrooms. Customers didn't need to shop from one dealer to another to get the best buy.

Saturn hired sales consultants from outside the industry with no previous car industry experience and trained them thoroughly in the art of the soft sell. Out of 63 Saturn stores in Canada, seven are owned by women, and there are double the industry average of women salespeople. As one general manager, Ernie Bugelli, says, "women are an asset on the showroom floor."

Saturn has also attempted to remove the barrier between service staff and sales staff. "We are a one-department store," Bugelli says, "not a building with four departments." Even Saturn's advertising seems targeted specifically at women, despite Airey's assertions. They use true stories that mostly feature women. There is a strong orientation to advertise company values, people, and process.

It's safe to say many companies don't have the resources or the will to use the green field approach. However, it can be done right even in those tough industries that women continue to wrestle with (and even by accident). It can be a stunningly effective method.

LOOK FOR GENDER INTELLIGENCE IN YOUR OWN BACKYARD

Another way to acquire gender intelligence is to look inside. You might have someone on board who recognizes what needs to be done and sets about doing it. The key is to find a way to align those personal values with corporate values in a way that creates an authentic connection to women. Gender intelligence doesn't only come from the head; the authentic kind that resonates with women comes from the heart. Whether in a big corporate setting, like BMO Financial Group, which could mine a huge organization for a champion or bring in people from outside, or in a smaller entrepreneurial setting like Magnotta Wineries, which does it because it's an extension of who the owner is, the results speak for themselves.

Consider Every Angle: Magnotta Wineries. There has been an emergence of women in the wine profession. Women everywhere are choosing some aspect of the wine business as a career. There are women managing major companies such as Corby's and Pernod-Ricard. The Liquor Control Board of Ontario has three management directors, all women. There are women sommeliers and masters of wine. In fact, there are now twice as many women product consultants at the LCBO as there were product consultants in total in the 1970s and 1980s.

Canada has its share of women winemakers, too. I went to meet one— Rossana Magnotta, co-founder of Magnotta Wineries. To get to her office, I had to first go through the store—a magnificent place, with a wonderful cathedral ceiling and a beautiful mix of wood and wrought iron with ample natural light. Paintings adorned the walls. Sculpture was everywhere. Off to the right, a bar offered free wine tasting. The aisles were wide enough for strollers, and the breakables, such as crystal decanters, were placed higher up. The store was busy but, with three cash registers, there were no line-ups.

Entering Rossana's office was like entering someone's home. It was splendidly furnished with family pictures everywhere. But we got right down to business: The first question I asked was, "Do you market to women?" Without a second's hesitation, she answered, "I have to market to women. It's in my blood, an extension of who I am. I know exactly what women want. I knew men weren't going to notice the plants, warm colours, wrought iron fixtures, the marble tables, unique items like copper oil decanters, art, chocolate, jam, but the women are ecstatic. That's why I have an all-women marketing team. We service and educate women and then they buy more from us. It's simple. If we take care of women, the money comes."

A biochemist and a microbiologist by training, Rossana started making juice for wine making with her husband, joining him full time at Festa Juice in 1986. "I took the medical lab approach," she says, "and set up my own lab to create and test wine." Festa's customers were 99.9% men. Rossana says wine making is part of the Italian culture, and she was not appreciated at all in this male-dominated business. Rossana even hid her female identity as a winemaker when she wrote a wine-making manual that was translated into different languages.

Instead of getting angry, however, Rossana got even. One day she met Mrs. Ferriera, a Portuguese woman who was fed up with her husband (who, because it's a bad omen in Portuguese culture for women to touch grapes, wouldn't let her make wine). Rossana secretly taught her to make wine. The quality of Mrs. Ferriera's wine was so good that not only did she win over her husband, relatives, and friends, but *The Toronto Star* ran a front-page piece on her.

Rosanna noticed a shift in the market, with people starting to come in and ask for ready-made wine. She and her husband responded to the demand and bought a winery—Magnotta Wineries. Their customers were still mostly men, but there were increasing numbers of women.

Today, in fact, the majority of wine consumers are women. "Most of the women do the cooking," says Rossana, "and they're the ones doing the shopping. So I designed the stores knowing women are buying. We blend science and art. Our gender is more focused on the ethic of care. We are more sensitive to needs. As women service and product providers, we intuitively give women what they need, even in shopping. Men do the market research. Women rely on intuition."

Though she in no way believes there should be "women's wines," Rossana believes women come to the consumer table differently from men. Magnotta's retail locations are by supermarkets to help ease women's time-crunch problems. There is an automatic carry-out service to the car. The design and packaging of all the products are coordinated. In fact, Magnotta was the first Canadian company to win a label design award, which raised the bar for the entire industry.

Rossana finds women are more patient than men when they shop. Women ask about the difference between one wine and another, and respond well to Magnotta's labels, which are full of information. Women also remember the wines by the art on the label more than men do. Displays include pictures of foods suitable for accompanying the wines, to help the quick shoppers—usually men, according to Rossana.

The gender balance of key management personnel was also an issue for the winery. The board of directors requested that Rossana become more visible, so she was prominently featured in the annual report in order to appeal specifically to women investors. "Women buy stocks," she says. "I want to encourage more women to be interested in the companies they invest in. I want to let them know a woman runs the company." Magnotta's strategy of gender intelligence—based on Rossana's intuitive reliance on her experience and values—permeates all aspects of the business, and its success is reflected in many awards. Magnotta has been named one of the 50 Best Managed companies for both 2000 and 2001, and Rossana herself has won several honours, including the Canadian Woman Entrepreneur of the Year for Innovation.

Setting Things Right: Tony Comper and the BMO Financial Group. One might be forgiven for wondering how you align corporate and personal values in a multinational corporation. It might not be quite as easy for, say, a major financial institution compared to an entrepreneurial enterprise like a winery. Ask Tony Comper, Chairman and CEO of BMO Financial Group. Turns out he took his own gender intelligence and made it company business.

"For me, it began a number of years ago with the nagging feeling that something was wrong here somehow," says Comper. "I was happy to be climbing the corporate ladder at the Bank of Montreal, but I couldn't help but notice that the other climbers were almost all white guys like me. Maybe the problem was that women weren't educated enough. Or maybe it had to do with the so-called fact that they were always quitting to have babies and maybe never coming back to work. Or maybe it was because they just weren't dedicated enough to the job or interested enough in building their own careers. Or maybe they just didn't, you know, 'have it.' The trouble with all of these explanations, though, is that they didn't fit with my experience. I'd worked with many women over the years that were at least the equivalent, in every respect, of the best of the men I'd worked with."

It occurred to Comper that the fault lay somewhere in the bank's corporate culture, a thought that surfaced once he became president of the bank. He was faced with daunting numbers: in a workforce that was three-quarters female in 1991, women comprised only 3% of the bank's senior executives and 9% of the executive ranks in general; when it came to senior managers—the natural source of the future's executives—representation was just 14%.

"The answer, when it came, was no farther away than an analysis of our own human resources database," says Comper. "Not only were Bank of

Montreal women as educated and loyal and dedicated as Bank of Montreal men, but they also scored slightly higher on performance reviews."

As for women customers, after thorough research, Comper concluded that the best way to market financial services to women was to create an equitable working environment within BMO Financial Group. Once there is a corporate culture in which equity (fairness), respect, and dignity are ingrained values, he believes, these values will be reflected in every business transaction.

In response to this information, Comper appointed the Task Force on the Advancement of Women. The bank's approach was to expose gender-based myths first, and all pat explanations for the non-advancement of women were the first to fall by the wayside. The Task Force then came up with 26 recommendations for change.

Comper says that the playing field was heavily slanted against women and many other people who didn't fit the age-old mould of middle-aged white guys, and that the bank had a moral obligation to level that playing field. But the people who needed the most convincing about removing artificial barriers to women's advancement weren't likely to be won over by how this would improve the bank's bottom line. "In an ideal world," he says, "every employee—and particularly every manager—would look at those recommendations and say, 'Yes, that's right, that's fair, that's a good idea.' But like just about every other large organization, ours was a culture that hadn't changed much in a century or two. We knew there would always be those who would not or could not accept the fact that women at the BMO Financial Group were as qualified and worthy of promotion as men, people who would argue that what we were really doing was setting up a quota system—to curry the favour of the government and the 'feminists.'"

Comper's view was not to have any part of BMO's women's initiatives as separate and distinct. He didn't want to see it as discretionary. "We're in it for the long haul," he says. "It can't be put at risk in times of downturn or the next new priority. So we made it a business priority—a core business priority—and in so doing, we made it irresistible. And we made it work."

How successful was Comper's approach? Today, the BMO Financial Group boasts that women are now 35% of executives (up from 9% in

1991), and women run three of the five Canadian divisions. They have a goal of gender parity by 2007.

Results from the bank's ongoing tracking study of retail customers support an image of the BMO Financial Group as an organization with strong relationships with its female customers. Women score significantly higher than men on customer loyalty, as well as on the measurements of overall relationship with the bank; they also score high in their view of the bank's professionalism and responsiveness. Women also report experiencing fewer problems than men (12% less) and have a larger share of assets with BMO (5% more).

In short, it would appear Comper's instinct was right on the money. "The bank must 'get it right' with employees," he says, "who in turn will get it right with customers, who in turn will reward the bank with more business, which in turn enables the organization as a whole to get it right with shareholders. The logic for gender balance is easily transferred to creating a workforce that is balanced in other respects as well—fully reflecting the society and the customer profile that are growing up around us. My dream is to have every language spoken here, every culture understood, every belief and tradition respected. Every base must be covered when it comes to understanding the full range of customers and responding to their individual needs with sensitivity and imagination and speed. By stressing the smart even more than the right, by pushing the utter logic of a representative workforce in an increasingly diverse and customer-driven marketplace, we have been able to start selling what had been unsellable."

This is what is known internally as "Tony's Logic Chain." Logic to Comper, and logic to us. Sadly, not logic in most companies.

FIND THE RIGHT BALANCE

You can also acquire gender intelligence by what I call "mixing it up." Regardless of what you sell and to whom you sell it, it can be disastrous if only Europeans, only tall men, only Protestants, only mothers, only straight folks, or only able-bodied people make all the marketing decisions. Especially as all the populations left out of this list likely represent a growing piece of your company's bottom line. This is, of course, true if you are trying to build up the number of women consumers, and especially significant in industries that have typically had a dearth of female input.

You need to ask two questions: Is your company operating on a dated paradigm? Is there a balance of x and y chromosomes throughout the decision-making process?

But first we must address another burning issue. In order to determine whether balancing x and y chromosomes in decision-making is effective, we need to answer the question of whether men can market intelligently to women. Bloody right they can, if the will and the focus are there. There are lots of thoughtful and respectful examples of inclusive advertising or advertising specifically aimed at women that have emanated from the grey matter of male creative types. In two of the country's largest financial institutions, the moving forces behind women's internal advancement and external marketing initiatives were men. But they didn't do it alone. They involved women in the decision-making process throughout their entire organization.

Having a balance of x and y works because it can be very effective in helping companies scrutinize their marketing worldview—what they sell and how they sell it—to see if it meets the needs of today's women. But don't interpret balance to mean just equal numbers—balance means considering both women's and men's perspectives to uncover the "full picture." For a better chance at successfully finding the right balance, start creating your own internal gender lens by contemplating the following questions:

> If men historically were the primary users of our product or service, is it safe to assume that it was designed, marketed and sold primarily to men?
> If women now use our product or service, have we altered anything in the way we design, market, or sell?
> If a critical mass of women use our product or service, does that affect the company providing the service and products?
> If we change the way we do business, does it affect the previous primary user of the product or service?
> Do these changes affect our employees?
> If we maintain the status quo, does it affect women consumers?

These are the questions RONA answered.

RONA Transformed. Home improvement stores used to be one of the last bastions of the man's world. But perceptions are changing faster than you can say "Mag Ruffman," and now there are many TV shows catering to a rapidly growing consumer force of women. One national home improvement company, RONA, has been transformed as a result, both at the customer end and at the dealer end. Sixty-two percent of its market is dealer owners and 30%—about 375 people—of the dealer owners are women.

A 1990s survey revealed 70% of all home improvement projects are decided by women. Sylvain Morissette, RONA's Director of Communications, says that women represent approximately 46% of home improvement shoppers. "Young, educated, single women are now the largest consumer group in the industrialized world. Women are generally the prime decision-makers on home decor and renovations. A recent survey indicates that 37% of women would prefer spending their weekend fixing up their houses over other activities. The most popular female do-it-yourself projects are painting, gardening, landscaping, and wallpapering. Women are more interested in working and creating with their own hands. They want to build. And a large majority look to their home improvement store for advice on how to complete their projects."

Morissette saw "an opportunity to respond on a larger level to women and deliver new possibilities to them. Our dealer owners and managers were also looking to offer more to women in response to what they were observing at store level." So RONA asked women how they wanted to be served by employees and by the store environment.

As a result of their responses and input from all of its women dealers, RONA reinvented itself. It created a welcoming place in an industry that was historically suited to the needs of guys in work boots and hard hats. RONA balanced x and y and got amazing results.

The home improvement industry is no different than many others: RONA's research showed that women wrestle with being taken as seriously as men. Claude Bernier, Executive Vice-President of Marketing, says, "Part of RONA's strategy to stay ahead is to break down the stereotypes. Women want to be treated with respect. It is more acceptable and necessary for women to make improvements to the home. We must acknowledge, guide, and provide superior customer service. As a result of this growth in the women's market and with the input of the women in our system, we added new lines of products to respond to the stronger presence of women in our stores."

When it opened its first big box store in 1998, RONA incorporated the "ambience" boutique, a store within a store for decor, paint, floor coverings, and doors and windows. These categories were the start of a large project. Thanks to the participation of the women dealers in the process, stores were no longer just hardware stores but "a store for the home." In stores of all sizes, entire sections were dedicated to decor-related products.

RONA created the unique "paint boutique concept"—a separate, serene environment where people can linger, discuss, and reflect on their choices before making their buying decisions. The paint preparation and colour mixing laboratory is separated by a glass partition to ensure quiet in the viewing salon. The format is based on colours rather than brands, and large colour chips are offered in order to test the true colour in the home before purchasing.

These steps, which have created products as well as places where women can feel more comfortable, are all thanks to the input of women. The steps extended to changes in the design of the main stores specifically to accommodate women: wider aisles, brighter and cleaner stores, price match guarantee, knowledgeable staff, product placement within reach of the average-sized woman. Their lumberyard is built into the store so people don't have to trek long distances outside to the back of the store. They stock lightweight power tools, including power saws and drills that are easier for women to use. They carry plastic gardening tools that are lighter, as well as a lightweight portable bench with wheels for gardening.

"This benefits men as well," Morissette says. "We're not all macho hulks, you know." Historically, men were the primary users of RONA's products and services, so this industry marketed and sold primarily to men consumers. "But with a critical mass of women consumers now using our products and services," he says, "we had to develop a new way to merchandise the products. Our employees changed by becoming much more aware of the importance of women's role in decisions around home improvement. We not only work with manufacturers to improve the products but, moreover, we also adjusted our customer service to provide better solutions and greater expertise to women. We improved the way we do business, and men enjoy the new opportunities that were created for women."

Since they reinvented the shopping experience in 1999, RONA's compound annual growth rate has been a staggering 39.3%, from $988 million to $2.3 billion for the last 12-month period ending September 2002. All this, Morissette says, because of a new customer service model and new lines of products in decor, seasonal products, paint, and flooring, to meet the needs of women. RONA was able to market intelligently to women, because it focused on their needs and concerns.

Teamwork: The LCBO. Though this next story is a brilliant example of what can happen when you bring women into what was historically a male bastion of monolithic proportions, it also beautifully demonstrates the green field principle. When Nancy Cardinal, Vice-President of Marketing, joined the Liquor Control Board of Ontario in 1989, the alcohol business was intimidating for women. There was still a hangover lingering from the days when it wasn't "proper" for women to go into liquor stores. Men were the ones who bought all the alcohol. A very conservative attitude prevailed, you couldn't shop on Sunday, and the industry was known as the "booze business." Gender intelligence was nowhere to be found.

In 1995, the LCBO set about a radical transformation. President Larry Gee saw a consumer split of 60% male and 40% female in the numbers and astutely concluded that, in all other categories, women were the majority shoppers. But it was also common knowledge that women were underrepresented in the alcohol beverage industry. So Gee's mandate became "Put the welcome mat out for women."

Gee wanted a concept that included women but didn't disenfranchise men. He put together a "women's marketing council" of the top 20 female experts in the alcohol beverage industry (specifically choosing to leave men out for the moment). In other words, he "hired" it. Gee asked women to look at the LCBO's world through a women's consumer lens. He gave them carte blanche—a green field—to make up an LCBO store, which opened in downtown Toronto later that year. They determined that if they could get an even 50/50 market split, it represented a $100 million opportunity for them.

The women's council began by asking women how they felt about the alcohol beverage industry and then asking what they wanted. To no one's surprise, women responded that they viewed the stores as a male enclave with a predominantly male workforce. Cardinal laughs, "Women felt that going into the LCBO was like getting caught in the men's washroom."

The council decided to attract women by "wrapping them in something comfortable," in something they could relate to. They reached a whole new level of gender intelligence by viewing women in the context of a much larger experience. They started with a new mission statement: "To be the source for entertaining ideas." It involved an entire line of entertaining solutions including music, food, and decorating suggestions, and applied that theme to all newspaper inserts, visuals, logo, store design, and colours.

The new store was designed by Nella Fiorino. Another woman, Jackie Bonnick, who worked closely with Cardinal, was responsible for the store design. Graphic artist Heather Cooper painted *trompe l'oeil* and frescoes all over the store (and still does).

The work of the women's marketing council produced a complete redesign of the brand. The LCBO looked at their business in a holistic and integrated way, and created a desire for their product by wrapping it in something special. Cardinal explains, "We create an 'aspirational' and engaging environment. The objective was to create the outdoorsy, fresh-air feeling of being in a vineyard. Even the new logo is softer and more elegant. We took the mystery and the 'booze' out of the bottle. The language is now 'fine wine and premium spirits.'" The result was a new lifestyle store linked to entertainment including related products such as music, food, glasses, tableware, and decorating elements.

Women also asked for more information to help them in their buying decision. Cardinal explains, "Women are more engaged at store level and they want information. Men are in and out. They don't ask questions. We also heard women ask for friendly and approachable staff and a consumer experience that is inviting and comfortable. So we made a conscious effort to hire more women and train our staff in product and service. We didn't want our staff to look like bouncers or wine connoisseurs. We wanted to recreate the environment of a grocery store where women were comfortable and many of the staff are women." To extend the life-experience marketing strategy, LCBO created its instore magazine, *Food and Drink*, full of music, decorating, and recipe suggestions. According to Cardinal, it receives positive comments: "magic made easy" . . . "not too Martha Stewart."

The resulting consumer response is a real curiosity about the product. "Women now want to know, 'Where do I start? What else can I learn?'" Cardinal says. "We have also been told that we now promote responsible consumption simply by the way we have treated the product—with respect." The result was also word of mouth that the LCBO has finally "got it." This redesign has been a resounding success.

The LCBO's wine appreciation classes are always sold out. The Retail Council of Canada twice awarded the LCBO "Retailer of the Year" for its store concept. Today, the customer split is now skewed in favour of women. The average transaction for men is still higher because men buy more spirits than wine, but women buy more wine than men. In terms of bottle count, women buy more than men. And Cardinal is very clear. "We believe that a team of men with the same mandate could never have produced the same results."

PICK THE LOW-HANGING FRUIT

Perhaps the easiest way to begin building gender intelligence is to go after the low-hanging fruit that's within reach. In other words, look for reasonable, inexpensive ways to address some of the things women look for in a consumer experience—ways that don't require massive overhauls or teams of consultants. The key to this step, however, is that it be viewed as a beginning. Real gender intelligence involves much more.

Let's use a car dealership as an example—there are a million things that can be done.

A very easy way to start is to create a place that is comfortable to visit. This can start with balancing the greeting process somewhere in between being jumped when you walk through the doors to being flat-out ignored. How about price lists and payment selectors that are available without talking to a salesperson? Get the women in your dealership together and ask for their input on what can be improved—this resulted in one dealer getting a different perspective on something as arcane as the washroom. The women's washroom was an ugly little room with cement walls; today, it boasts terracotta treated walls, a shelf with tissues, hand cream, scented soap as well as flowers and pictures. A grease-ridden, dirty place—whether it be the washroom, service reception, the parts counter, the showroom, or the waiting area—neither welcomes nor encourages anyone to spend any extra time or money there. Look around the workplace with this new worldview. Do the salespeople hang around out front smoking? Have staff smoke behind the building instead. Think kids. Make it easy for parents to look after them. Provide a private place to change an infant. Get some toys and have a safe place for children to play while parents discuss purchasing a new vehicle. Is it easy to navigate your premises with a stroller?

Other examples—there are hundreds—of easy-to-pick fruit are keeping public areas clean, offering expanded hours or online shopping, providing seminars for women, including women in advertising and marketing materials, recruiting women, and sponsoring events that support women's health, sports, or charities.

Now, will these minor improvements earn you dramatically more market share? No. But each is a small step that has a degree of visibility that makes it appealing. And with every step, it gets easier to go even further.

Our Four Principles

If you were to ask women what they want in a consumer experience, all the many different roads would lead home to our quartet of principles. That's certainly what years of research have shown us and every other company that has focused on women consumers. It's fascinating to see how these four fundamentals emerge as common themes in just about every piece of proprietary research done by corporate Canada on this particular consumer group.

So, instead of analyzing these in a vacuum, sit back and let me tell you a story.

Discovering Women: Air Canada

Not that long ago, I had a travel experience that illustrates how so much of our world is viewed through a dated male lens, and also reveals opportunities to adjust that view. Picture this: I entered the business class lounge, a frazzled, exhausted mother in blue jeans carrying a baby seat containing—gasp—a two-month-old child.

And she's awake.

I was flying from Toronto to Ottawa to visit my parents for the weekend. I had brought Kate into the business class lounge, which I anticipated would be a pleasant, peaceful place to wait for my flight. Now, business class lounges have testosterone as their central decorating scheme, not surprisingly since men used to be the predominant inhabitants. But despite all the travel I do, I'd never quite noticed before the sheer number of suits, ties, briefcases, and cell phones. The place was packed. As I stood there, looking out over this sea of suits for a quiet, private spot to feed my now-starving daughter, I felt as though every pair of eyes was fixed on us.

You might imagine that I'm not easily intimidated, and you'd be right. But even I don't relish the notion of sitting beside a group of grey-haired businessmen, whipping open my top and fastening a howling Kate to my breast to wait patiently for her to finish slurping her way to a blissful slumber. I beat a hasty retreat into the nearest washroom.

There was nowhere to sit, nowhere even to lean, no place to go except down, so I sat down on the floor and Kate settled peacefully into lunch.

Suddenly, where I am dawns on me. In my frenzy to get out of an area where Kate's crying was an obvious disturbance, I'd settled on the first place where I could find a modicum of privacy and back support: the floor of the women's restroom. To my left was a garbage can. To my right was the toilet. Above my head was the sink. And my rage was instantaneous.

In my anger, my mind filled with images of me marching out of the washroom, breasts bared, Kate slurping happily as I stride up to the front desk to complain loudly. But alas, I remained where I was, fuming.

My resentment grew when I entered the business class cabin. I noticed the expectant looks from the passengers, all of whom I'm sure were silently praying I'd keep moving right on through the cabin. When I sat down in the second row, the temperature in the cabin dropped 10 degrees.

After a few minutes, a flight attendant genially informed me that I needed to remove Kate from her car seat in the empty seat next to me and hold her on my lap for take-off. There was Kate, snug in her safety-regulated car seat (required by law in all moving vehicles on the ground), secured in place with the aircraft seat belt. I pointed out to the flight attendant that Kate was significantly safer buckled in eight ways to Sunday in that seat than she would be held in my arms. The flight attendant insisted that airline regulations specified that children sit on their parent's lap for take-off and landing. I patiently repeated that Kate is better off where she was. She repeated the airline policy. I declared Kate is not going to move.

Meanwhile, several pairs of bespectacled eyes peered over newspapers, mildly curious at the scene that was unfolding. Another flight attendant moved in. Cornered, I prepared to battle to my death to protect the safety of my child.

These two flight attendants appeared unaware of the "Mama Bear" phenomenon that occurs when a mother perceives an action that puts her child at risk. This Mama Bear, now ten feet tall, teeth and claws bared, snarled in her best Mama Bear voice, "Airline regulations require passengers and flight attendants to be seated with seat belts fastened securely during take-off and landing, am I right? These same regulations require all loose cabin baggage to be secured under seats or in the overhead compartments during take-off and landing, do they not? Do you not require pop cans in the galley to be secured? Surely you're not telling me that the safety of a tin of ginger ale is of more value than the safety of my daughter?" Mama Bear reared up and roared, "Tell me again what it is that you want me to do with my child?"

By now, everyone in the cabin was watching this drama unfold. After an interminable silence, the flight attendants wisely chose to acquiesce.

I sat down, exhausted from the protective surge of adrenaline. Kate gurgled blissfully, trying to fit her entire foot in her mouth. In my altered state, I dimly heard some faint applause, but when I stood to put my jacket in the overhead bin, I saw nothing but balding heads bobbing behind their newspapers.

I must have been imagining things.

My experiences on this particular flight reveal a serious systemic flaw. The issue is not insensitive flight attendants—most of whom are consummate professionals, who have been known to take Kate into the galley so that I might eat a hot meal in peace and have magically appeared to help when I was struggling with something baby-related. But they don't make up for a system that appears to be working against you, as a woman and parent. It's a system that views the world through the dated male lens that is prevalent in so many corporate cultures and business practices. It's revealed in the way corporations develop and offer their products, which is translated into the customer experience, which is translated into sales figures and customer satisfaction numbers—which is translated into the genesis of the 80% minority.

When business class was first offered, the people travelling in it tended to come from a narrow sample of the general population, middle-aged white guys who travelled for one reason—business. The environment obviously needed to support its major constituent—businessmen. Business class offered amenities such as male-oriented magazines and newspapers, large seats with lumbar support for tall people, washrooms devoid of any facilities other than antiseptic soap, and a crew accustomed to one type of traveller. And it was this way for a very long time. Consequently, a whole set of unconscious preconceived images and expectations developed about people travelling in business class.

But today women are a large and growing segment of the business class travel market. So why wasn't there a comfortable place for me to feed and change my baby? If your answer is there aren't enough women travelling with infants in business class to warrant the changes, my reply is that would be a good point—if it were 1971, when only 1% of passengers were women business travellers. Today, women account for half of all business travellers and make $55 billion in purchases of pre-trip equipment.[9]

In 1999, Air Canada sponsored a study called Frequent Female Air Travellers. Women business travellers were identified as one of five potentially important target groups. The report begins with the acknowledgement that airlines have overlooked this segment of the market and found what I've been saying all along: Until you ask questions specifically comparing their experience with men, you'll never get to the heart of what women encounter with your company. What women revealed to Air Canada was that they felt like an 80% minority. Not surprisingly, the results revealed that women want to be treated on an equal footing with men, but feel the airlines do not consider them as important as men. The study said this perception is reflected by airline counter and lounge personnel who constantly question their frequent flyer status and travel class, by in-flight personnel who jump to serve men and ignore women, and by amenities and services that cater to men rather than to both sexes. Indeed, the survey participants—frequent travellers who had taken 1,022 round trips in the previous year—told the researchers what we've been advocating for 15 years: Women wanted to be acknowledged as valued customers and shown respect without having to ask for it.

They specifically asked for a consumer experience that could be summed up in our principles:

> Be intelligent about gender differences.
> Get through with intelligent communication.
> Recognize that women live multidimensional lives.
> Live your corporate soul.

BE INTELLIGENT ABOUT GENDER DIFFERENCES

Air Canada's study exposed women's unhappiness with countless details that made flying a very male-oriented experience. In addition to the masculine interior design of the lounges and the seats designed for bodies bigger than the average female, women noticed that the amenities and services tended to overlook women's needs (up-to-date feminine hygiene products would be appreciated, for example).

This is not about airlines for women. Being intelligent about gender differences means you do something about why women are made to feel invisible, and you recognize that women aren't men in skirts. They have preferences and need space and amenities that are relevant to them.

GET THROUGH WITH GENDER INTELLIGENT COMMUNICATION

Air Canada's study said women wanted reading material more appropriate to their needs and reality than the materials typically found in the lounges and on board. They also spoke of wanting to see women depicted in airline-related communication materials, not just men.

But their concerns went well beyond magazines and brochures. The "getting through" part referred to the communication skills of the staff.

The study spelled out some of the things so many women notice when they travel: Men's trays are cleared away faster than women's and attendants rush to hang men's coats up; and airline counter and lounge personnel constantly question women's frequent flyer status and travel class, and appear to pass judgement on their legitimacy as frequent flyers, especially since women don't usually wear a suit and tie.

There is a significant difference between providing information on a website or in a brochure or seminar and the art and method of communication. Nothing will stop success faster than the breach that directly results from women and men's different communication styles. Or the unspoken communication—the quiet but deadly vibes that women often speak of, the ones that are difficult to articulate but have been felt at one time or another by most women. In keeping with the airline example, it goes something like this: The smile is quick and professional, but the eyes say, "Good heavens, what extraordinary circumstance or accident enabled you to fly business class today?"

Women get this feeling in airplanes, stores, car dealerships, and bankers' offices all over the country. There has been much research quantifying the differences in communication styles and rituals and gender-biased attitudes, all of which reveals they have a huge impact on the quality of the face-to-face experience. This is as true in the boardroom where a woman may decide on a multi-million dollar computer technology deal as at the airline counter. (Oh, and by the way, it's the same woman.)

RECOGNIZE THAT WOMEN LIVE MULTIDIMENSIONAL LIVES

The women in Air Canada's study saw air travel as a disruption and a poor use of their time, and said men viewed air travel as a natural part of their business life and an opportunity for networking. For so many men, there is a woman around somewhere taking care of the rest of their lives, but when women travel, chances are they are still managing the home front. I can't tell you how many times in those last minutes before boarding I've called home to check that the dentist's appointment isn't missed and the school forms are filled in, and have called my assistant Rosa to make sure the package has been sent to the client and the meeting is confirmed.

In our study, a staggering half of all the women respondents indicated that companies didn't understand the complexity of their lives. One-third said companies are out of touch and don't understand the needs of women today. Consider my mother's job description of her life as a homemaker:

Nurse; doctor; cook; hostess; gardener; decorator; chief researcher of vacation spots, schools, children's programs, contractors, car dealers; shopper of food, clothes, gifts, toys; teacher; mother; wife; psychologist; housekeeper; laundress; seamstress; maintenance worker; family chief financial officer; social secretary; family historian; environmentalist; volunteer; chauffeur.

Now add a full-time paid job on top of it. Welcome to the world of the majority of Canadian women today. This has profound marketing ramifications. The first is easy: Do anything and everything to make women's lives simpler. This applies to product engineering and development, how and where you market, your delivery channels, the hours you are open, customer support, and whether you make house calls.

The second is tougher but equally important. Some universal realities hold true for almost every woman: Women are busy, health-conscious, ethically minded, and holistic in their consumer approach. If you can find ways to create products, services, advertising, and marketing that incorporate these concepts, you'll have a higher chance of meeting the multidimensional needs of more women at some point throughout their lives.

LIVE YOUR CORPORATE SOUL

The Air Canada survey respondents spoke loudly and clearly that the airline's sponsorship, which is one of the many elements that make up corporate soul, is "predictably male-oriented and promotional, rather than philanthropic." They wanted to see the company support health-related, social, cultural, and educational initiatives.

Women rank being a good corporate citizen as high as good customer service. We found that 75% of the women we surveyed said that a company must care about the community and its employees and be a good corporate citizen if it wants their business. They don't want to deal with large, anonymous companies any longer.

But the gender intelligent variety of corporate soul also understands the concept of "different worldviews" and life realities. It ensures the consumer experience and the internal company culture actually support what the marketing promises—in other words, the inside matches the outside. What you promise is experienced on the floor of the store. No small order, especially for those companies with a history rooted in a male-based paradigm. To do it right, you need an internal culture where every single employee not only understands and believes, but actually lives and breathes what the marketing is saying. It's a place where everyone is part of the company hierarchy—from the mailroom to the executive suites. And that kind of respect and integrity are reflected in the company's advertising, which takes a responsible position on how it relates to and portrays women.

Air Canada was faced with the realization they were a company with low gender intelligence. Charles McKee, Senior Director of Marketing for Air Canada, remarks that it's cheaper to keep a customer than acquire one. "To do that," he says, "it comes down to the emotional connections, and the way to increase connecting is to meet needs. Customer satisfaction is the number-one factor correlating to profit. The issues of women and travel are very important, whether in terms of product design or staff training. Companies like Air Canada need to be focused and diligent in dealing with them."

WHAT AIR CANADA DID

Air Canada chose to start by picking the low-hanging fruit—a good, inexpensive choice for the first step in creating a gender intelligent process, especially for companies with a long product cycle that can't reposition their product or service quickly. For Air Canada, with a product cycle of 8 to 12 years, it meant starting with smaller innovations. In some business class flights, travellers can choose the amount and type of food they want from fresh, healthy choices. There are change tables in the large aircraft and there are more feminine types of toiletries and reading material available. Emergency feminine hygiene products are available on long-haul flights. Business class lounges have been redesigned in a more neutral style and include mothers' comfort stations. Their marketing materials reflect more diversity. (In fact, on Air Canada's marketing communications team, 14 of the 17 members are women, and half the product design group is women.) Air Canada has increased its arts sponsorship portfolio and has, in the past, sponsored events such as CIBC's Run for the Cure, the Canada/USA Businesswomen's Trade Summit, and the Canadian Women Entrepreneur of the Year Awards, as well as the International Federation of Women Travel Organization.

Air Canada still has a way to go before it is out of the woods, and not only with women. Some of our team members were disappointed to find that all that resulted from Air Canada's research on women's experience was a better selection of toiletries, magazines, and a change table. Advertising expert Mary Koven said, "I feel it's a bit like a pat on the head and they said, 'There, there, dear, here's some hand cream and a *Vogue* magazine. Now, sit down and fasten your seat belt.'" The Air Canada story illustrates the dramatic effects of plucking the low-hanging fruit, but it also reveals how you need authentic gender intelligence to tackle the real attitudinal issues that must be dealt with: All the goodwill garnered by picking that low-hanging fruit disappears in an instant when women encounter the negative attitudes of staff that were revealed in their study. It's a start, but it's clearly not enough.

What waits for you in the following chapters is a look at each principle through our eyes, and through the eyes of companies that are successfully reaching the 80% minority. We start at the beginning, with the intelligent recognition of gender differences.

2

Two different worlds

Frankly, I don't need scientific proof women and men are different, I'm married. There isn't a person who graces this planet who doesn't understand, even if only intuitively, that women and men see the world through different lenses. I am a firm believer that these differences manifest themselves in many ways. The following true story, in my estimation, provides sufficient proof of gender differences.

Vive La Différence: Women and Men

My friend Judy and I share much in common: We are both authors, mothers of seven-year-old daughters, married, and we are both dedicated trail walkers. On these walks, Judy and I regularly marvel at the profound gender differences in our husbands' worldviews. If not for us, we've concluded, they would starve, be penniless, and live unnoticed and unloved in a cardboard house in some ravine. Like many married people, we can be pretty judgemental. However, one day last summer, Judy and I came to deeply appreciate the most fundamental of differences between us: man as hunter, woman as nurturer and gatherer.

We were engrossed in conversation when we happened across a fatally injured chipmunk in the middle of the path. It must have been hit by the cyclist who had roared past us just minutes before. Its back was broken, and it was convulsing. We stood there, stunned by this unimaginable suffering. We both hold a reverence for the natural and spiritual, which made what we had to do both infuriatingly harder and easier. Our eyes locked for a brief instant and the message that passed was clear.

A quick check yielded little in the way of suitable weapons, unless, of course, we wanted to drown the poor thing with our water bottles. We grew agitated when we realized our only option was a violent one. We dithered deciding on a plan, hoping our chipmunk would expire before we had to commit this horrific act. But it continued to twitch, and it was utterly heartbreaking.

In despair, Judy headed into the woods to secure a suitable weapon, and returned with an impressively large stick, but not quite large enough. "Judy," I said, "we have one swing in us. If it doesn't work the first time, we're in trouble." We both went back into the woods, this time on the lookout for a weapon of mass destruction. Judy burst into laughter as I emerged, groaning under the weight of an enormous log, half a metre in diameter and at least two metres long.

I almost dropped the log while Judy, giggling uncontrollably, spontaneously burst forth into a eulogy: "Well, little chipmunk, I'm sure you had a good life and we need to send you to a better one now." We clenched our eyes, raised the 15-kilo log as high as we could, and let it drop on a 250-gram chipmunk. Then we fell, gasping, into each other's arms.

The results were predictable. (For physics-challenged readers, the term "explode" may help.) When we peeked under the log, we were flooded with relief rather than remorse. We took this as a sign we had done the right thing. We scraped the remains of the chipmunk off the path and resumed our walk, feeling very "Me-Woman."

For the rest of our walk, we talked about how our husbands would have handled this situation. We concluded the story would have been much shorter: Michael and Terry see injured chipmunk, feel compassion, go into woods, get big stick, hit chipmunk on head, throw it in woods, keep walking. No angst, less suffering. Total time? Two minutes.

Judy and I? See injured chipmunk, feel compassion, engage in heart-wrenching pleading with God to get us off the hook, indecision, go into woods, get big stick, dither, get bigger stick, pronounce eulogy, explode chipmunk, supportive hug, throw remains in woods, keep walking. Much angst, more suffering, but profound reverence. Total time? Twenty minutes.

Yes, we conclude, the chipmunk may have fared better physically with the men, but under our watch, it died knowing it was cared for. But we're left with a niggling feeling—what if the chipmunk had to choose? We quickly agreed it was sometimes good to have a man around.

Women and men react to and perceive the world differently. You may have heard the analogy of a man and a woman sitting side by side in the same theatre but walking out having seen entirely different movies. A wonderful example of gender-based worldviews is a study done by Linda Duxbury, from Carleton University, who looked at women's and men's perspectives in the workplace.[1] (Incidentally, these study results have been replicated in a variety of North American corporations.) These people worked for the same company and had the same bosses, peers, and subordinates. Yet their impressions of the work experience were as different as day and night. When it comes to whether both genders have the same opportunities in Canada, for example, 75% of men said they did, and 31% of women concurred. And while half the men believed men have better opportunities for career development, 75% of women said it was men who have the advantage. Only 8% of men reported encountering assumptions about their commitment to their job because of their gender, compared to 30% of women. Another study—the "Closing the Gap Study," conducted by Catalyst/Conference Board of Canada—produced similar findings: Senior women cited the top issue as being "male stereotyping and preconceptions of women's roles and abilities," while chief executives (overwhelmingly male) identified "lack of significant general management or line experience."

Different movie.

CORPORATE ANGST ABOUT
GENDER DIFFERENCES

I've heard it a million times. "Women and men want the same, and current marketing is equally effective with both." I have two words for this: ba loney. There is no shortage of studies proving gender-based consumer differences in perceptions, attitudes, priorities, and communication styles. What is particularly fascinating is the pervasive outright fear of marketing anything that even remotely hints of gender differences, a fear I've seen exhibited by many senior corporate types. Often, these people tell me that "marketing to women" is discriminatory and anti-male. These would be the same people who drop a fortune going after the retirement market. I'm quite fond of asking them if they have experienced any agist backlash.

Fear of all things gendered, whether that means gender parity within an organization or external marketing, can only be partly attributed to unevolved or uninitiated thinking. Gender anxiety has its roots from a time not that long ago when many feminists feared gender-based research would relegate women to stereotypical boxes. But recent advances in brain and technological research methodology have sent this thinking the way of the Dodge La Femme. If your company still resists the notion that women and men are different, get out the metaphorical two-by-four and prepare for a thwack to the back of the collective head.

It is true, of course, that both women and men want a consumer experience that resonates, but research proves that what connects with women can be different than what works with men. And although we dedicate an entire chapter to revealing the multidimensional nature of women and the importance of not treating all women with the same brush, there are universal truths that hold. Martha Barletta, president of the TrendSight Group, says, "Men respond better to competitive or hierarchical ideas, such as 'bigger,' 'newest,' 'highest return,' and so on." Women tend to respond to messages focused on similarities and affiliation. "These differences can be used in marketing to great advantage," says Barletta, "or they can be ignored—at the marketer's peril." At a recent marketing seminar for one of Canada's largest mutual fund companies, the vice-president of marketing told me, "We don't segment anyone because invariably someone will always get pissed off." "And," I replied, taken aback, "what you are doing now doesn't annoy anyone?"

Another belief I often hear is that it's unnecessary to recognize women as a specific segment of the market, since women will respond negatively if there is any hint of lumping them into some kind of pink-collar ghetto. "If we spend resources on improving levels of service for everyone," say some executives, "women will be happy. We've asked our women employees and they agree." Intelligently recognizing that women respond differently from men and have different consumer experiences should not create the impression that women are victims or need special treatment.

Let's address the improved customer service argument first. As our research shows, women still fight to be taken seriously—something shown to be true in research done within the airline, home electronics, computer, home improvement, financial services, travel and hospitality, health services, liquor, and automotive industries.

As we know, both women and men complain about bad sales experiences, but it is women who often perceive this to be a direct result of who they are. It becomes about "me as a woman" rather than a "stupid salesperson." For women it's personal; for men, it's someone else's problem. Avoiding gender bias or even achieving gender inclusiveness is usually not even on the radar with standard customer service and sales training. And even though it helps, it still won't address women's experience of not being taken seriously. Generic customer service training has failed spectacularly in this regard.

As for the pink collar argument, there is good evidence that many of the female detractors of so-called "marketing to women" within Canada's corporations have been "raised" in the male model. Recognizing that men and women are different would undermine what they have worked so hard for—especially in those industries that are male bastions, like automotive and financial services. One example is Anne Nurse, who owns a couple of Saturn dealerships; she has enthusiastically resisted being singled out as being a woman in any context of her business. As she put it, "I have no intention of wearing my bra outside of my clothes." There is no shortage of similar stories from women in the top ranks of corporate Canada. "I got here just fine by playing by the rules," they say. "We don't need to shine a spotlight on women just because they are women."

These women aren't rabid anti-feminists or heartless. In fact, many are dedicated feminists who believe women can and must do anything they choose. However, these women often perceive their personal experience as the same as everyone else's, and since they did it "their own way" (which historically meant the male way), so should everyone else. They also believe marketing to women is often some kind of separate program that might appear inferior to what would be used normally. Nothing could be further from the truth.

If the women in an organization fear they (or more importantly, the clients) will be made to feel marginalized in any way, that company's gender intelligence is extremely low. I defy you to show me a woman who doesn't want a bias-free sales and marketing experience. What woman doesn't want a product that she doesn't have to modify or accommodate in some way so she can use it effortlessly? Think about sports and exercise equipment, insurance and financial products, public restrooms, airline seats, cars, erotica, tools—the list is exhaustive. Who wants to pay as much as 50% more for the same goods and services that men use just because they're women? Who doesn't want to see advertising that resonates with authenticity and actually reflects what's going on in her life? I'd be curious to meet the woman who doesn't care about corporate responsibility, inside and out. If a company's women are resisting a proposed gender-based marketing strategy, it's not them, it's the strategy.

So, while many men in decision-making capacities within corporate Canada regularly consult with their women colleagues before venturing out into this market, there are some who do so without considering women outside their organization. Big mistake. The women of "Bay Street" are not necessarily the women of "Main Street." The women consumers your company wants to reach may not look, think, act, perceive, feel, and respond like the women in the company, especially in traditional male-dominated industries. Imposing your company's or personal worldview on your market is never successful.

Liz Torlee, President and CEO of Kaléidovision Inc., used to be one of those executives who railed against gender-based anything. The people she worked with tried hard to keep pace with the needs, the hopes, the ever-changing frames of mind of the people they were trying to reach, no matter what demographic or other arbitrary segment they belonged to. "Ham-fisted communication and clumsy stereotypes insult and discriminate against all kinds of different people," she explains. "Our work was based on the fundamental belief that the principles of good marketing apply to everyone. Whether I was working with clients, international colleagues, peers, or staff, discrimination against me personally was simply never an issue. If I ever felt a smidgen of it, I dismissed it as an irritation and moved on. I can't stand 'victim' talk and grandstanding. As the first woman to become chairman of what is now the Institute of Communications and Advertising, I was told that 'chairman' would be changed to 'chair.' It was a nice gesture from a group of very liberated guys, but to me it was not only unnecessary but almost regressive. We will only make progress when things like this don't matter."

Torlee, and many women like her, believe women have made progress by what she describes as "wielding formidable customer savvy, threatening bank managers, Internet providers, and insurance sales reps with imminent extinction, airily dismissing those marketing dinosaurs still lumbering about in Jurassic Park swinging their Swiffers." However valid, this simply isn't the point when it comes to gender intelligence. After many long and enthusiastic debates, Torlee finally relented. "Alas, you're right," she says. "There still remains an alarming number of marketing campaigns where the lofty ideals of a brand that has been crafted with soul and sensitivity have met an ugly death at the hands of those with biased behaviour and stereotypical ideas."

GENERALIZATIONS—CONVENIENT BUT INACCURATE

Part of what rankles people about "marketing to women" may have its genesis in the term itself. The phrase "women's market" is laden with risk because it appears, at first glance anyway, to suggest homogeneity and a nice, neat, tidy market. But if women were such a homogeneous lot, how do you explain their representation in all four of the country's major political parties, or their participation in Catholicism, Judaism, Islam, or Buddhism? What about lesbians, or women who happily choose child-free lives? Plus-sized women (anyone over size 8)? Unless your address involves a cave, you are probably aware that women represent every body type, race, age, religion, sexual orientation, education level, and socioeconomic level. "Women's market" suggests a generalization.

More importantly, the term is a misnomer because it implies women are separate and distinct from the rest of the market, which may not be necessarily accurate. In fact, it is common within corporate Canada to hear women described as a niche market. A niche is a specialized, profitable corner of the market, likely small. That's an odd way to describe the 51% of the population who make 80% of the consumer decisions. Women aren't a corner of the market—in most cases, they *are* the market. "Marketing to women," for many companies, simply means being inclusive, virtually the opposite of separate and distinct.

Many would also argue that there are as many differences within this group as there are between women and men. In fact, there are tremendous variations in needs, attitudes, and consumer power simply within one woman's life, let alone among 15.4 million Canadian women, or between 15.4 million Canadian women against 15.1 million men.[2] However, recent research results have revealed characteristics universal to and dominant within each gender that influence how women and men behave, think, and communicate with the world around us.

Even so, we are still feeling the reverberations from the early controversial years of research into gender differences. This area of research is a minefield due to its complexity. But it's tough to avoid when you are writing a book about meeting the needs of women consumers. And it is what makes women different that must be known in order to market to women effectively and—more importantly—authentically. So, it's down this road we tread, but very carefully.

WHERE THOSE DIFFERENCES COME FROM

One piece of good news is that the raging debate about gender differences has shifted from "Do they exist?" to "What exactly are they?" and even "Are they innate or are they taught?" But it's not really an either/or answer. In fact, I suspect both biology and socialization have strong influences. Here's a vote for biology. I remember my friend Cheryl's son when he was a toddler. Cheryl and Dave tried to offer him a gender-neutral environment. They didn't allow him to watch television, in order to try to minimize stereotypical and potentially damaging influences. They gave him a wide variety of toys, including cars and trucks, and also dolls. And the fate of Nicholas's first doll? He immediately pulled the arms off and made a gun out of it.

Here's a vote for socialization—what's the first question asked when a baby is born? The process of gender identification begins with little pink or blue booties, and research shows how we physically handle and speak to our babies has an effect as well. It includes the choice of toys that we as parents make and the stories we tell. I grew up hearing children's stories that had a boy as almost every central character and where the top two occupations for girls were housewife and witch. Debbie Gordon, our resident Mediac, is an expert in the end result of how socialization (read: media) and biology play themselves out in our behaviour as consumers. She spends her days talking to kids and working with teachers and parents to help sort out this brand-consciousness-saturated world.

"Our society raises our sons and daughters to assume different roles, led in large part by the mass media," says Gordon. "We make men and women different by socializing them differently from a very young age. We teach boys and girls to behave differently and, since mass media and marketing culture play to stereotypes, we teach them to live in a marketing world that works best when brands play to those differences. Rare is the boy with an Easy-Bake oven or the girl consumed by Hot Wheels or an ad showing a male or female child with these toys. We continue to stereotype and pigeonhole girls and boys into sex-based roles led in large part by gender-based marketing."

Gordon points out that we are still far from gender-blind, despite the protestations and achievements of feminists. Gender continues to limit people's opportunities and choices. And as long as we still have widely popular influences like half-naked under-age pop singers whose version of female empowerment is based on their sexuality, women will continue to be seen as objects and body-obsessed creatures. As she says, "It takes strong parenting and independent, forward-minded individuals to move beyond those stereotypes."

Mallika Das, marketing professor at Mount Saint Vincent University, agrees with Gordon and goes even further. "Since women are the major purchasers of household items and food, general household shopping is considered part of a woman's role. As a result, girls are given more purposive consumer/shopping training than boys. Men, on the other hand, are considered more specialist shoppers."

HOW THOSE DIFFERENCES SHOW
UP IN CONSUMERS

Let's face it, the debate is fraught and risky. But there is one area of universal consensus—at some significant level, women and men are indeed different. Biology and socialization both dramatically influence the lives of women and men. Understanding gender differences plus having a cursory sense of how they may have come to be can be useful for marketing. Having gender intelligence about the nature/nurture debate means you can translate this knowledge into your marketing. It can make the difference between those who lead and those who follow. So let's look at how some of these differences play out in the consumer experience.

Case in point: Is it biological reality that women be size 2 and wrinkle-less, or is it social conditioning (i.e., media and advertising) that contributes to this desire? Understanding the difference between what's real and what's a societal expectation has led some companies to lob direct hits at their own industry for unrealistic advertising. Some have consciously avoided portraying women as a pack of tittering fools who buy a lipstick to transform themselves magically into fashion models.

In fact, some of the finest advertising targeting women has been produced by Benjamin Vendramin, classically trained artist and graduate of the Ontario College of Art. His work has garnered more than 150 awards around the world and is even included in the permanent collection at the Royal Ontario Museum. He says being an artist is why his "feminine side" is so evolved.

Vendramin says, "Cosmetics are very personal to women. When we were re-launching Shoppers Cosmetics, it was critical that our message ring true. Instead of playing off the physical benefit of cosmetics—looking good—we focused on the emotional benefit—confidence. The spot opens on a woman in her 40s applying makeup. As she peers into the mirror, she is confronted with society's 'beauty judges': a dietician who claims he has a new miracle diet, a supermodel who exclaims 'You will never be as beautiful as me' and a 'typical guy' who says, 'Sorry, I'm into blondes.' Each one of these reflections she blows off literally or blows up with a piercing look. Finally, the reflection is of only her, and she finishes applying her makeup, smiles, and walks off. We then cut to a super that says, 'Confidence is beautiful.' Vendramin sums up his intention: "We went out and challenged the superficial, societal view of beauty because we wanted to drive home a greater, less superficial meaning of beauty: 'Empowering versus enslaving.'"

Cosmetics companies are, of course, not the only suspects in creating an unrealistic image of femininity. But some women's magazines notorious for perpetuating unnervingly thin body ideals are starting to give their heads a collective shake. In 2000, a British voluntary body made up of editors, stylists, and photographers established a voluntary code agreed to by editors to "banish anorexic models and girls of a certain age." In the U.S., *YM* has chosen to stop using models whose malnourished bodies would alarm any mother. Rona Maynard, Editor-in-Chief of *Chatelaine*, told us, "We insist on healthy, womanly models, and many readers have complimented us on our choices. No jutting hipbones or stick arms allowed (we like toned, muscular arms). We will go out of our way to book full-figured models—quite a challenge, given manufacturers' blind spot about cutting sample sizes to fit a range of body types. We keep pushing the fashion industry, but the old attitude that the only stylish look is skinny has been tough to dislodge." These examples of gender intelligence acknowledge what's real and what's taught, what's healthy and what's not. It's this kind of intelligent interpretation of gender differences and gender-based consumer research that should get translated into marketing, advertising, product design, and the sales process.

When it comes to the major gender differences that marketers need to integrate into everything they do, however, it turns out that a big issue may in fact be gender identity. Das explains, "There are, obviously, differences between males and females in brain structure and information processing, but how much influence they might have on consumer behaviour has yet to be determined. Until a few years ago, marketers did not focus on them very much. It is only recently that they have started examining these influences more carefully. Most researchers now agree that it is not the biological sex that matters, but more the gender identity and gender-role attitudes of the person."

We see this in advertising now. Old-school advertising is giving way to the notion of targeting messages to people's perceived gender-role identity—masculine or feminine—rather than their actual biological sex. There is increasing evidence that this gender identity and subsequent gender-role attitude (attitude towards what is appropriate for men and women) may be more important in advertising than biological sex itself. However, biological gender differences remain critical in terms of the sales process and product development.

In general terms, this relates to identifying the values and attitudes of your target market. For example, Das explains that ads and products aimed at men who are more traditional may emphasize conventional masculine, gender-appropriate roles, while those aimed at men who are less traditional may focus less on those kinds of masculine roles. The same would apply for women. So, for example, if you are catering to professional or managerial women who can be expected to have less traditional and more egalitarian views, it might be appropriate to show a woman engaged in a non-traditional activity or behaviour. In an ad for the same product aimed at an older, traditional female target market, the woman might be shown engaged in more conventional female-appropriate behaviour or activity (but remember—it always pays to be wary of stereotypes). To make it even trickier, the motivation for purchasing could be different. For instance, both male and female business owners identify with the characteristics and needs of decision-makers and consequently have more in common than if one considered them only in terms of gender. We'll talk about this more when we look at the nature of women's multidimensional lives in Chapter Five.

Also, women are considered more emotional than men. However, studies suggest that emotion is driven by context. Women are more emotional in an interpersonal context and men are more emotional in an achievement context. Look at shampoo ads. Feast your eyes on a wide array of images such as damaged, tortured hair that magically morphs to smooth, shining tresses, with technical-sounding explanations of hair DNA and some snazzy European guy named Alberto. Or those ads that are designed to evoke distinct and rich images such as women having orgasms in public washrooms as a direct result of washing their hair. Or the ones that guarantee women a better shot at getting their man or that put them on sun-drenched beaches in Hawaii. Now look at men's shampoo ads. Under a picture of a Super Bowl quarterback standing confidently in the centre of the page, there's a shot of a single shampoo bottle next to a slogan about winning. It's simple and direct, and it tells the reader that a champion uses this product. According to Chicago marketing professor Joan Meyers-Levy, successful advertisements aimed at men often tout self-expression, adhering to one's own values and beliefs in the face of adversity, or overcoming obstacles through determination and persistence.

Author of *Secrets of Customer Relationship Management*, Jim Barnes teaches relationship marketing at Memorial University of Newfoundland and is former Chair of the Bristol Group. "Customer relationships are not about repeat buying, share of wallet, loyalty, or dollar value alone," he says. "It's about how you make your customer feel, and the emotional connection the customer has with the company. Women are more likely to connect emotionally and be open about it. My experience has shown men tend to disavow emotional connections. Women will talk about comfort level, friendliness, while men will talk of functional issues." It comes down to this: Consumers, both women and men, prefer products and a sales process that match the gender attributes that they perceive to be characteristic of themselves and important to them. Frankly, someone has simply got to talk to the shampoo companies.

A GENDER-BASED CONSUMER BEHAVIOUR HIT LIST

I've come up with a list of some of the basic ways women and men differ, and put them in context for reaching that 80% minority, illustrated along the way with a few success stories. (Remember my caveat from Chapter One: For every one exception, there are five people that support the general contention of the finding.)

Women and men differ in the way they process information. After examining decades of gender research, Joan Meyers-Levy has come up with what she calls the "selectivity hypothesis": Men eliminate and women integrate when they process information.[3] Men focus selectively on a few cues and make their decisions based on general guidelines and categorical concepts. They often use simple decision rules, such as price or a salesperson's recommendation. They tend to be self-oriented and geared towards achieving their own goals. Men tend to focus on objective claims, and their stripped-down processing may frequently be fast and efficient.

Women tend to pick up all kinds of information, including what may seem to be irrelevant details. They tend to be communal, concerned both about themselves and others. They consider more angles and use more sources of information to make their decisions. Women process subjective and objective claims and respond equally to both. They also change the way they process those claims, depending on the situation. When there is more risk involved, such as investing in the stock market, they respond to subtle signals and focus more on objective claims. They try to get all the information they can before they decide, and give equal weight to their own experience as well as others'. Women are comprehensive processors who approach information holistically by using a range of cues and all available information.

"Women tend to be more intuitive and sensitive and possess the ability to decode non-verbal cues," says Das. They recognize, consciously or unconsciously, if they are being represented in advertising and marketing claims. They respond to colour, pictures, and charts. In other words, they look at not only what is being sold, but how it's being sold. Women pay close attention to the salespeople.

In fact, women notice absolutely everything. "Females generally attempt to engage in an effortful, comprehensive, piecemeal analysis of all available information," says Meyers-Levy. "Men are more selective processors of information, who tend to pick up on single, highly salient, or personally relevant pieces of information that are quickly and easily processed. They disregard the rest."

Why does this happen? Meyers-Levy believes that these processing differences exist for any or all of three reasons. One, the origin of these gender differences dates back to the dawn of humankind, when sex roles were established. Men were hunters, charged with completing a single, clear task, while women were primarily gatherers, focusing on multiple, simultaneous tasks including foraging for berries, watching children, and preparing meals in a communal environment.

Two, there are alternatively structured environments for both genders. As we've already seen, boys and girls are still socialized in different ways, and their resulting behaviour supports the gender differences in Meyers-Levy's selectivity hypothesis. Data suggest that these processing tendencies are maintained in adulthood. Three, biochemical and physiological factors may contribute to the differences between men's and women's processing. Scientific evidence suggests that hormonal factors influence the formation of different brain structures among males and females, which hard-wires males and females to process information differently.[4]

Meyers-Levy maintains that advertisers need to recognize that men and women process information differently, because the success of their ad campaigns often depends on the judgements and knowledge that consumers assimilate from ads. Men are less interested in taking in every detail and they may not be as prone to process layers of mixed or complicated messages and images. With women, advertisements can provide more information, encourage inference, and need not be literal. Women are likely to read between the lines, and to read an ad or watch a commercial all the way through, and they tend to remember and retrieve the message easily, assuming that they'd made any mental associations in the process.[5]

Reflecting Real Women: Shirmax Ltee and Addition-Elle. Some companies have already designed successful campaigns that recognize how women integrate everything. About 10 years ago, Shirmax Ltee started to look at market research and saw that sizes were growing upwards. They considered this a viable market for their Addition-Elle stores, and indeed the plus-sized segment of the market was not served well at all. Statistics Canada says that 46% of the current population is plus size—that's a market of 7 million women typically relegated to shop at Joe's Tent and Awning. You'd be hard pressed to find a store, advertisements, salespeople, information of any sort that represented these women.

Daniel Langevin, Shirmax's Vice-President of Marketing, says, "There was no relationship between the plus-sized woman and the fashion industry. There weren't any books or magazines that reflected her lifestyle. There were no images in magazines or the media of plus-sized women. Even when the first boomers hit 40, they were portrayed as trim and fit. Most of the salespeople who sold fashion were small. A plus-sized woman had to resort to buying t-shirts and sweatshirts in the men's department. If she wanted to wear jeans she had to buy men's jeans in her waist size and hope the rest of the pants fit. She'd wear housecoats, menswear, or muumuus. Often she would have to sew her own clothes, and there weren't even patterns for plus sizes. She would have to buy a regular-sized pattern and modify it."

Addition-Elle's website trumpets, "Awaken the goddess within." It's adorned with beautiful pictures of a naked Rubenesque woman. It breaks all the stereotypical images we see in fashion magazines: There is a buxom black woman in a sexy, lacy bra and panties; active wear is updated, colourful, and hip looking; a plus-sized woman reclines in a sexy satin teddy. There are sleeveless and low-cut tops rather than the "hide fat arms" variety. Low-rise, hip-hugging jeans, tight-fitting tank tops, hip belts and swimsuits. All the images portray women as sporty, sexual, and active— living full and exciting lives, just like everyone else.

Langevin describes today's plus-sized buyer as being no different than any other woman. "She is always making a time/money/relationship compromise," he says. "She is fit and aware of her health and body." But if you suggest that the way Shirmax represented women gave plus-sized women the opportunity and permission to be themselves, Langevin will object: "We did not give women anything—they gave it to themselves. We are not creating aspirations or fantasy in our marketing. We are merely reflecting reality. Historically, the plus size was treated as a special size. In fact, the plus-sized woman should be considered a mainstream customer, because her needs and wants are not different than any other woman."

"Your message needs to be part of your culture. So I am a big believer in making sure your message touches everything, because women notice these things. We produce an internal magazine that covers trends, styling, current fashion items, and design features to make our sales staff more knowledgeable and current. The store image and sales experience also has to be consistent with the culture. We hire plus-sized staff to create a comfort level, and because they are better able to understand the concerns of other plus-sized women. We also produce a magazine for our customers that is the only plus-sized magazine on the market.

"Our role as marketers is to talk to the customer in a language she understands. Traditionally, marketing has been considered advertising, but it is really the communication of information. It is education. We need to communicate information regularly at all levels and in all manner of forms to help her understand our brand and what it stands for."

Where did this understanding of women's comprehensive consumer approach take Shirmax and Addition-Elle? Their market share increased from 5.7% to 9% and sales increased over 150% in three years.

Details: *The Globe and Mail.* The way something is presented can have as much impact on women consumers as the thing itself. Look at how *The Globe and Mail* integrated this information in order to get more women reading the paper.

During a focus group, a researcher asked the women if the *Globe* were a person, who it would be? The answer: "A white male, 55, business executive in a suit getting out of a limo." Richard Addis, then editor of the *Globe*, kept this in mind when he and his team led a redesign of the newspaper in order to attract more women readers. He understood that if you make the *Globe* women-friendly, then the net casts wide and you end up making it more appealing to a much wider group of people.

Das says that in addition to using an appropriate model and message, even the colours, font, and background should indicate the suitability of the product for its target group of professional women. The newspaper's management recognized that to reach women better, the paper needed to introduce more colour, better photo essays, more human interest photos, coloured graphics and charts, and better visual direction on how to get through the paper.

The newspaper changed the content as well. More space was given to women—journalists such as Jan Wong, Margaret Wente, Leah McLaren, Heather Mallick, Johanna Schneller, and Janet McFarland are much more visible. There are more stories about health and science and about people. There are more features, more focus on home and relationship, and more humour as well.

The response from women was overwhelmingly positive. This huge investment in graphic design has garnered many awards and the *Globe* has maintained its market share and fended off competitors. The percent total of "Globe Weekly Cumulative" women readers in major markets rose from 38.8% in 1994 to 45.7% in 2002.

Women and Men Process Metaphors Differently. Some research suggests that men are oriented to the left hemisphere of the brain (the concrete, linear side), and women to the right (the abstract, creative side). Both abstract and concrete metaphors are processed better by people who are integrative processors (their right and left hemispheres "cooperate"). If women are more integrative, they might be better at processing metaphors.

What does this mean in terms of advertising and sales? It provides different opportunities for marketers.

According to Meyers-Levy, an advertiser can use ample cues to evoke positive associations. Women tend to use these positive feelings later to define the product. Meyers-Levy looked at a couple of ads for Evian bottled water. In one, a beautiful picture of the French Alps is accompanied by the words "Our factory." The text underneath runs for several paragraphs, filled with elaborate descriptions of this refined "factory." Meyers-Levy says this ad is oriented to women because it uses a metaphor, which requires a fair amount of processing. All the imagery, too, she says, encourages the viewer to build up the image of this brand. The text describes the French Alps as "one of the most pristine places on earth." To get the message in this ad, the viewer has to integrate all the elements, rather than pick and choose. In another Evian advertisement taken from a men's magazine, a picture of Olympic gold medal swimmer Matt Biondi dominates the page. The caption reads simply "Revival of the fittest." There is a total of 29 words of text. The other ad has 119.[6] Nonetheless, Meyers-Levy says that it's possible to reach both men and women with the same advertising campaign, but it will present a more challenging endeavour. (More on this in Chapter Six.)

Gender differences impact not only how one constructs advertising messages for women and men, but also the face-to-face sales process. Mr Muffler has created a strategy to attract more women consumers through its doors. We'll hear more from this company later, but one thing it has done speaks specifically to this point. Mr Muffler has trained its mechanics to use metaphors when talking to women customers. Mechanics are instructed to compare the car or part to something women would be familiar with, such as a lawn mower or a bicycle. Luc Charlebois, Mr Muffler's marketing director, reports that "women have really responded well to this and feel that they understand the problem better. They also told us they felt they are being respected and not treated like idiots."

Women and Men Are Motivated by Different Factors. For example, in the case of gift giving, when faced with a lot of information and alternatives, both men and women seek sales help. However, men are often looking to reduce time involvement (as a short cut), and women are often trying to make sure that the purchase will be a suitable gift. Training salespeople to understand these different motivations could be useful in their response to male and female customers. Another example comes from Linda Lee, who led Ford's efforts to improve the product and experience of women consumers for 15 years. She says women and men talk differently about safety. A woman thinks of safety for herself and others and, if asked about an SUV, will say she likes being high up and able to see everything. She means it makes her feel safe. A man will talk about the size and height of the vehicle, too, but he means it looks good and powerful. Neither view is mutually exclusive, but the top-of-mind issue is different. Lee says, "You need to listen to find that out." For other products, finding out what motivates men and women and catering to these underlying motivations is critically important.

As we've seen, things aren't always as they seem.

THE BIG ENCHILADA

So we know that women process the "little things" to a greater degree and frequency than men. When political scientist Roger Masters of Dartmouth College asked men and women about their political views and then showed them videotapes of politicians with various facial expressions, the sexes responded noticeably differently. He concluded that "information about a leader and the non-verbal cues of the leader are integrated more fully by women than by men."[7] Women notice the creases in your clothes, the tension in your voice, your tapping foot, the faint annoyance on your lower lip. They pick up more messages from posture, gestures, emotional expressions, and voice. Then, with their uniquely constructed brains, women are more apt to assimilate all of these disparate little facts faster, achieving what appears to be a clairvoyant view. Puts a lot of pressure on you if you're a salesperson (or a husband).

Women, on average, do not think in a linear, step-by-step fashion as many men do. Women tend to think in webs of interrelated factors, not straight lines. They explore the multiple interactions, the multidirectional paths, all of the permutations of the puzzle. Women consider more options and outcomes, recall more points of view, and see more ways to proceed. They integrate, generalize, and synthesize, and they tolerate ambiguity better than men do. They visualize more of the factors involved in any issue. And here's the big enchilada. The attention to detail and way of processing contribute to why women are more likely to elaborate on any negative emotions at the time they make a purchase rather than on any positive emotions. Research points to this factor translating into greater trend effects (the negative is emphasized more over time if the process or evaluation is repeated), with women showing greater trend effects for negative emotions and men showing greater trend effects for positive emotions. Simply put, it appears women may be more inclined to look for the downside of the experience. Besides being treated generally worse than men, women have their radar finely tuned to pick it up—what people call "women's intuition."

WATCH OUT

Since women show greater trend effects than men for negative emotions during the purchase process, while men show greater trend effects for the positive side of the ledger, it's crucial to check on customer satisfaction with women consumers to ensure that any negative feelings are dealt with immediately. Torlee weighs in: "Category by category, brand by brand, the quiet but seething anger of many patient women is going to detonate, and when it does, it will destroy far more than the female franchise. If marketers don't listen very carefully indeed, they will one day wake up and realize it's too late." Said another way, when women have a negative experience, 96% don't complain to the source—they just don't go back.[8] If for no other reason than this, the old expression of *caveat emptor* had better be extended to include "marketer beware."

There are countless areas where you could use a gender differences lens to create a gender intelligent product or service, but for the purposes of this book, we are going to look at three areas: market research, product development, and pricing.

Market Research—Best Friend or Worst Enemy?

The first step to creating a gender intelligent product or service is to ask the right questions. This includes making sure your interpretation is checked through an authentic reality—a women's consumer lens.

WE KNOW IT WORKS

Let's start with an excellent example of how shining a "gender differences" lens on market research can improve gender intelligence. It begins by acknowledging that women have a different reality than men while travelling. Half the world's business travellers are women, yet nearly two-thirds would rather order room service than face a hotel restaurant, according to a survey of UK customers by Carlson Wagonlit. Only 9% were prepared to eat alone at restaurants outside the hotel. Just over a third said international hotel chains didn't do enough to make them "feel safer and more confident" and 28% levelled the same criticism at airports. Safety was a main concern: lighting and security in garages, spy holes in room doors, preferring car rentals instead of taxis. Again, it's a different movie than the one men are watching.

Toronto's Holiday Inn on King used market research to find out, when it came to staying in hotels, what made women different from men (I suspect it went beyond preferences for being called "Sir" or "Madam" in an ad). In fact what they found was that women were more likely to add a weekend to a trip, value late check-out, incorporate leisure time away from home more often, view business travel as an opportunity to network once at their destination, and are more demanding for responsive service.

So the hotel introduced a travel program for business women with spa and safety features. They designated an underutilized restaurant for women business travellers, with round tables so individuals could talk easily with one another. They offered a separate express check in/out in a private priority club, with a security escort to and from the garage or room and, of course, valet parking. They offered a private women's lounge. They assigned women travellers rooms closest to the elevator.

Interestingly enough, many of these initiatives didn't cost any additional money. Was this enough to get women to come? Apparently. Holiday Inn on King didn't advertise in the first year of the program, yet the occupancy rate increased from two women per night to ten per night, a 400% growth. And it was strictly through word of mouth.

GET MARKET RESEARCH RIGHT

Market research is "the systematic design, collection, analysis, and reporting of data and findings relevant to a specific marketing situation facing an organization."[9] (Public domain polls and research are different animals—there is always more to those stories than the screaming headlines.) To do all that, you need to go through four stages:

> Define the problem and research objectives;
> Develop the research plan for collecting information;
> Implement the research plan—collect and analyze the data; and
> Interpret and report the findings.

Gender bias can factor in at any one of those stages, resulting in research that doesn't capture the gender-based influences. Innumerable companies remain blissfully unaware of the nature of the problem they have with women consumers, simply because they're unaware of the need to understand them. They may know something is wrong without knowing the specific causes, but if the problem is misdiagnosed, all the research in the world won't expose the missed business opportunity. Or, as Ian Lightstone says, "it all starts with the questions. If you ask a silly question, then you will get a silly answer." Lightstone is a director and founding partner of Maritz: Thompson Lightstone and past president of the Professional Marketing Research Society as well as the Canadian Association of Marketing Research Organization.

But because the "women's market" is relatively new, no one dares move until the market has been researched to death. This, as we shall see, creates a whole new set of headaches. You need to be sure your market research methodology acknowledges women. This might mean online polling or even just reviewing the feedback that comes in regularly through your customer service channels. But what and how you ask are only a small part of market research. Interpretation is the biggest piece, and if not done carefully, can be littered with landmines. There is some evidence that unless you surround yourself with the right people, market research questions and results are often filtered through a male lens and don't reflect women's reality accurately.

The same goes for the sources of your information. For example, a lot of market research uses administrative details such as warranty registration. But that information can often be skewed male. I recently came across a good illustration of this in the marine industry, which has trouble tracking the trends of female customers because the husbands or male partners tend to put their name first on the warranty cards. That means that the data are processed in a way that leaves out the people who likely have at least 50% influence over the decision to purchase a boat.

There's an added benefit to market research, incidentally. Beyond helping to identify how to make your products and services better, feedback from women can also help you refine your processes, because they tend to notice friction and suggest ways to improve sales or customer service delivery.

ASK THE RIGHT QUESTIONS

The key is to start with the assumptions about the problem. If gender isn't considered properly, the market research may miss the mark. If people know little about how to get and interpret gender-based marketing research, they may end up with the wrong information, accept wrong conclusions, or spend more than they need.

It can be as simple as the surveys used. With close-ended questions—the ones that offer all possible answers—people can't respond in their own words. These can be leading questions, or might completely miss gender-related issues if those issues aren't built into the offered answers.

Our research showed abysmal numbers for women's customer satisfaction levels with car dealers. But not according to Dennis DesRosiers of DesRosiers Automotive Consultants Inc. Now, he generally "gets it" about women consumers, and offers lots of solid data on the different purchase patterns and behaviour between the sexes. But one of his surveys showed no gender difference among the high customer satisfaction numbers regarding where people bought their car.

"How do you explain the lack of gender difference in satisfaction levels?" he asked, with a twinkle in his eye.

"The wrong question was asked," I countered. "Given what we know about women's consumer experiences with the automotive industry, the question ought to be about the "shopping" experience rather than the "purchase" experience. How many dealerships did women have to visit to find one where they felt comfortable enough to buy a car? In fact, once they finally find one that takes them seriously, they're likely so relieved that they rate the experience in the stratosphere." We knew the questions to ask.

Linda Lee, of Ford fame, offers an additional perspective. "Women always respond more positively on surveys than men. You should always be looking to have women happier than men as a true measure. I spent my last 10 years at Ford dividing and comparing research by gender and age and we never looked at the whole. It's meaningless. Women can be happy with the car but if you talk to them, chances are they may not be happy with the dealer or service."

"The very nature of the profession is to be able to ask unbiased questions that are not leading," says Lightstone. "They need to be relevant and sensitive to the target audiences' reality, and of a nature that a respondent can understand and answer honestly."

Unless you walk like a duck, talk like a duck, and swim like a duck, how can you know what questions to ask when a duck buys a car? By looking through a duck's lens. It doesn't mean that only women can do the asking and interpreting, but you do need to look at the world from their perspective. That's why you need gender balance and intelligence both in deciding what to ask and in interpreting the answers.

INTERPRET THE RIGHT ANSWERS

Interpretation is critical. People may blindly accept research assumptions without question, or may start with a bias that colours whether they accept or reject the results. In fact, people tend to accept research results that show what they expected and to reject those that don't meet their expectations.[10] However, as Lightstone points out, "there is a discipline that comes with the profession that one hopes should eliminate bias. If you are an honest broker, the impact of personal bias should at worst be minimized." Still, you need gender intelligence in the belief system of the decision-maker, as well as in the belief system in which the research process is founded.

The nature of research is to take properly gathered information, and to digest it and use skill in the interpretation. Skill comes with understanding the subject, knowing the sector and the audience, experience, and ethics. The facts have to be right first. Then, as Lightstone says, interpretation is just that—interpretation. You draw conclusions based on experience and what you know. You can always challenge interpretation. You have to make sure research and interpretation are done carefully, with integrity. One area where marketers get into trouble all the time—and, for the most part, the problem is unconscious—is the notion that male and female traits are polar opposites. But being different doesn't necessarily mean being diametrically opposed. An example from the investment business—one of those industries that typically has difficulty understanding women— illustrates just what kind of trouble this can lead to.

So many studies conclude that women have a more cautious investing style. This kind of statement drives me batty. It's in the same category as those claims that women are less willing to take risks because of their biology[11] or are more timid by nature.[12] The truth is women are calculated risk takers, which is hugely different from being unwilling to take risks.

In fact, this truth is borne out by lots of research. Studies on investors show that when male and female samples are identical, women's portfolios perform better. Once educated, women are just as likely to invest in the high-risk realm as men are. One Swiss Federal Institute of Technology study found that women are not more risk averse than men and concluded that gender-specific risk behaviour was more likely due to "differences in male and female opportunity sets rather than stereotypical risk attitudes."[13] Becky Reuber at the University of Toronto's Rotman School of Management agrees: "Stereotypes are so strongly held, but [attitude towards] risk has nothing to do with being male or female."[14]

A Bishop's University study quizzed 303 workers enrolled in a large company's employee savings plan and found that women employees had put 37% of their assets in high-risk investments, just short of 38% for men.[15] It concluded that women in the workforce are often sophisticated investors, compared to brokerage customers—likely the source of information in studies that skew women as cautious, and likely to be elderly widows.[16]

I think you get the point that in real life women aren't risk averse. But the notion persists. Researcher Penelope Wang says that "women are expected to be the more conservative investors and are consequently offered investments with lower risks, and therefore lower expected returns, than males." A gender-based study by *Working Women Magazine* found women are sold investments too conservative for their needs based on the incorrect assumption that women fear risk. And there's the rub.

Women's frequent inexperience and their information-gathering process make it appear as though it is an innate trait. Risk aversion is not about gender, but about people's individual situations. In fact, this assumption that women are timid and conservative investors is downright insulting to most women.

But the assumption is often corroborated by the way surveys and polls are interpreted. It's common for investment companies to survey their women clients, find a large percentage are investing primarily in guaranteed investments, and assume therefore that this means women fear risk. There are two things wrong with this interpretation:

> Chances are good their sample may be skewed. Some evidence suggests that many women who invest with stockbrokers or trust companies (the ones likely to do most of this research) are older, retired widows. Therefore, the conservative profile fits, but it isn't representative.

> The researchers didn't ask why women have chosen conservative investments. In studies that did ask this question, the number-one reason for seeking financial advice was having enough time. (This response tied with death of their partner.) Another compelling reason that women may choose investments like guaranteed investment certificates and Canada Savings Bonds is that they require little time and no maintenance.

Honing Instincts: RBC Investments. Graeme Harris, Senior Advisor of Corporate Communications at RBC Investments, hired a market research company to poll women investors and suspected something wasn't quite right when the report came back claiming—you guessed it—"Women Have a More Cautious Investing Style."

"While this data seemed quite juicy and suggested lots of potential from a publicity point of view," he said, "I was wary of leaving the interpretation of the data to myself when writing the news release. It seemed to me that we should validate these findings from the perspective of someone outside the organization who understood women and money." He came to me for advice.

One of the things Harris wanted to know was whether the data could be interpreted as women being more conservative investors than men. Although the results showed that men had a higher risk tolerance, the corollary didn't necessarily point to the conclusion that women were therefore conservative.

"The whole notion of risk is the degree to which one accepts it," Harris says. "And to understand any market you need to see it for its own attributes rather than in contrast to others. After all, you don't appeal to children by starting with the premise they are not adults. Women are a definitive market for financial services and our views on serving this market are shaped by our ability to seek advice on key elements that define it. This notion of comparing and contrasting in such a polar methodology gets you into trouble in any debate, and we took pains to avoid it when releasing our data to the public.

"The RBC Financial Group's annual RRSP poll in 2002 also showed that women were more likely than men to feel concerned about their plans for retirement and economic uncertainty," Harris says. "Despite their feelings of concern, women were not about to stand on the sidelines. Nearly 40% stated they were more inclined than in the past to look for professional advice, compared to 25% of men. So, how were we to interpret this data? With help, we learned that a strong gender difference may exist when it comes to the way women and men define retirement goals or financial security, and that men may simply feel more financially secure than women, regardless of the state of their finances."

RBC Financial went on to release the poll and framed the results precisely as they should have: "Women More Concerned than Men about Retirement Plans." The press release included a statement by Anne Lockie, Executive Vice-President of RBC Royal Bank: "Whether it is to meet long-term retirement goals or to help manage the family finances, Canadians are increasingly seeking professional financial advice, and women are leading the way." It mentioned women's financial competency and intelligent concern for financial matters. Nowhere was there even the slightest hint of women being 'fraidy cats.

Harris says it worked. "We knew that we were on the right track when our news release set a new highwater mark for publicity at RBC."

There are some major lessons here. I have seen dozens of surveys released in the last couple of years expounding blatant stereotypes that women are conservative and low risk takers based purely on the fact that men take more risk. As Harris also pointed out, it is important to stretch beyond your enterprise's worldview and talk to people to avoid interpreting consumer data flat-out incorrectly.

THE LOWEST COMMON DENOMINATOR

Finally, here is one last thing to watch out for in market research: working towards the lowest common denominator. According to Jen Bermingham, President of Strategic Navigator, "researching a piece of advertising often shaves the edges off an idea, leaving it accessible to the greatest number of people in the target audience but often less provocative and motivating than it might have been. This is particularly problematic when conducting creative research among women, because a great deal of the advertising targeted to women is specifically designed to evoke an emotional response. Yet creative research tends to work on a rational level, forcing respondents to intellectualize their response to the creative presentation of an idea. As a result, women's true, emotional responses to an idea are vastly misrepresented."

SO, HOW DO YOU DO IT RIGHT?

The first step to solid market research is to acknowledge that there may be gender differences in how your product or service is perceived. All too often a company claims its product or service offering couldn't possibly be gender specific. This is a common theme in financial services. On one level, it's correct—a stock or bond doesn't care about the chromosome makeup of its owner. But are you assuming too much? You need to ask if your external message is correct or whether the distribution of your product or service serves the needs of both genders. Until you specifically ask, you'll never know.

There are six basic aspects to gender intelligent market research.

1. Call in the Professionals. A professional can make sure the questions and research project are free of bias, and can help with the analysis. Hire independent market research professionals to work on the design, execution, and interpretation phases with your company's market research team. Bobbie Gaunt, former CEO of Ford Canada, says, "When I was asked to run market research in North America for Ford, there was not one research professional with a degree in market research on staff. Eventually retaining professionals and, in the meantime, using consultants were immensely helpful in improving the quality of the research and getting the organization to be open to the results."

When you consider the investment and the value of proper market research, it would be irresponsible on the part of the company to its employees, customers, and shareholders to skimp in this area.

There are a few general tips for developing high-quality market research:

> Get advice from your target group. You need to know how the target group views the product and the brand, what emotional attachments people have, how they use the product or service, what benefits they derive—and you can only do that by finding ways to get close to the consumer.
> Use full immersion. Use people—employees or advisors—who know the culture, whether that be gender, ethnic, or age.
> Always use appropriate interviewers, namely people with whom the respondent feels comfortable and is willing to talk openly and honestly. You need people who understand how to look for the innuendoes and who can pay attention to sensitivities, historic or otherwise.

2. Find Creative Ways to Listen. Expand how you interview women. Don't just interview them over the telephone—you can't read their body language or facial expressions. Plus they're probably doing two things at once and are not focused on your questions. Ask them to tell you stories, not answer yes/no questions.

Depending on your budget, there are several ways to listen to your market. One way is what Andrea Learned, creator of ReachWomen, calls "the listening event gathering." Listening events are structured to draw out feedback and feelings unlike anything you've ever heard in a traditional focus group. ReachWomen works with small gatherings of no more than 10 participants in intimate settings like day spas or bookstores.

Debbie Gordon shared a story about a wonderful insight gained from a piece of "grandmother research" done by her former ad agency. It was a very informal chat in her living room, the kind of research that would never be officially sanctioned because of its very loose design. A bunch of women were brought together to talk about their lives as women, mothers, and consumers. Gordon says, "These were all highly intelligent women who knew nothing about the brands in the category and their claims, mostly because their lives were spent on a treadmill, just trying to cope with the day-to-day. One woman, Renalda, confessed that her frenetic life had led to an ongoing lie to her husband. She had taken out a gym membership, with his support and encouragement, because it would allow her to get out, clear her mind, escape the kids, and get healthy. But Renalda couldn't summon the energy to work out, so she'd kiss her hubby good-bye, gym bag in hand, and then go sit in a coffee shop and just veg. When we met in this very informal research setting, she still hadn't confessed. This confession represented an intimate moment of bonding for the eight women in my living room. How can you pull that kind of an insight out of a quantitative study or a sterile research room discussion?"

In intimate gatherings you can zero in on specific brand challenges. You can avoid some of the set-up hassle and join in with a pre-existing women's gathering (book or investment clubs, for example). Don't forget the incentive, in all cases. Even a $30 day spa gift certificate can be enough of a thank-you for participation. Whatever the environment, and whatever the size of the company seeking insight, a relaxed, comfortable atmosphere generates the most authentic discussions among women. This open, all-female group shows respect and encourages participants, whether among friends or strangers, to delve into a deeper level of sharing. Furthermore, what a randomly chosen, 43-year-old Canadian woman, sitting in a comfortable environment with others, can bring to light about a product can be rather astounding.

3. Transfer Control. Research is usually done on the researcher's terms. The researcher decides when, where, and how to ask the questions. Some of the best research, however, is conducted on the respondent's terms. It takes time, confidence, and money (three elusive traits in today's marketing world) to allow this transfer of control to take place. The respondents choose the location and time and may even have some control over the discussion itself. Bermingham recently conducted in-home interviews with women who suffer from depression. "Only by entering these women's homes on their terms was I able to fully appreciate the closed curtains, daytime sleeping aids, and fear of the telephone ringing," she says. "They trusted me enough to show me the truth because I handed them control of the research situation." Shop-along grocery research is another great example of transfer of control.

Bermingham is often hired by manufacturers to shop with their consumers—what Ian Lightstone calls "accompanied shops," when the researcher can discuss the decision-making process right at the "moment of truth." Bermingham explains, "If I were to stage these shopping expeditions, conducting them when and where I choose, I would never fully appreciate why women spend more time shopping end-aisle displays next to the toy section of a large supermarket (where kids are occupied) or why they ignore the plethora of choices in the deodorant aisle (because of decision overload)."

Lightstone also conducts intensive in-home interviews/observation sessions to observe a busy individual who has just come home from a trying day at work and has to prepare dinner for a demanding audience. "No wonder so many households eat frozen meals or Kraft Dinner," he says.

4. Walk Like a Duck. The recent explosion of ethnographic research is beginning to address gender bias on the qualitative side, but many wonder how to ameliorate the misrepresented female perspective on the quantitative side. Bermingham says, "The only solution I have found—and employ when affordable—is to ensure that quantitative research is always designed after an insightful qualitative research undertaking. An astute qualitative researcher is indispensable in the design of quantitative research. Perhaps Internet-based surveys will be the solution. I like using them for women because they allow women to complete the surveys when they choose. Working women [is there any other kind?], in particular, are often willing to participate in a survey after the kids have gone to bed, yet they don't want to speak with an interviewer at that time."

5. Interpret Creatively. Top-ranked creative director Chris Staples was charged with redesigning the marketing campaign for Finesse shampoo. "The advertising for this product had always been about male affirmation—woman at the centre of a man's attention," he says. "Early commercials showed women catching men's attention in all sorts of exotic situations, from yachts to the polo field. We decided to focus on a more defined target group of women between 30 and 49, with average household incomes. In focus group after focus group, the message was loud and clear: Stop showing pretty models with no relation to real life."

To understand the role that hair plays in a woman's look and her relationship with men, Staples and his team decided on an unconventional research approach. First, they talked to men about women and hair, and videotaped their responses. The men told them that although hair is an important part of a woman's overall look, they rarely say anything about it. Instead they'll compliment her by doing something they think she'll like, something they considered romantic. Often these romantic gestures were less than truly romantic. ("On her birthday one year, I surprised her by hand-waxing her car.")

Then they got really creative. They showed the men's tapes to women— and the women were touched by what they saw. The women admitted they fuss over their hair because it's one of the ways they attract their man— "When my husband compliments me, that's worth gold." They knew that men aren't very good at romantic gestures, but they still appreciated the gesture. For these women, it truly was the thought that counts.

To update the strategy of male affirmation, which had worked for Finesse in the past, Staples decided to show a more realistic form of affirmation between average women and their "romantically challenged guys." As one woman said: "My guy's a goofball, and he doesn't really know how to compliment me. But he tries, and that's what counts."

The campaign broke virtually every rule in shampoo advertising. There were no pretty models, because the research said the target couldn't relate to them. There were no glossy hair shots, because the research said they were too divorced from the reality of middle-aged moms. Instead, there were men, with no women in sight. Goofy, fumbling men who love their women (and their hair), but have trouble expressing themselves. The TV commercials focused on a support group for romantically challenged guys, and the radio spots featured women's takes on men's attempts to compliment them. Tags on the shampoo bottles told real-sounding stories and invited consumers to send in their own.

The results from this innovative research were rewarding. More than three-quarters of women said the advertising made them laugh. Two thirds said the people who made the advertising understand the relationship between men and women. Over 90% who saw the advertising said it was a humorous example of how men sometimes have difficulty expressing their feelings. As for Finesse's declining market share, sales for 1999 tracked at 13% above projections. The campaign attracted a lot of media coverage, from daily newspapers and trade publications across the country, to production companies around the world that included the advertising in various "World's Funniest Commercials" programs. One TV spot brought Canada its first Gold Lion at the Cannes Advertising Festival since 1981.

6. Remember Perspective. Combining qualitative and quantitative research is ideal, as the qualitative provides the colour and dimension lacking in the numbers while the quantitative helps us apply our learning to a broader population. But one without the other can be dangerous. Jen Bermingham, for example, finds that in surveys women are much more likely than men to agree that they look for an appealing label when choosing a wine. "One could assume this suggests men do not rely on appearances when selecting wine," she says. "Only because of my experience conducting focus groups and shop-along wine research among men and women was I able to understand that men rely just as heavily upon labels. They simply aren't comfortable admitting that their wine expertise doesn't extend beyond finding an 'appealing' label."

Controlling the variables in market research can be daunting, but it will ensure that the product or service that you create reflects the needs of women. Considering the size of the opportunity, it's money extremely well spent.

Product Development—Yes, Virginia, There Is a Difference

During a hot day in the summer of 2002, my aerospace engineer husband burst through the door brandishing a sporting goods catalogue. (For those of you who know the engineer archetype, the level of excitement is indicated by how high the right eyebrow is raised.)

"Look, here's something I've never seen before," said Michael. "Lifejackets for women."

He described the details of the jacket designed to accommodate the contours of a woman's chest and torso. Of course, being Michael, he was more interested in the quick-release chest harness with a D-ring and the 500-denier Cordura® outer shell with the 200-denier oxford nylon lining, and the contouring made of bevelled resilient Winboss® PVC foam, not to mention the thermo-moulded padding and Hypalon™ surfaces. I, on the other hand, was stunned by the concept of a lifejacket that has space for boobs. What took so long?

I can't think of a more glaring example than this lifejacket of why gender differences need to be considered in product development. Here it is the beginning of the twenty-first century, and I'm seeing a lifejacket designed to accommodate women's "unique physical characteristics" for the first time. Could it be that women have just begun to venture into that strange substance called water? Was it only recently that they sprouted breasts? More to the point, women were invisible in the product development sphere. It's another example of the unisex debacle—one size fits almost no one.

Typically, the product development process consists of eight steps: idea generation, idea screening, concept development and testing, marketing strategy, business analysis, product development, test marketing, and commercialization.

The time to be on the lookout for gender differences is at those first two steps. Sources for new product ideas can be internal, such as engineers, manufacturers, and salespeople, or external, from customers, competitors, distributors, and suppliers. Ideas come from people, and if your people source is not representative, then you're missing the opportunity to address a market need. The objective of screening ideas is to develop ideas that will turn into profitable products. You need to be conscious of possible personal values and judgements that may filter out ideas of products or services that women consumers want.

So just how do you integrate gender intelligence into your product development? Depending on the business you are in, it can be incredibly simple or very complex. You consider all aspects of the features and benefits—including pricing structure and market research—of your products and services through a women's lens. It requires equal parts will, imagination, and brain cells. A budget might be required, but it needn't be huge.

There are all kinds of examples of gender intelligent product development. It could mean adapting an existing product or service to create a gendered product that is inviting to women, or it could be repositioning that product or service so it appeals to women. It could be starting from scratch, too, designing a gender intelligent product on the drawing board. When it comes to existing products or services, they may have historically been based on a unisex model or a male model (arguably the same thing). Or they may have been predominantly used by men, but women have been using the male version all along or would use the product with the right modifications. It's not about being only for women, but being for both women and men when it makes sense.

It has been happening in all kinds of places. I feel in my bones that we are at the cusp of major change. Compared to when I was growing up, women today can choose from a far wider range of products and services that actually acknowledge them as users. We're witnessing the genesis of a shift from the murky world of unisex to truly enlightened gendered product development. I never thought I'd see the day when the business class section in aircraft would include seats that comfortably accommodate an Asian female as well as a North American male. Or when critical care insurance products would be based on women's unique health characteristics. There are banks that sponsor international trade missions for women entrepreneurs, and movie theatres that offer matinees to moms and their infants, complete with lower sound and change tables. Did you think you'd ever see a sex shop with women-only shopping hours and erotica written and produced by and for women? There are tools and bicycle seats, both designed to accommodate women's smaller frames.

Take fitness equipment, for example. It was designed for men, and women's bodies just didn't fit. However, the newer generations are based on ergonomics and the amount of physical strength required to use the equipment. It uses pneumatic resistance and smaller increments, with a wider range of motion and settings. Seats on stationary bikes are broader and more comfortable. Interestingly, what started out as a way to make the equipment accessible to women has benefited a full range of users, such as older people who may not have exercised in a while.

An open, expansive approach to marketing and product development includes the possibility that a different reality might exist for women. And when you compare women's needs to how things are currently being done or made, the resulting changes can have quite an impact on your company's bottom line. Especially if those changes improve the experience for the male chunk of the market—as they often do. According to Paula Jubinville, co-founder and President of AQUEOUS Advisory Group Inc., gender must always be included in the definition of a company's market. "Different product features will carry varying weights, be more or less emphasized by women and men," she says. "Because women value something highly doesn't mean men don't. Other factors may have a higher priority, depending on who you talk to."

Though gender intelligent product development isn't exactly what I would call status quo yet, it's definitely trending upwards. Any way you look at it, having an intelligent view of gender differences in order to offer gendered products and services almost always nets the same results. Satisfied women customers and, often, satisfied men who have somehow benefited from the innovation. At the risk of sounding like we're beating you over the head, if you get it right here, you'll get it right in pretty much every other market out there.

STARTING FROM SCRATCH

Though there is no one solution for everyone and there isn't a detailed road map to follow, we can hitchhike a ride with some others so we can see examples of gendered products and services that work. Let's start with two examples of creating something new.

Time Out: The Supermom & Dot Canoe Trip. When Caryn Colman and her family moved to Temagami to found Smoothwater Outfitters & Ecolodge, they missed the choice and culture they'd had when they lived in the city. To satisfy her own interests—and to provide extracurricular enrichments for her daughter—Caryn started inviting artists and artisans to the lodge. Soon it became clear that these artistic, heritage, and recreational activities were good for business. Caryn and her husband, Francis, were invited to speak at conferences and sit on panels, and newspapers and magazines wrote about them.

"We had never worked harder in our lives," she says. "Like most working mothers, finding a balance between job, husband, kids, and oneself is a daily challenge." Caryn came up with the concept of women's programs: Women's Quest by Canoe, with yoga and painting, and Holistic Spa Retreats. Guests came running from across the country. One of the nice features of Caryn's concept was that not only did it not put any burden on her budget to offer these programs, but they also succeeded with almost no promotion—women's proclivity for referrals spread the word like wildfire.

"While I spent most of my time nurturing others and the business," she remembers, "I felt guilty about not finding enough time for my daughter. It is a fact: one has to make special time for family. It doesn't just happen. So I organized a personal canoe trip for a small group of friends and their daughters, and it was just what the doctor ordered." Surely, she thought, it would be medicine for other mothers, too.

"Here's the demographic: busy working mom, loves nature, unskilled canoe tripper, looking for meaningful activity with daughter, desires all-inclusive, convenient packages. Solution: the Supermom & Daughter Canoe Trip. Just arrive with your personal clothing and curiosity. Add water, gear, talented guides and four days of fun, loving nature, learning activities."

Caryn has thought about duplicating the success of these women's programs with similar programs for men. "But it is not about switching genders. I cannot imagine men being interested in a weekend of psychic readings, massage, pedicures, painting, and a bit of canoeing. I've asked male guests what they would like—they joke about trail clearing and construction. We see more independent groups of men going on trips than all-women's groups. Men like to be the first ones on the water, earlier in the season. Physical challenges and flirting with invincibility are tied into their psyche. Women are generally not as confident in their physical abilities, yet on our organized canoe trips, they rediscover their strength in body and mind through physical challenges. Women are surprised by these accomplishments. Perhaps men expect it. But bragging rights and a feeling of pride are real for both genders. And rightly so."

Assuaging Women's Guilt: Looneyspoons. In 1994, Greta Podleski moved into her sister Janet's very tiny house, into the basement, in fact, a week after Janet's wedding. She began cooking daily for the newlyweds, who were culinarily challenged.

Several months later, Greta broke the news that all of the meals she had been preparing were low in fat. Janet's husband (who had "mysteriously" lost two and a half kilos while enjoying Greta's flavourful meals) said, "If this is low-fat, you should write a cookbook. This is the best food I've ever eaten!"

And so began the Looneyspoons legend. Janet and Greta thought that others could also benefit from tasty, healthy, easy-to-prepare meals, and they were convinced that combining humour with great-tasting food was the secret recipe that would get Canadians on the healthy eating bandwagon. They knew that women were looking for real-life solutions that solved everyday problems. They intuitively understood that women wanted scratch cooking that didn't have to take a lot of time, yet still addressed their concerns about health and wellness. Greta says, "At the time, most low-fat cookbooks were the same: bland, sometimes clinical and intimidating. We felt that people didn't want to read a nutritional encyclopedia just to provide their families with healthy food."

So the sisters quit their full-time jobs on the same day, and went 14 months without incomes in order to work on Looneyspoons. Janet, the "domestically challenged sister," did the research and writing while Greta, the "food genius," as Janet calls her, spent $10,000 on groceries while developing more than 150 low-fat recipes. Unfortunately, when they shopped it around to prospective publishers in both Canada and the United States, they met with rejection. They weren't celebrities, they were unknown authors without a track record, they didn't have a literary agent.

Janet and Greta were devastated. At that point they were $80,000 in debt, they had exhausted their credit cards, cashed in their RRSPs, and even held yard sales. (Janet sold her car and her wedding dress at their "everything but the kitchen sink sale.") Instead of throwing in the towel, they turned to their mother for solace. "She said she would pray to God that he would send someone to help us," explains Janet. "Well, that's exactly what happened. A three-page article from *Saturday Night* magazine appeared on our coffee table. No one could figure out who brought it home. But the article chronicled the self-publishing success of David Chilton, author of *The Wealthy Barber*. We were so inspired that we taped it to our wall."

Janet eventually called Chilton, who, after tasting the cheesecake, decided to get involved. The three decided to form Granet Publishing Inc. to publish *Looneyspoons*.

The first print run, a whopping 10,000 copies, sold out in two weeks, and then went on to set a Canadian publishing record by selling 325,000 copies within the first year. Today, *Looneyspoons* has sold an astonishing 850,000 copies. In 1999, they wrote a second book, *Crazy Plates*, which has already sold half a million copies.

Then the phone calls and letters started coming. "I love your recipes," they all said, "but I'm so busy during the week, I don't have time to cook from scratch." Greta explains, "I was stunned by the number of women who told us they were defaulting to fast foods to feed their families because they were so time-pressed. But they told us they didn't want to serve their families microwave dinners, and began to ask, 'When are you bringing out food products?'"

Hence, the next stage in the evolution of their business—Crazy Plates Meal Kits. Greta says that women don't want to take food straight from the freezer to the microwave, because it makes them feel guilty, justified or not, if they don't provide their family with nutritious, home-cooked meals. "When we ask women what is the most stressful part of the day," she says, "the most common answer is 'What am I going to cook for dinner?' With our meal kits, we've solved that problem. All of the components are in the box and you assemble the meal, so you still have a hand in the cooking. That way, it's fresher and better tasting than its microwave cousin, and it only takes 10 to 15 minutes to prepare. We say 'It's cooking from scratch, but we do the scratching!'"

"Today, fewer than 50% of meals are eaten together as a family," Greta continues. "Mom might be working late while Dad is taking the kids to their soccer game. Families are eating on the run. This time-starved family is our target market. The time issue is not so much about time available to cook, but about wanting to eat right away because everyone is hungry. People are working longer and getting home later so they want to eat as soon as they get home."

The Podleskis realize that educating the public is critical. "Women typically read everything in the grocery stores," says Greta. "I've seen women take 10 minutes to read the directions, scrutinize the ingredients, and then taste the product. The man immediately tastes the product and if it tastes good, into the cart it goes."

Janet and Greta have targeted the evening meal since most people consider it the big, hearty meal of the day, the one that ought to be homemade. "People tell us they fool their spouses with our meal kits, passing them off as something that was made entirely from scratch," says Greta. "We get emails from men who are cooking for the women in their lives, much to the delight and appreciation of their spouses."

But could healthiness, good taste, and convenience alone create the overwhelming success these sisters have enjoyed? Chilton says no. "It's because this brand has an authentic face behind it." Greta agrees. "What helps makes our brand successful is that women can relate to us. Eighty percent of all grocery purchases are made by women and they're into establishing relationships. Our job is to make a connection with women, and we do this by emphasizing our 'sister relationship.' We are the faces behind the product. We're not an anonymous company. We answer every single phone call and email that we receive from customers. We do in-store promotions every Saturday, travelling across Ontario and talking to customers in the frozen food section of the grocery store. We connect with hundreds and hundreds of women. Everyone who buys one of our meal kits while we're in the store gets a free, autographed cookbook."

Greta points out that this is also a great way to get feedback from customers. They also use themselves, their families, and their friends as "test kitchen dummies." In fact, they use a local little-league baseball team—kids, parents, and all—to test new meals. "I send them home with my own makeshift meal kit, and ask them to tell me what they think," she says. "Did it taste good? Was it easy to prepare? Were the directions clear?

How were the portion sizes? Did your family love it? These are all questions that I want answered. But taste is my priority."

"Our goal is to help Canadians eat more healthfully," she explains. "When people meet us, they tell us they see two things: passion and sincerity. We're honest. We want to be authentic, real, and truthful. We would never make a claim about how we could single-handedly change your life or provide some kind of miraculous instant weight loss. We prefer to underpromise and overdeliver. I want to wake up every day and be part of a business that adds value to people's lives."

"Women trust Janet and Greta," adds Chilton. "People believe them because they've experienced the quality of their recipes."

The Podleskis' successful formula of saving women time coupled with brand authenticity has paid off in spades. Their meal kits recently won the Canadian Grand Prix New Product Awards in the Best New Entrée and the Best All-Canadian Grocery Food Product categories. They are also the first frozen entrée to meet the criteria for the coveted Heart and Stroke Foundation's Health Check program.

Women on the Radar: Lester B. Pearson International Airport.
Women air travellers represent almost half of the people travelling through Toronto's Pearson Airport. They're at the centre of the radar screen of the architects—two of whom are women—in charge of building the airport's $4.4 billion new terminal. As a result, says Lloyd McCoomb, Pearson's general manager, "women are favoured in the design. The lead architect travels all over the world and she knows the needs of women travellers. I fight and lose to these women all the time."

Laura Ettleman, Associate Partner, Skidmore, Owings & Merrill, part of the joint venture Airport Architects Canada, says that having women on the team means they instinctively include things that are important to women travellers and employees. "Women think differently than men about some things and we integrated those things into the design," she explains. "Baggage carts are plentiful, well located, and easily accessed and returned. There are more moving walkways, big enough for strollers and carry-on luggage. All space has been very well lit, because women in particular are uncomfortable when lighting is inadequate, especially in staircases and secondary corridors as well as the garage. Every check-in counter and public phone has a purse shelf. Of course, women and men use it for briefcases and the like."

There's more space between seats and aisles in waiting areas—good for people travelling with children. They're making the terminal oriented towards families, with an art program and children's activity centres.

"As a father of grown girls and a grandfather," says Lou Turpin, the airport's CEO, "I've experienced travelling in airports as a family man and have first-hand experience with safety. I panic at the thought of sending my granddaughter into a washroom without any adult supervision, while I have to stand outside waiting." After studying hundreds of designs from around the world, he decided on a separate family washroom concept where everyone is welcomed. Washroom areas are easily located and well distributed throughout the terminal area, with careful consideration of the number of fixtures, particularly for women. Facilities are designed to accommodate baggage carts, and washroom stalls have room for hand luggage. Women's washrooms have a continuous shelf above the sink and counter areas for purses and other personal effects. All washrooms contain space for baby changing, away from the main counter areas, as well as an additional family washroom. This addition can easily accommodate two adults, in case one requires aid, and provides a more private location for changing or nursing babies. Washrooms are located on every level in the parking garage.

Even the wayfinding system (the signs and system for navigating through the airport) was heavily tested with a wide variety of potential users, including men and women of all sizes, disabilities, and age (an aging population was also identified as primary users of the airport). Electric carts, comfort, and space were all very important to the design. Ettleman and her colleagues considered the distribution, location, access, and variety of everything from telephones to retail areas to ensure the overall goal of making the terminal "passenger friendly." As she says, they "went in wanting 'better than average' in terms of the usual airport standards and worked to meet or exceed that goal."

THINKING DIFFERENTLY

Caryn Colman, the Podleski sisters, and the architects working on Pearson's new terminal have come up with successful gender-inclusive products from the ground up. It's not hard to find stories of companies coming to realize that it might only take a little shift in thinking to reposition their products and services so they're more useful and appealing to women.

A Wide Product View: Schleese Saddlery. A horse show judge was having recurring painful bladder infections from riding. When she went to Schleese Saddlery for help, the light bulb went on. Women are 95% of this company's clientele, and women's anatomy hindered them from riding properly in a conventional saddle, which is designed for men. Because of the angle of women's hip articulation, the width of their pubic bones, and the depth of their seat bones, women fight the saddle—the very tool that is supposed to help them to achieve the proper position.

The Schleeses came up with a design that allows women to maintain the proper position so they can concentrate on riding properly, rather than straining to avoid pain. They used their plaster cast method, which takes each individual's anatomy into consideration, to design a saddle with a specially located air pocket. Did it work? Sales for the Schleese saddles have increased over the last five years by almost 150 percent, and they have quadrupled their workspace. They supply saddles to the U.S. and Canadian Olympic equestrian teams. They won an Award of Merit from the Ontario Chamber of Commerce in 1997. Even the *Wall Street Journal* and the Discovery Channel have found their story compelling enough to profile them.

And here's the additional bonus: Not only did women find this innovative design feature attractive, but men also loved it.

Chocolate for Women: Nestlé's Aero Bar. Imagine the prospect of spending a couple of hours researching one of my favourite food groups, chocolate. I love my work.

Elizabeth Frank, Nestlé's marketing manager, says there was a loud "Aha!" when they studied heavy users of Aero bars and discovered that women eat theirs piece by piece, savouring the "effortless melting" of the bubbly chocolate. (They define "heavy" as a habit of up to five a week.) When they asked what they would choose if they couldn't have an Aero, many women had difficulty answering. "Woman want the warm, melty experience," explains Frank. It requires patience. Men, on the other hand, tend to consume for hunger and like chunky or chewy bars. Women also like products in pieces, like Smarties or small, wrapped bars, so they can—allegedly—portion it out to share or save for later. Nestlé's research shows they usually eat the whole thing anyway.

Nestlé recently launched the first new Aero commercial in 10 years. It features two women eating an Aero, with one admonishing the other when she tries to bite it rather than let it melt in her mouth. While the campaign doesn't suggest men can't eat Aero bars, it does specifically highlight one of the reasons women said they liked eating the chocolate bar: It provides a brief respite from a busy day. Nestlé purposely avoided suggesting it will change your life, transport you to another world, or make you more sexually attractive. Instead, it portrays eating a chocolate bar realistically, as something for the moment—part of a balanced lifestyle—without implying it's sinful or something to feel guilty about.

In fact, most chocolate products are split relatively evenly between men and women consumers; a 60/40 split is considered heavy skewing. Among the top 10 bars, Aero has the highest level of "over-development of women." Ted Rideout, Director of Visual Properties for Nestlé, says that "the target and the user have always been women for as long as I have known the product. The bubbles have always been the attribute used as a means of talking to the consumer. Also, the curving movement to the logotype has a natural appeal to women. We all have a natural affinity to objects and visuals that have similarities to our own basic physiology. This holds true in industrial design, architecture, and fashion, and in packaging. The project here was to rejuvenate, update, and strengthen the look of the brand on the shelf. If the new logotype emphasized the sensory/sensual nature of the product, the next logical step in design was to build on that. Thus, the colour saturation speaks to a greater taste expectation. We were able to emphasize whom the product was for, the taste experience, and the unique product attribute (the bubbles), all the while making the package more modern and giving it greater shelf impact—particularly when merchandised in a sea of graphic design maleness."

Aero's results have been terrific. They coincide with a dramatic increase in brand awareness among the target audience of adults between the ages of 18 and 34. Sales went up 42% within the first three months of the redesign, and the total brand ranking increased from the eighth position at the end of 2001 to the second position behind Kit Kat.

MAKING THINGS DIFFERENT

There are plenty of products out there that may have been intended for everyone, but are really designed for men. But as companies are recognizing the differences between the sexes, they are going back to the drawing board.

Clear the Air: Tim Hortons. Here's a short, clear tale of taking something that already exists and expanding its appeal in a breath. Tim Hortons wanted to attract more women in its coffee shops. However, having to flail your arms to create a tunnel of breathable air through the clouds of smoke (produced, incidentally, by the 99.9% male clientele) and high-fat fare were major obstacles to women. Tim Hortons went no-smoking, introduced much healthier food choices, and gave the stores a more open, friendly, and clean design. Women came en masse and they brought their children. Of course, more men weren't far behind.

On the Road: Ford Windstar. As Linda Lee, formerly of Ford's Women's Marketing and Product Office, says, "Automobiles are not like running shoes—you cannot design a car just for women. Instead, you need to find ways to create adaptability and adjustable features of the product." Things like height adjusters on shoulder belts, increasing the range of seat adjustments, and adjustable pedals. You need to get close to the woman consumer to find out how she uses her car and what she wants. This includes moving the glovebox latch so she can reach from the driver's seat, designing running boards on SUVs so they're easier to get in and out of, installing exterior security lighting, making lift gates and grab handles effortless to use.

The Windstar team serendipitously had a higher proportion of young women on it than most of Ford's product teams. Several happened to be pregnant, too, and they integrated product features they thought "Windstar Moms" would appreciate. "You don't always get people assigned to a product team who would be potential customers," says Lee. The result? Soft lighting that won't waken a baby, storage bins that can hold diapers, power ports for video/CD players, a personal safety system with sensors for crash severity, personalized settings for the positions of seat belts, driver's seat, and even tires.

Men benefit from these features, too. Says Lee, "Being flexible has enhanced our ability to compete globally—if you look at stature, for example, many men from other parts of the world are more likely to want the ability to adjust seats, belts, and pedals."

Before she left Ford, Lee worked on a future concept car/van to reflect a familiar reality. Families are often on the go from morning until night, kids in tow, mealtimes on the run. They're in the car at all times of the day or night. In a joint project with Maytag, Ford developed a Windstar model that had a small refrigerator, a microwave, heated and cooled cup holders, and a wet-dry vacuum cleaner. The response at the auto shows was "incredible." It might be some time before these features become commonplace, but road warriors, families, and people with special needs alike see great advantages in being able to keep food or medicine hot or cold, to vacuum up a spill, or heat up a nutritious meal instead of stopping for fast food.

Pricing—Fair Is Fair

Another area to focus a gender difference lens on is in the realm of pricing. Case in point: David Liu, a Chinese-born Canadian, walks into a downtown Halifax hair salon. The stylist is ringing up the charge of $30 for Patrick White's haircut. Mr. White is a Caucasian with straight, short hair, which took about half an hour to cut and blow dry. Mr. Liu settles into the stylist's chair. His hair, straight and short, also takes about half an hour to get cut and blow dried. After, the stylist charges him $45, explaining that there's a different charge for Asians. Unimaginable? Perhaps. But a huge number of companies charge particular groups based solely on a similarly irrelevant characteristic. That characteristic is gender.

Women in North America pay as much as 50% more for goods and services such as haircuts, alterations, cars, cosmetics, contracting services, and dry cleaning. According to consumer advocate Aaron Freeman, "Gender-based pricing certainly falls within the legal definition of discrimination, and the practice is completely inconsistent with contemporary attitudes regarding gender and equality." More obvious forms of sex discrimination—denied job opportunities, or inequal pay for equal work—may seem to have a greater economic and social impact, but each nickel and dime of gender-based pricing has a huge impact in the aggregate. Canadian women comprise nearly two-thirds of the market, spending nearly $2.5 billion on hair services each year. Gender-based pricing costs women up to $750 million annually, and that's just for haircuts. And of course, women pay again in many other sectors where gender-based pricing has been shown to exist—new and used cars, dry cleaning, alterations, clothing, and others. When all sectors are considered, the total for what I call the "gender tax" in Canada must be billions of dollars. In the U.S., the Assembly Committee on Consumer Protection reported that adult women pay a gender tax of US$1,351 annually; that adds up to about $15 billion for all women in California.[17]

A SAMPLING OF GENDER-BASED PRICING

In 1996, The Thomas Yaccato Group surveyed hair salons in four cities. We conducted random surveys in 243 salons in Toronto, Montreal, Saskatoon, and Vancouver. Each one was asked how much the top stylist charges for a basic wash, cut, and style for a woman with short hair; then each was asked for the price of a cut of identical specifications for a man.

GENDER-BASED PRICING IN CANADIAN HAIR SALONS

	Saskatoon	Vancouver	Toronto	Montreal
Number of salons surveyed	45	29	99	70
% of salons using gender-based pricing	76%	55%	84%	79%
% difference between prices*	35%	29%	54%	55%

*Women were, of course, charged more than men.

Clearly, gender-based pricing is widespread. Moreover, while you might think gender-based pricing would be more prevalent among more expensive salons, we found only a slight rise at the higher end of the market.

I remember a story told to me by the late Shaughnessy Cohen, who was Vice-Chair of the Federal Liberal Women's Caucus and a criminal lawyer by training. "I took on a dry cleaner's a few years back when I discovered I was paying 'women's pricing' to have my court shirts cleaned. What made this so ironic was that court shirts only came in men's sizes. My male counterparts were charged 80¢ to have their shirts cleaned and I was being charged $2.50. Even after I explained this to the cleaners, they still refused to lower the price. I ended up giving my shirts to a male colleague who took them in with his shirts."

The well-worn argument used by many places is that it costs more to provide services to women. But when such arguments have been challenged by regulators or in lawsuits, they usually haven't prevailed. In a settlement with the U.S. Office of Human Rights, the Metropolitan Drycleaners Association wrote that it's "inappropriate" for its members to "charge separate or different prices for the laundering or finishing of shirts and blouses based in any way on size, placement of buttons, whether it is a man's or woman's shirt or whether it is brought in for service by a man or a woman."

Even so, the same thing happens with all kinds of services. Research has found that department stores hem men's pants for free but charge women to do the same thing.[18] Car dealers have been found charging discriminatory pricing: Women are quoted higher prices at the beginning of the bargaining process and end up paying more than men—with women of colour paying the most.[19]

Speaking of cars, there is a one-in-three chance of women overpaying for auto repairs, according to the Automobile Protection Association. APA president George Iny believes unequivocally that "vulnerability" plays a part and says some people working in the repair industry think that seniors and recent immigrants are also vulnerable. "Given that most people working in large chain store repair shops are on some sort of commission or incentive program, they can be acutely aware of how to assess the insecurity level and economic resources of customers—often based on appearance. If you're uncertain or inexperienced, if your car isn't in running condition, if you're unknowledgeable, you may find yourself paying more or paying for unnecessary services."

Even when it comes to deodorant, women can pay up to 50% more. My local drugstore offers 11 different scents of Lady Speed Stick at 50 grams and 15 different Mennen Speed Sticks for men at 75 grams, both priced at $2.99. A representative of Colgate-Palmolive Canada told me that the wholesale costs of women's deodorant are higher because they use more expensive fragrances. (Women's "Country Fresh" costs more than men's "Fresh Surf"?) She said that the unscented version was "price equalized" with the scented versions, and that the "ergonomically designed" Lady Speed Stick was smaller because women use less (men's armpits are larger and have more hair). "Men and women thus use up the deodorant at roughly the same rate," she said, "so they get equal treatment." I don't buy it—and neither do most women I know. They use men's rather than women's deodorant, and get much more for the same price.

I've heard some ridiculous excuses for gender-based pricing over the years. Apparently women don't understand complicated mechanics or technology. Evidently they're poor negotiators. And they come in different shapes and sizes, but one size fits all men. Anyway, since women's appearance is so essential to their well-being and status, they're prepared to pay far more for anything that will make them look more attractive or appear thinner.

Get real. A dollar in the hands of a woman should buy the same as a dollar in the hands of a man.

PRICING FACTORS

Of course, many factors determine price. Some are internal, such as marketing objectives, marketing mix strategy (target market and position), costs of bringing the goods to market, and organizational considerations. External factors are the nature and demand of the market, competitors' products, and the general environment, which includes resellers, the economy, and government influences. It gets tricky in the nature and demand of the market, where gender-based pricing flourishes. However, an example of where one could legitimately charge gender-based pricing is disability insurance—companies charge according to gender, based on sound actuarial principles. Women become disabled more frequently in certain categories and so pay a higher risk-adjusted premium. But for the most part, legitimate price differences are based on the amount of time, difficulty, or cost of providing the service or product. They are almost never legitimate if they are based solely on the chromosomal make-up of the consumer.

Many people believe the marketplace is a democracy and regulations that restrict gender-based pricing are unnecessary intrusions. Brian Doherty, editor of the Cato Institute's *Regulation* magazine, argues that if there's no legitimate reason for charging women more, merchants who do so "are only hurting themselves and will perish in a free market." However, the *Wall Street Journal* observed that "consumer markets don't always punish irrational behaviour. Some retailers can get away with charging more based on convenience rather than price. And many consumers don't have time for comparison shopping." Robert Kerton, an economist at the University of Waterloo, says that "price discrimination exists in the marketplace any time you can get more from one group than another, whether it's based on their wealth, or their degree of information, or their urgency. The question becomes, when you raise the price, does the person pay it or leave? It depends on the priority the person places on the item, how important it is to them." We've just gotten used to it because it's the way it has always been. "Until you have people asking the difficult questions," says another industry expert, "you won't see any change."[20]

THE LAW AND GENDER-BASED PRICING

If your industry is known for gender-based pricing, I strongly advise you do what it takes to separate your company from the pack. The heat is building.

California has passed the *Gender Tax Repeal Act*, the first law banning gender-based pricing as part of civil rights legislation. The act specifically states that "no business establishment may discriminate with respect to the price charged for services of similar or like kind, against a person because of the person's gender."[21] It's now illegal for Californian dry cleaners to charge women more than men to launder shirts that are the same size and require the same procedures. The penalties for violating the state's civil rights laws are being increased to as much as US$25,000—a significant deterrent to businesses that too often simply factor in the fines as a "cost of doing business." Victims can seek damages up to US$4,000. Other states are considering similar legislation.

We're not there yet in Canada, but I know the issue is burning in the hearts and minds of Canadian women consumers. I've been campaigning against gender-based pricing in Canada for more than 10 years. The momentum is gathering. For example, responding to the pressure (from me), Toronto's Alan Davis Salon not only dropped gender-based pricing but advertised it—and witnessed an immediate jump in traffic. Do as Mr. Davis did. Review your price structure with the view to seek out and destroy any hint of inappropriate gender-based pricing. You may be pleasantly surprised by the results.

PUTTING IT ALL TOGETHER

Once you have acknowledged gender differences in market research, product development, and pricing, you will find your path to gender intelligence. It will take you exactly where you want to go—to establishing enduring relationships with women consumers. As we will see later on, the incentive to do this lies in the rich referral opportunities that are characteristic to these consumers.

Clearly the trend line is heading where it's supposed to. Check out the following list of standards for evaluating products through a women's consumer lens and see how your products or services stack up.

WOMEN'S KEY CONSUMER STANDARDS: EVALUATING PRODUCTS THROUGH WOMEN'S CONSUMER LENS

Biological Criteria

Does the product need to be gender-specific?

Is colour your main point of product differentiation? If so, ask yourself why.

Can the product be modified or created to more specifically "fit" women's physiology?

Where appropriate, can it address women's longer life span?

Does it affect or address women's unique health concerns?

Does it support or interfere with a woman's life while pregnant, on maternity leave, or caring for children?

Social Criteria

Does it satisfy women's demand for information?

How can it save women time?

Can it support her many roles or does it serve only one need?

Does it respond to women's concerns for the environment?

Does it address women's safety concerns?

Does it reflect women's view of money as medium of exchange or tool to purchase rather than source of power and status?

Does it consider that women control 80% of the purchase decisions for the household?

Does it help women share information?

Does it pose a win/win outcome or an ethical solution, or does it "do good"?

General Product Criteria	Is it truly useful to women consumers?
	What primary benefit will it provide women?
	What existing products compete with it?
	When and where will women use it?
	Can it be positioned as a personal finance/small business solution (if appropriate)?
	How can it offer flexibility and choice?
	Can it be positioned to support women's self-employed status?
	Can the benefits be communicated in terms of its impact on issues important to women?

Market Research Criteria	From the outside: Are you talking to women consumers?
	From the inside: Do you have a gender intelligent team to interpret the research?
	Are you asking gender intelligent questions?

| **Pricing Criteria** | Is the cost structure based on sound math? |
| | If there is a flexible price policy, can you justify the criteria for charging different prices? |

Internal Company Criteria	Is it good for the company? Does it match the company's objectives and strategies?
	Does it deliver more value to women customers than competing products?
	Have you checked out magazines, television, stores, and websites targeted to women consumers?
	Have you observed women's experiences in settings similar to yours?
	Do you have the people, skills, and resources to make it succeed?
	Does your company's leadership demonstrate diversity awareness?
	Does your sales and marketing department include users of the product?
	Are women involved in the design process?
	Can you assimilate consumer information from various sources in your organization?

Does your system allow frequent innovations to address a constantly evolving market?

Can your product cycle be shortened in order to accommodate market changes?

Is it easy to advertise and distribute?

Putting Gender Neutral Products Through a Gender Lens: Ford Credit Canada. This is a classic story of what happens when you take a so-called gender neutral product and filter it through our gendered product lens. We were hired by Ford Credit Canada to create marketing strategies and product enhancements to benefit women entrepreneurs. At first pass, there couldn't be a more unlikely candidate for gender intelligent product development than car finance products. However, when we looked at the company's products through the Women's Key Consumer Standards for evaluating products, we saw that Ford Credit Canada had a couple of things going for it. Because it was strictly the finance arm of the industry (an industry with a terrible history with women) and had the right product, Ford Credit could actually help drive sales. Plus it had a marketing department and a president, Peter Sinuita, with the will and the vision to look through a gender lens.

We determined three main focal points for Ford Credit. The first is the paradox that although North American financial institutions are currently witnessing unprecedented demand for personal finance information, especially by women, car financing is right off the radar of most women. Our research showed that car financing is not viewed as a personal finance issue.

The second trend to consider was that 80% of Canadians work for companies employing 10 people or fewer. Small business is the engine of our economy. Ford Credit could easily capitalize on the strong tradition of entrepreneurship in Canada by repositioning leasing as a small business solution. Especially since Canadian women are opening their own businesses at three times the rate of men. Industry Canada reports that young women start four out of five small businesses today.

According to Statistics Canada, the one single event with the most dramatic impact in the 20th century was not the invention of the automobile. It was, in fact, women's participation in the workforce. This leads to the third focus for Ford Credit's consideration—women. Women are not only the common link, but also a major catalyst for both the personal finance and small business trend. As David Foot, author of *Boom, Bust, and Echo*, says, "It's actually remarkably simple. Companies only need to know three things about how their customers make decisions—gender, income, and age."

From this, we extrapolated the following: Take women's (gender) relatively new but significant economic clout (income), mix in an overall aging population of which women make up the majority (age), and you have a personal finance and entrepreneurial revolution.

We recommended that Ford Credit change its direct marketing campaign to offer more business or personal finance solutions, rather than create financial products specifically for women. By default, it would appeal to women. In other words, take the personal finance and small business approach, filter it through a gender intelligent product lens, and create very tangible programs that women can sink their teeth and money into.

When we compared Ford Credit's product features to our list of standards for evaluating products through a gender lens, we added two criteria for providing business and personal finance solutions. We could frame each product feature in either context. We were able to see the strengths and weaknesses of Ford Credit's product as it related to women consumers in general, women entrepreneurs, and women's demand for personal finance information.

It was very encouraging to see how well most of the existing features fit into what women typically look for in their overall consumer experience. The product also rated very high in the criteria for personal finance and small business solutions.

We suggested product enhancements such as deferred payment options when people took family leave, especially welcome since most women entrepreneurs have no access to maternity benefits. Since most start-up entrepreneurs don't know how many kilometres they'll run up, we recommended an option to buy additional kilometres at preset times within the first 12 months of the lease or each year at preset prices, rather than setting prices at the beginning of the lease. This disproportionately affects women simply because so many are in start-up positions, and research shows women consumers value flexibility more than men do.

In the gender-specific category, we reviewed Ford Credit's marketing material for gender-friendly images and language, and tested all the marketing material in focus groups. We got a clear sense of women's priorities for the product enhancements and could determine in what order to begin the process of implementation.

Ford Credit Canada recognized that a "lease for women" would have gone down in flames. Instead, they opted for an authentic understanding of how women's needs differ from men's. Now, anytime Ford Credit goes into a product development phase, they'll know the criteria for meeting those unique needs, which will—by default—improve their products for men, too.

ARE GENDER LINES BLURRING?

Yes and no. Though an intelligent acknowledgement of gender differences is healthy, in many other realms, it's actually good news that gender lines are beginning to blur. We see more and more of this happening as women and men continue to cross over into previously unimagined territory. Specifically, gender differences in language and styles will become less of a problem in marketing, advertising, and the sales process as people become more aware that they even exist in the first place. In this case, just having an awareness there is a difference can go considerable distance to smoothing the lines of communication on all fronts—the office, store, and at home. I know of what I speak.

I remember a moment when I was eight-and-three-quarter months pregnant. I was standing in the kitchen (good Lord, I think I may have even been barefoot) when my husband, Michael, came to the front door. He was wearing overalls, covered in grease from head to toe, as he'd been working on his car out in the driveway (a favourite pastime). He said, "Can you give me a hand? I need some help with the car."

I stood there stunned. I was actually being asked to enter the inner sanctum of guy stuff? I was thrilled at the prospect of what had historically been a male domain being opened up to me. Perhaps those lines of distinction were really becoming more blurred. I pictured being some kind of surgical assistant, handing him tools to help him do whatever it is he does while lying under a couple of tons of machinery. I was smiling as I waddled out to the driveway. Michael turned to me. "I need extra weight on the front of the car," he said. "Would you mind sitting on the hood?"

We're still married.

Communication: Relevance through gender intelligence

I can't pick up a newspaper or watch TV without seeing some kind of women-oriented advertising. I go online and there's a proliferation of women's websites. Not a week passes that I don't receive an invitation to a women's conference, women's speaker lunch/breakfast event, or some kind of women-targeted direct marketing. Everywhere I look, there are women salespeople where none existed before.

Many hail this flurry of activity as the dawn of a new consumer era for women. Alas, to do so would ignore that cogent point continually raised by researchers and women consumers alike. Why, in spite of all of the welcomed and legitimate efforts of so many companies spending major dollars to reach this audience, do women still have to do battle with corporate Canada to get noticed? Follow the bouncing ball:

> Women control 80% of the consumer dollar spent in North America.

> Advertising is big business in Canada—in 2001, the cosmetic/toiletries industry spent $170 million, the alcohol and related beverages industry $145 million, the automotive $918 million, the financial services and

the insurance industries $319 million, the book/stationery industry $4.6 million, the hair products industry over $74 million, and the apparel industry $27 million.

> Educating themselves about their purchasing decision is a top concern, according to 77% of women consumers.[1]

> The two most cited sources of information used by women are the Internet and sales staff, and 7 in 10 Canadian women online use the Internet to shop.[2]

> Half of Canadian women say companies need to improve their selling approach to women, and that they have felt discriminated against when purchasing a product or service or treated differently simply because they were a woman.[3]

> Women are more likely than men to elaborate on the negative rather than the positive emotions experienced at the time of a purchase.

> Women tell more people about their consumer experiences than men do.[4]

It follows that less money should be spent on inanimate information sources like advertising, brochures, and websites, and more spent on developing gender intelligent people. We continue to see many companies pummelled by women's experiences, transmitted by word of mouth. Service or sales forces that operate on a dated or biased paradigm cost big money in lost sales opportunities, often without companies even knowing it. So much is spent on advertising to bring women consumers through the doors, but it may be the company's salespeople who are responsible for flushing that expensive ad or direct marketing campaign down the drain.

Companies that don't address the face-to-face experience stand to lose considerably more than those that do nothing at all. It's ten times harder to go back and get it right a second time. Gender intelligence in marketing is valuable, but it must be put right into the hands of the people dealing directly with the consumer.

And if the economic power of women doesn't motivate companies to figure out how to sell to them, this will: Not only are women getting riled, but so are the men in their lives—the same men who also buy cars, mutual funds, stereos, and beer. Remember, our study showed an equal or slightly higher response from men in terms of their desire to see corporate Canada improve marketing to women.

It begins with creating a gender intelligent or women-friendly sales force. How do you clean up the inside to match the experience to what your advertising is selling? How do you change women's consumer experiences in order to stem what seems to be a never-ending public relations nightmare? We have evidence that if you do this right, the dividends are tremendous.

Is Recruiting Women the Answer?

It's a common refrain—get more women in the business and consequently create more women customers. Why are so many strategies to recruit women unsuccessful? Because in almost all cases, very little has been done to effect change within the work environment.

If, in concert with recruitment efforts, companies don't examine the gender messages contained in their internal processes—what gets rewarded, who gets promoted, what image is acceptable, how decisions get made—there is an increased chance that the women who are recruited into the environment will not be as effective as they could be. Many may leave, not because they didn't have what it takes, but because they don't find the environment a comfortable place where they could be successful. Underperformance and high turnover are costly in themselves, but other costs are just as real and affect corporate reputation and the inability to get a wider gender- or diversity-based worldview.

In my experience in training corporate Canada, particularly in male-dominated businesses, I've often found that women need gender awareness training as much as men do. In most corporations, male-style behaviour is the norm and is overtly or covertly rewarded. To succeed, women must assimilate into that environment. They need to become more like men. I often hear women in certain industries, most notably the investment and automotive industries, say, "I get so tired of having to be a man all day." So it's more complex than simply having more women staff in the business.

But does this mean companies don't need to create and position products and services for women as long as they have a diverse workforce?

They don't have to if there is systemic recognition that treating everyone equitably doesn't mean treating everyone the same. Companies don't have to if they're in an industry that doesn't have a challenged history with women consumers or if there isn't the perception that the industry doesn't take women seriously. They don't have to if the sales force doesn't labour under gender-based stereotypes and biases about women investors, entrepreneurs, and consumers. They don't have to if there is inherent understanding of how women and men's worldview and biology can influence what and how they buy. They don't have to if the company's sales force is representative of the market it serves.

But they do if their industry has ever dealt with even one of these issues.

Which brings us back to my earlier point about creating a gender intelligent sales force. It isn't recruiting women first or in isolation. It's creating an environment where women will not only want to come and work, but also to stay and progress. It's acknowledging the need for change, dealing with the attitudinal barriers, and recruiting wisely. It's fostering a gender-inclusive atmosphere that stems from having people who have an open and responsive worldview in critical roles. Combine all this with proper insight of women's consumer reality and your workplace will be somewhere where women will intuitively want to do business. And remember our mantra: If you make it women-friendly, you make it everybody-friendly.

Industry research from a variety of sources, including RBC Royal Bank and the Canadian Automobile Association, makes it clear that women don't care about the gender of their salespeople. However—and it is a big however—this assumes that the salesperson's approach includes gender intelligent communication and is free of gender bias. Case in point: According to the 2000 Canadian Automotive Retailing Industry Report, "Men believe that they can sell well to women and the comments we have received from consumers suggest that women have no gender preference from their salesperson. Perhaps this supports the contention that men can sell to women, but few have the necessary gender sensitivity."

Communicating Through a Gender Lens

A cornerstone of gender intelligence is understanding differences in communication styles and rituals. It also comes down to seeing the difference between information and communication, terms often used interchangeably, although they mean quite different things. Information is something given out and does not imply a direct connection to the consumer. Communication is getting through, and this means recognizing there are big differences in how women and men communicate, negotiate, and process consumer information. These differences play out in how consumer decisions are made and affect what information marketers choose to provide and how they provide it.

Let's take a look at the main criteria for gender intelligent information and communication that affect the method, quality, and type of information that you provide. These have a profound impact on your most important information distribution channel—your sales force. We'll also look at how to give out gender intelligent information through two means in particular that resonate with women consumers—seminars and the Internet.

The first step is to get through to women consumers by understanding gender differences in communication and negotiation rituals in the face-to-face sales experience. We mentioned in Chapter Two that there is evidence supporting the theory that women are affiliation-oriented—they are concerned with people's feelings, seek approval from others, want to create nurturing relationships, and strive to maintain interpersonal balance. Men are often described as achievement-oriented—driven to accomplish external goals, achieve success, and be assertive, independent, and self-oriented. Women want to get along while men want to get ahead. This is an incredibly condensed version of a warehouse full of academic research on gender differences. These particular characteristics are of interest because they have considerable impact on interpersonal interaction. In other words, the sales process.

My colleagues and I saw ample evidence of these differences in the interviews we conducted for this book. It was a struggle to keep the men on topic during the first 45 minutes of the hour-long interview and we invariably ran out of time. We would have to cram an hour's worth of material in the last 15 minutes. The beginning of each meeting was always spent on their biography and achievements. It often felt as though they were holding court. In the interviews with the women, however, we were always able to get down to business quickly and there was a more collegial sharing of information rather than a lecture. Just before each appointment, Judy, Barbara, Rosa, and I would bet on how the interview would unfold, depending on whether it was with a woman or man. We were never wrong. Soon we simply booked extra time with our male interviewees.

After 10 years of training salespeople, we have seen that a big source of gender bias stems from women and men misinterpreting each other's gender-based communication styles and rituals. The problem often disappears when salespeople recognize that a lot of the disconnect results from communication miscues, as we can see if we look at one example in the financial services industry. But let's look at this industry's "environment" first.

In the 1960s through to the 1990s, people within the financial services industry believed that women and men were socialized to think, act, and feel the same about money. They created a sales and service experience that was based on women and men having the same historical experience with the financial services industry. This meant that everyone apparently had the same power, the same experience, and the same education about money. Yet, when *Money Magazine* sent market testers into a variety of financial institutions in the mid-1990s, they found that women received advice that was too risky or too conservative for their needs. Advisors spent on average 50 minutes with men, 38 minutes with women. They explained investments more often to men, plus they told them about a wider range of investments. According to the researchers, advisors believed that women with less investing experience would be confused by the explanations. None of the men were asked to go home and discuss their investment decisions with their partners, yet all of the women had the request made of them.[5] In much of the advisor training, there was barely any acknowledgement of the financial price tag paid by women for their contribution to society as unpaid caregivers to children and seniors. This included the career cost of having to jump in and out of the workforce and the consequences on retirement savings. There was little recognition that women are avid consumers of advice and information and use advisors and salespeople as sources of information significantly more than men do. There was a long-held belief that the "know your client" rule would take care of complex sociological, biological, psychological, and communication gender differences, which put an inordinate amount of pressure on the sales force.

However, one financial institution decided to put its money where its mouth was.

RBC Royal Bank. As a new entrepreneur needing an operating line of credit I turned to my bank. Like most women entrepreneurs, I didn't have a warehouse full of widgets to secure the loan. In fact, the only real collateral I had was what went down in the elevator with me at the end of the day. I was prepared to do battle around getting credit.

My account manager, Kathrine, was honest and said there were no guarantees; she would have to circumvent the system in order to get me credit. However, a big step in my favour was that she was targeting women entrepreneurs so I didn't have to convince her of the viability of my business plan. To my surprise, within 48 hours, my request for an operating line was approved. When I went to see Kathrine to sign the paperwork, she suggested I also meet the credit manager. I'll call him Chester to protect the guilty.

"Chester," Kathrine began. "This is Joanne Thomas Yaccato, one of the bank's newest customers." Chester stuck out his hand and said, "Terrific to meet you, Joanne."

"Hello, Chester," I replied. "I'd like to thank you for your vote of confidence in our endeavour. I realize you had to go out on a limb to approve us and I'd like you to know I really appreciate that."

"No problem. You know, that's quite a nice little hobby you've got going for yourself there."

The word hung in the air. "Hobby?" I thought in disbelief. Kathrine and I both knew that had I been a man standing there with the same business and the same plan, that word would never have crossed Chester's lips. Both feeling incredibly patronized, Kathrine and I stood there stunned, shifting uncomfortably. I, for the first time in my adult life, was rendered speechless. On his way to meet another client, Chester said a fast farewell and quickly departed.

Everything crystallized for me at that moment. The issue at hand certainly wasn't discrimination; I had got our line of credit. It was gender bias in the sales experience. Chester certainly had no intention to insult or patronize me. In fact, he didn't have a clue that he had. Gender bias isn't some nasty overt prejudice. In the vast majority of cases, it's unconscious. The financial services industry and others are filled with Chesters.

It so happened Royal Bank was in the process of evaluating a gender-based sales and marketing training program developed by my company and the first pilot was to be held in a couple of weeks. Chester was going to be there. I scheduled a meeting with him beforehand with the view to help him understand how patronized I'd felt. I started by telling him my perception of the meeting. His reaction was swift. He was astonished and appalled by his choice of words. "I have no idea why I would use the word 'hobby,'" he said. "I have three daughters, for Pete's sake. I would never want them to feel put down like that."

He gave me permission to tell his story and went from zero to hero in 12 seconds flat, becoming my star pupil.

Next I met with the Executive Vice-President of Business Banking, Charlie Coffey. On the outside, Charlie is all banker. On the inside, no greater advocate for women and Aboriginal people exists. Feeling pretty cocky after my encounter with Chester, I wasted no time. "Mr. Coffey," I declared, "contrary to what you may think, your bank is no different from any other bank. You need serious help dealing with women entrepreneurs."

He roared with laughter.

At that time, Charlie was unfamiliar with this concept of a defined "women's market," but having come from a family that included five sisters, he appreciated the business case I set before him. It supported meeting the specific needs of women entrepreneurs through the usual means, beginning with a strong economic business case. But when I mentioned my personal experience with Chester, Charlie got very quiet. When Charlie gets quiet, I've discovered, run.

Charlie asked me to tell my story to the Senior Vice-President of Business Banking, Anne Sutherland. She understood the problem went beyond just Chester. How many Chesters were there? Sutherland approved a national rollout of the training program on the spot. With Coffey's support, almost 1,600 account and credit risk managers went through a day-long gender-based sales, marketing, and communications training. Though the Royal Bank has always provided top-drawer training to their account managers, it recognized non-gendered customer service training would do little to eliminate any gender bias and stereotypical mindset that may come into the sales experience. As Chester illustrated, it's tough because in almost all cases, gender bias is unconscious.

How do you fix something that you don't know is broken? By building a company-wide gender awareness filter into the system. We began the process of developing a gender intelligent sales force for the bank by helping employees acknowledge that gender-based stereotypes and biases about women consumers may actually exist in their system. The staff learned that women and men can, in fact, speak a different language, which affects how work get done. Staff came to understand the crucial distinction between information and communication, something women are very much attuned to.

Coffey credits The Thomas Yaccato Group with revolutionizing the way the bank does business with women. Why?

In 1997, one year after the first four years of training, the Royal Bank's market share of women entrepreneurs rose 10 points and the bank experienced the largest increase in customer satisfaction in the history of business banking—a 29% increase in satisfaction levels of women entrepreneurs with their account managers.

Language: Creating a Gender Intelligent Sales Experience

More than any other channel of information distribution, the face-to-face experience on the floor of the store is often the black hole for companies when dealing with women consumers. Some release a cargo net of brochures upon her head when she walks in to address her information requirements without first figuring out how to get through to her. Well-intentioned companies that provide veritable tons of information through every conceivable channel often see it all amount to a hill of beans. They didn't get the most important source of information right: the sales force. Unless this works, no amount of women-friendly anything—women's conferences, websites, women salespeople, women-centred advertising or marketing, no matter how expensive—is going to change one immutable fact: The whole thing can implode the minute a woman consumer sets foot into your establishment and turns to face the salesperson.

One of the biggest pitfalls for salespeople and marketers is in the realm of language. Though language is crucial in advertising and marketing, it can be responsible for completely making or breaking a deal when women speak with a salesperson. My advice? Go inclusive, or go home.

THE POWER OF A SIMPLE WORD: GENDER-INCLUSIVE LANGUAGE

Words are the basis of all thoughts. A complex idea or image can be created merely by uttering a single word. Individual words can pack a lot of power because of this ability to create very specific visual images. Let me use an exercise from our gender-based sales and marketing training program to illustrate.

We ask the group to reply "male" or "female" spontaneously when we say specific words.

"What do you think of when you hear the word *wimp*?"

The unanimous answer is invariably male.

"Battleaxe?" Female is always the answer.

Research, as well as our little exercise, shows that we often think in pictures and that there is strong gender identification with our choice of words. So if people react so strongly to apparently non-gendered words like wimp and battleaxe, what about words that are strongly gendered?

We then ask a true-or-false question: "People assume that words such as *mankind* and *he* apply to both sexes."

Surprisingly, most people reply "true." Historically, and even today, terms such as "mankind," "man," and "he" are supposed to be generic and are presumed to include both men and women. But research shows that this isn't really the case. Studies with elementary, secondary, and college students show that when the term "man" is used, people envision males, even when the content implies both men and women. This is why there is a movement to change the words to "O Canada" to be more inclusive in the phrase, "In all thy sons' command."

REWRITING TRADITION: THE UNITED CHURCH OF CANADA

The United Church of Canada put everything it did under a gender microscope, resulting in a wide-angle worldview lens. This exercise was spearheaded by Anne Martin, who heads the Ministry with Women at the church's head office, spurred by the results of a 1996 survey conducted by the Committee on Sexism. As Martin says, the gender-based Just Language survey found that "language was the top issue primarily because our male-based language set men up as 'God.'" What resulted was a thorough examination of the language used in all aspects of worship, including bible interpretation, hymns, sermons, and prayers.[6] It doesn't take much to see how the church's recommendations can apply to the business world as well.

As a result of the survey, the church now recommends using texts in prayers and sermons and even bible translations that use inclusive language—"humanity" instead of "mankind," or "someone with a disability" rather than "afflicted or lame"—or using a variety of materials that show the diversity of interpretations. People tended to be uncomfortable changing text that came directly from scripture, so the church recommends using background material to provide context. The point is always to choose language that includes all members of the community.

The church suggests keeping three main principles in mind—principles that work well applied to almost any situation, in business as well as in places of worship:

> Consider whose story is being told, and whose is being excluded. What does it say to women, children, people with disabilities, people who are being abused, and so on?
> Talk about texts that serve to oppress others. Don't deny the reality of sexism within the text; address it directly.
> Challenge texts that promote or praise sacrifice, suffering, or passivity.

It certainly speaks to the importance of gender-inclusive language when an institution as traditional and sacrosanct as the church takes steps to address this issue.

TIPS ON GENDER-INCLUSIVE LANGUAGE

Here are some tips that we've gathered along the way.

> The word *man* as a generic term to describe men and women, or sometimes women alone, is inaccurate, offensive to some, and unnecessary when you can use words such as people, humans, human beings, and individuals.

> Eliminate the pronouns *he, him,* and *his*: "The customer wants knowledgeable salespeople" or "Customers want their salespeople knowledgeable" instead of "The customer wants his sales representative to be knowledgeable." As a last resort, use *he or she* and *his or her.*

> Avoid such terms as manpower, the common man, and man in the street. (But don't carry this to extremes by avoiding such terms as boycott and manufactured, which have different roots.) Avoid *manned,* as in "the store is manned by part-time workers tonight."

> Where appropriate, use neutral terms. For *man-made,* use *engineered, manufactured, artificial, custom-made, handmade,* etc. Use *police officer* instead of *policeman, firefighter* instead of *fireman, sales representative* instead of *salesman,* and *letter carrier* instead of *postman.* Use generic terms for occupations, such as camera operator, dairy worker, cleaner, room attendant, housekeeper, bartender, bar worker.

> Avoid female suffixes such as *-ess* at all costs. Terms such as manager, author, and waiter cover both sexes.

> If gender is not relevant, don't point it out. We are way past mentioning "male nurse" and "woman doctor."

> You're safe being gender-specific when referring to a specific person with terms such as spokesman or spokeswoman. The suffix *person* is acceptable, but use it sparingly. *Chair* is fine.

> Refer to husband and wife, not man and wife. Only call a woman a "girl" if she is under 16. For those 16 and 17, say "young woman." My dear 80-year-old friend Ruth has a view that those under 16 and those over 70 should all be called "girl."

> Watch for traditional expressions such as "old wives' tales." Find a substitute, such as, in this case, "superstition" or "popular misconception."

> Be wary of sports and military terms. There is a preponderance of sports and military metaphors in the business world: the front line, making a killing, penetrating the market, team player, the whole nine yards, step to the plate, playing in the big leagues, ball park figure, getting down to the short strokes. The key is to use a mix of topics and metaphors (although not in the same paragraph). Constantly talking about "a targeted marketing campaign" or "fighting in the corners" is not motivating to people who function by building relationships rather than by competing and fighting.

Learning Different Rituals for Different Cultures

In *Talking from 9 to 5—Women and Men in the Workplace: Language, Sex, and Power*, Deborah Tannen examines how women and men talk and get work done in the workplace. Women and men have two different cultures that manifest in different types of communication rituals being used. It is in our different gender cultures that we learn our "conversational rituals." We learn these rituals from the children we play with, often the same sex. So when we talk to the other sex, if the conversational rituals we have learned are not shared, we tend to interpret them literally. But when we do this, we can end up completely misinterpreting the speaker's intentions and abilities.[7]

To illustrate women and men's different styles, I gave Chester at the Royal Bank a little quiz.

I asked him, "Did a man or a woman say this: 'I was wondering if I could possibly get a loan for new computers'?"

"A woman," he said, without hesitation. "'I was wondering' . . . 'if I could possibly'—those are things a woman would say."

I continued. "What about this: 'I need an operating line for $50,000.'"

Chester started to laugh. "Definitely a man. He's direct and assumes he's going to get the money."

"So the first style is indirect?" I asked him.

"Absolutely," he said.

"How does that style sound to you?"

Chester thought for a moment. "To be honest, it sounds hesitant, tentative, not very confident. Actually, it sounds pretty weak."

"Would you agree many women speak in that style?" I asked.

"Sure," he said. "My wife and daughters, to name a few."

This was going exactly where I knew it would go. "What percentage of the credit-granting process is based on gut feel or subjective evaluation of the person asking for money?"

He was surprised by my question. "Not that long ago, as much as 50% of an account manager's decision was based on the gut feeling of the person sitting across from the desk. That's changed with centralized credit scoring, but it's still a factor."

"Are tentative, hesitant, and lacking in confidence character traits that bankers look for when deciding to lend someone money?"

Chester smiled. He knew he'd been had. "Absolutely not."

"Is it possible, Chester, that bankers confuse a conversation style with a character trait?"

I pointed out that many women have a communication style that is based on politeness, not weakness. Chester agreed that this unconscious bias might have historically had a big effect on granting credit, even if the banker wasn't aware of it. However, I told him about a recent ground-breaking study that reported women entrepreneurs say their greatest challenge is not access to capital, as everyone assumes. It is being taken seriously.[8]

BODY LANGUAGE

There are limitless examples of how communication styles differ between the sexes. In terms of the sales process, this next one wins hands down. We have worked with countless numbers of men in sales who say they don't have as much success selling to women as they do to one of their own. They usually say something like this: "I do everything right. I give her tons of good information, I answer questions, and I listen. She gives me all the right buying cues, and I go in for the close. She walks out of my office and I never see her again."

So we ask how they knew the woman prospect was so in synch with their sales presentation. The number-one answer is: "She clearly agreed with everything I was saying. She nodded in agreement throughout my whole pitch. That's when I decided to close." A classic example of communication style misfire.

Most of these men are good salespeople. But they were way off in terms of understanding women's readiness to close. They have misunderstood a classic feminine communication ritual: When a woman nods, it is merely a listening cue, not a sign of agreement. In fact, it is entirely possible that a woman can be nodding her head and thinking, "And the door would be where, exactly?"

For valid reasons, men may interpret "affirmative" head nodding as a sign of readiness to close. That may be what happens when the prospect is a man, but research proves this isn't necessarily the case with women. If you attempt to close before a proper sales or business relationship has been formed, especially with women, you've blown it. This also might be a contributing factor to why women constantly complain that many salesmen are too aggressive and "hard sell."

A senior banker once told me her experience as an account manager. She'd listen intently, nodding, to small business owners explaining why the bank needed to fund their entrepreneurial dream. She noticed that men often reacted with more surprise and anger at being declined than the women did. At first, she thought it was merely an "ego" thing but then realized she may have inadvertently given the impression of "buying in" to the business case by nodding. I see this play out constantly with life partners (my own included). Without understanding the different styles and rituals women and men have in communicating, this kind of miscue will continue to happen unabated, and can have serious consequences.

Another miscue occurs when men tell us they're always accused of not listening. One day, I told a male insurance agent I felt he wasn't listening to me. He was shocked and then proceeded to repeat the gist of all I'd said. Puzzled, I couldn't shake the impression that he hadn't been paying attention. I began to recognize that the cause may have been nothing more than his body language—the way he positioned his body and directed his gaze. He rarely looked at me. He was always looking down and taking notes.

Tannen says this is a common male ritual in communicating. Her research shows that men can be uncomfortable with direct eye contact, perceiving it as a challenge from someone of the same sex or as flirtation if made by the opposite sex. Women, on the other hand, don't view it in that light and will often go out of their way to ensure it is made.

Think of yourself as a salesperson during a client's visit. Is there direct eye contact, and how did it make you feel? Are you sitting or standing facing each other directly, at angles or side by side? How close or far apart feels right? Think of the times you have been accused of not listening when you heard every word, or when you felt you weren't being listened to. Could your body language have played a role? What was the position or posture of the other person?

If you haven't thought about this until now, watch out for it for the rest of the day. It's a very revealing exercise.

DEVIL'S ADVOCATE

I've been in meetings where men seem to beat the crap out of each other, then go off for a friendly game of squash. This totally baffles most women as their conversation rituals involve maintaining an appearance of equality, by avoiding boasting, downplaying their own accomplishments, or including others by asking for their opinion. Tannen's research shows that conversational rituals common among men, in fact, often involve opposition that is not meant literally. This includes banter, teasing, or discussing an idea by playing devil's advocate.

Playing devil's advocate can be one of the most effective ways to test the validity of ideas. But, as Tannen says, it's "a classic area where, if not shared, it can be construed as a literal attack." It's not uncommon for a man's first response to be 18 reasons why something is a bad idea, but it's his way of processing the information. If it stands up to a nuclear attack, it's a good idea.

Many women who work in sales report that men often challenge their recommendations. Consequently, the women believe the men were attempting to undermine their "expert" status. In fact, the men were likely expecting the women to defend and push right back and are thrown off when women back down.

In selling to mixed-gender couples, just because the man may be more vocal or dominant in the process, he's not necessarily the decision-maker. It is often communication rituals that create the impression. Remember— women control 80% of the consumer dollar spent. The most hesitant-sounding, apologetic-sounding women may be the hardest to close, and the most direct and abrupt men may buy in during the first appointment.

Communication rituals can create an impression that isn't accurate. Tannen says, "If rituals are not shared, what you say may be taken literally. Things like using verbal opposition to explore an idea can be construed as a literal attack. A playful insult can be taken as a literal one. An expression of sympathy can sound like a put-down. An expression of concern may be regarded as an apology. The missed opportunities lie in not recognizing and interpreting how men and women do business differently."

DIRECT AND INDIRECT COMMUNICATIONS

Ask yourself: Male or female?

"I would put a sign on the door so no one slips on that spill."

"Put a sign on the door. Someone's going to slip on that spill."

Each statement differs in its directness. The first can be taken as simply an opinion, but not actionable. The second is direct. Then there is a third method, the one I use that drives my husband mad.

"There's a spill on the floor," I say. To which my husband invariably replies, "I assume that means you want me to clean it up." Many women subscribe to this form of vague instruction. The number-one reason given is that direct statements sound bossy and no one wants to insult anyone's intelligence by having to ask directly.

Women may not use a direct style in personal interactions, but they certainly do use it in professional settings such as the trading floor or operating rooms. Imagine this: You're a woman surgeon and the patient is going into a cardiac crisis. Would you say to your colleagues, "Excuse me, if you're not busy, could you hit Code Blue?" Or would you say, "You know what I would do if I were you? I'd start CPR"? Or perhaps you'd say, "Could you do me a favour, please? Inject a milligram of adrenaline."

Not likely. It would be more like: "Bag her. Get her pressure up, stat. Give me a clamp."

I've learned that women can adopt the more direct style of speech when the situation warrants it, even if it's not their natural style. It's situational. While working with the Ontario Medical Association, I spoke with many women physicians who said they would revert back to their more natural style when they left the medical setting. I saw little evidence that men changed (it is more likely already their style).

Let's assume you're a woman talking to a male client. You're going in for the close. "I was wondering," you say, "if you possibly had a chance to consider my proposal for your landscaping services?" This may sound wishy-washy to a man who prefers direct communication.

Let's assume you're a man closing a woman prospect. "What have you decided on for your landscaping requirements?" you say. This may sound abrupt to a woman prospect who may prefer a more indirect or polite style of speech.

The truth is women may benefit by adopting a more direct style when warranted and men may benefit by using a less direct style if the need arises. These differences in style really play out in the world of negotiation.

GENDER DIFFERENCES IN NEGOTIATION

Sociological studies indicate that women are taught to please as many people as possible, an attitude that seems weak to male negotiators. Based on the language of the male business model, women's negotiating style isn't considered as effective as men's style. In *Is It Her Voice or Her Place That Makes a Difference? A Consideration of Gender Issues in Negotiations*, Deborah Kolb notes that both men and women are taking more active roles in each other's traditional domains, giving rise to gender questions. Here are the highlights of her research:

> For men, the primary matters to be dealt with are the substantive issues. For women, the quality of the relationship is most important, and they look for agreements that enhance relationships. In other words, women look for a win/win rather than a win/lose outcome.

> Women see negotiation as a part of an ongoing relationship with a past and a future.

> Women often learn through dialogue—a sharing of concerns and ideas —rather than through challenge and debate.

> Because a woman's status in negotiations is not automatically assured, she often has to be tough and aggressive to establish her place. However, women are generally expected to be passive, compliant,

non-aggressive, non-competitive, and accommodating and to attend to the social and emotional needs of those present. A great example of this was reported in *Frank Magazine*: When the woman vice-president of a major client of a bank walked into the boardroom, one of the bank's vice-presidents said, "Oh good. The women are here. That means the coffee has arrived."

> Men and women often find that different meanings are attached to their behaviour, even when they say or do the same thing. For example, aggressive women are thought of negatively (ever heard the terms "ball breaker" or "man in a skirt"?) and aggressiveness is admired in men.

This is not about men learning to talk or negotiate like women and vice versa. But we have seen first hand what can happen when people are merely enlightened to the fact there are differences. Incorrect assumptions diminish, communication pathways open up, and success rates in closing business increase.

According to a JD Power survey, more men than women like to negotiate. This likely contributed to the not-so-surprising answer when Toyota Canada asked women whether dealerships need to change their selling approach. Watch what happens when you pull your sales process through a gender lens.

Jumping for Joy: Toyota Canada. Judy and I met with Access Toyota's Kevin Olfert, National Manager, and Jennifer Barron, Manager, and told them that according to our research, women rank car dealers second to last in terms of understanding their consumer needs. To our surprise and delight, Olfert and Barron "high-fived" each other, exclaiming, "At least we weren't last!"

In 1995, Toyota Canada's research told them only 16% of women car buyers—an astonishingly low number—wanted to keep the current car-buying process. Olfert wryly noted that 58% of men claimed to be the primary decision-maker when buying a car, and 62% of women reported making the decision in combination with their spouse. Toyota Canada quickly recognized incongruent and differing gender worldviews.

Yoshio Nakatani, Chair of Toyota Canada, recognized that to survive and excel in the competitive marketplace, the company would have to find a way to connect with women, who are increasingly active participants in the vehicle purchase process. He challenged his project team to find a way to meet the needs of women and also keep all consumers top of mind. The only conditions were that there be no new products or high-cost incentives. The team decided to focus on the sales process. This is quite different from Saturn, which had the opportunity to work from a green field—a whole new dealer network and new products. Toyota Canada's challenge was to find answers within the same dealer network and the same products. The good news was that both men and women trusted the Toyota name for a quality product. What they didn't trust was the sales and negotiation process.

With that in mind, the team, which included Olfert and ten other men plus four women, set out to transform the way they sell cars—a novel idea. "Let's do it the way the customers want and let's get the dealers to feel good about it," they said. They began by asking 1,000 people what they were looking for when buying a car.

They tested ideas specifically with women and at one point considered that there should be a separate "female-friendly process." Sixty-eight percent of prospective female buyers liked the ideas that the team came up with and were excited to see an auto manufacturer take on such a major undertaking. In fact, out of women polled, 67% claimed that if their first experience in this "new world order" was satisfactory they would stay with Toyota. When the team reported back what women wanted in the sales experience, the men around the table said, "Huh? But I want that." Of the 44 initiatives approved, 17 related specifically to improving the sales process. And thus Toyota Access was born—and only in Canada.

Toyota Access alleviates customers' concern with shopping around for a fair price. My own research on the car-buying process has shown that, for women, this issue tied with boorish salespeople as the worst part of buying a car. Toyota Canada found it was also frustrating for the dealers, who would lose to another dealer who undercut them by $100, regardless of how long was spent with the customer. Besides, it didn't help customers establish a relationship with their closest neighbourhood dealer for after-purchase service, which is the dealer's real goal. According to the company's research, one of the common problems was that people were worried they would be taken advantage of because of their unfamiliarity with the automobile purchasing process.

Access turns that process around. The website offers full disclosure of pricing and feature information, including competitive comparisons and trade-in values. You can print out the information and walk into your local dealer and the price will be the same as the dealer on the other side of town. Salespeople are now product advisors who can focus on your questions about the product features and benefits. It's called "hassle-free best pricing." The manufacturer's suggested retail price is set by the company; the dealer price is set by the regional dealer group—it might fluctuate by market—and the dealers determine the discount and everyone gets it. So your neighbour who buys the same car gets the same price. And because Toyota Canada changed its pay-plan structure, the salespeople are now paid according to volume of sales rather than the dollar amount, so they can focus on offering the best choice for the customer, not the best commission.

All sales staff received special training to learn the new philosophy. For a few it has been a big leap from the old hard sell, upsell, and price games, but Olfert and the dealers remain confident. "This is the new world order because it is what most of our customers want," says Olfert.

Did you notice how many of these tactics reflect the way women function in the marketplace, with the emphasis on information and education, and on eliminating competitive negotiations? Toyota Canada actually listened to women when it revamped its sales processes.

It's not hard to be committed to the change when the numbers back you up. According to the Maritz annual new car buyer survey, the results in Manitoba after the first year showed the percentage of customers "completely satisfied" scored in the top category. In most categories, the scores exceeded the national average by around 15%. And 40% of customers were "completely satisfied," compared to 22% in 2000, and a national average of 31%. Toyota Canada's market share went up half a point compared to the national average. That's about $175 million. And the first reports back from Quebec, where Access has just been introduced, confirm these results.

No wonder Olfert and Barron are giddy.

Using Gender Intelligent Information Channels

How you get information out to women is limited only by your imagination. Among the countless ways two are growing in prominence for women consumers: seminars and the Internet. Let's begin with the ever-popular seminar selling approach.

SEMINARS

Over the last 15 years, I've seen the full range of events, from the best of the best to outright cataclysmic failures, and from both sides of the speaker's podium. In this section, you'll benefit from my hard-won wisdom about this very popular style of providing information and connecting to women.

Many industries use seminars extensively to reach women consumers. Why? Because women go. One Canadian study showed seminars are women's preferred method of marketing.[9] Women hate hard sell and love information. No one likes cold calls, especially women, which is the principal reason that seminars work so well. Seminars really warm up what would otherwise be a cold call. Women appreciate the focus on education and the soft-sell approach, and it builds on the relationship dimension.

Seminars are also a particularly effective way to market to women entrepreneurs. If done in a way that showcases their businesses and promotes active networking, there can be stupendous results. Introducing a woman entrepreneur to a large number of prospects at one time and providing a place where she can network and build relationships cannot fail.

What Should You Talk About? The key is legitimate content for women presented in a way that has relevance. If you market the seminar directly to women, be absolutely sure the content is truly for women and not simply generic content packaged for women. For example, if you are going to offer a seminar on RRSPs, the speaker ought to understand the very real and unique challenges faced by women saving for retirement and offer appropriate investment strategies.

However, it need not be a straight-line connection to your business. For example, I have conducted seminars on gender differences in communication for industries as diverse as financial services and the daycare industry and a whole host of organizations from the Ontario Hospital Association to the Prince George Chamber of Commerce, all with the common element of providing an added value for the audience. The possibilities are endless, depending on your industry—think personal finance, small business, how to use digital cameras, home renovations, car maintenance, and wine classes.

Another important consideration is associated topics within your field. Say you are a real estate agent. Rather than focusing primarily on rates and economic projections, bring in an expert to speak on the ins and outs of getting the right mortgage or how to make moving easy and pack properly. Include topics such as what you need to know about your new neighbourhood before you move in, and what are the most desirable places in town to live.

Keynote Networking Event. Another very popular form of seminar marketing is the keynote networking event. Though the cost is higher than holding small seminars in your boardroom, the dividends can be greater. You can help ease the pain inflicted by the required human and financial resources by seeking alliances with other organizations, for example a charity. A charity typically can't contribute money, but it likely has an immensely valuable database. Charge a fee for the event, but have the proceeds go back, all or in part, to the charity. Look for a charity related to something women care about, such as family shelters, and be on the look out for one that doesn't get much public or corporate funding. Invite the head of the charity to speak for a couple of minutes after your company has presented the cheque from the proceeds raised by the event. This is an excellent way to demonstrate the corporate soul that is so important to women. There is also an issue of perceived value at play here: The admission fee, especially if it goes to charity, actually encourages attendance and attracts more serious prospects. Attendance is usually higher for events people have to pay for than at freebies. And don't forget these charities after the event either—establish an ongoing relationship and remember them at the holidays as well. My company donates money every year to our favourite charity in lieu of sending out holiday cards.

Getting a big-name speaker, with proper marketing, can yield several hundred people, possibly thousands. Companies often go this route to establish or reinforce their brand with a targeted audience. However, I'm always astounded by the amount of money spent by companies that then let people walk out into the street, never to be heard from again. Sure, the companies can promote their brand to large numbers, but it's a waste of time and effort if there is no follow-up to begin the sales process. For very little extra effort, they can have the added benefit of paying customers—quickly.

The purpose of a keynote address is simply numbers. But how do you contact all those individuals for follow-up? You invite them to a more intimate seminar with no more than 10 to 20 people—where you can start establishing a relationship. Place a response card or flyer on each seat at the big keynote event detailing the date, place, and topic of the smaller seminars, hosted by yourself or by an expert on a relevant subject. The card should explicitly ask if people are interested in attending future, small seminars on a variety of topics related to your business. (For example, if you're a financial advisor, offer a selection of topics such as estate planning, insurance, or investment strategies.) It should ask what specific days and times are convenient, and it should be very easy to fill in. It should include a fax number and email address so people can confirm their attendance. Be sure to have a draw prize to create incentive to return the cards.

Remember: The purpose of seminar selling is to get access to all these people that you've attracted and not to let them leave before you know who they are. It's not unusual to fill up six small seminars at your own location from one big keynote event.

The keynote event is only as good as the marketing machine behind it. Here are some pointers to ensure maximum return on your financial and time investment.

> Sell tickets in advance so you know what your numbers are. People generally procrastinate, so keep the momentum up right until the event.
> "Guerilla marketing" tactics work well for big keynote events. Use all the media at your disposal, from radio spots and newspaper ads to calling organizations. But advertising alone won't bring people out—you must call, confirm, and get commitments.

> Try to get a radio station, cable television station, or newspaper to sponsor the event—and get free media coverage and advertising.
> Call organizations that may be interested in the topic. Ask if you can use their membership list or ask to put a notice in their newsletters or include a flyer in their next mailing.
> Advertise in community newspapers two weeks ahead. Run advertisements at least twice. Be sure to mention that space is limited.
> Post notices in daycare centres so parents can see it when they drop off or pick up their children.

There's a lot of good advice out there on how to conduct successful and effective keynote events, but having spoken at hundreds of events over the years, I've learned a few tactics that work especially well when it's women you want to reach.

> Hold the seminar at a convenient time for women, for example, breakfast or lunch time, weekends. Keynote events work well on Tuesday or Wednesday evenings starting at 7:00 or 7:30 p.m.
> Women like an interactive environment. If possible, avoid theatre-style facilities, which separate the speaker from the audience. Target your audience appropriately, including size of group so you can choose the location carefully. If it's a small group, use a library, a health club (especially if daycare is available), a corporate location, or even your own premises. Use hotel conference rooms and restaurants for large groups.
> Aim for a location that has access to public transit, major roads, and safe, adequate parking.
> Consider providing child care during your seminar, though regulations may make this prohibitive.
> Any event is more appealing when it can be combined with a social outing, so encourage people to bring a friend. Many companies offer both customers and their friends discounts on the price of admission.
> Think networking. This is easier for a smaller seminar or focus group; for bigger events, consider holding a small "trade show" by having women entrepreneurs showcase their wares in the main lobby.
> Figure out a way to rally the group to do a variety of good works. Can you get a group to repair a building at a camp for children with disabilities or sponsor an inner city children's sports team? Get a golf game going for women and get prizes donated for a silent auction; part

of the fee can go to a local charity. Sell tickets to a boat cruise and have part of the proceeds go to a women's shelter.

> Provide take-away material for all those consumers of information. Women also appreciate copies of speakers' books. Book sales can help you recoup some of your costs—buy them from the speaker at a low bulk rate, and charge a special seminar price that's still lower than the bookstores'.

Host Regular Intimate Seminars. Let's assume you were successful and now have six small seminars planned. You can invite your favourite expert to speak. If you're comfortable, do it yourself. Bill the seminar as a networking event and invite no more than 20 people, and hold these seminars every other month.

Here's where you can have fun with venue. Try a restaurant or bookstore. One enterprising salesperson did a singles night with a tag line that said, "Single? Don't have anything to do Friday night? Join us at Starbucks for some learning." Filled in an hour.

Create opportunities that facilitate the networking. Give people two minutes to introduce themselves and then, for example, if they are entrepreneurs, give a quick synopsis of "Who is my perfect client?" Be sure you meet each person and introduce your guests to other women.

Company "Lunch and Learns." For six years, I was a financial advisor dealing primarily with women. From my first year in business on, I qualified for every award there was, and my salary reflected my success. Yet not once did I make a cold call. My success was a direct result of my personal educational approach and the "lunch and learn" method of seminar marketing.

I concentrated on a specific group—women lawyers. First, I got to know their business thoroughly. I learned of their concerns and challenges with money and made it my business to understand their business vernacular.

Then I began a formal marketing campaign. I contacted the human resources departments of the top 50 firms in my area to sell them on the idea of free lunchtime seminars designed specifically for their women employees. I always positioned the seminar as a no-cost value for their staff. Some law firms provided an elaborate lunch while others didn't have a budget so we billed the event as "bring your brown bag lunch," which proved to be just as much fun.

I was also upfront about being a commission-based advisor and positioned it in advance that anyone interested in a free consultation could contact me afterwards.

The seminar would last anywhere from an hour to an hour and a half. I'd make sure it was always lively and entertaining. After all, these people were giving up their lunch hour. There were response cards evaluating the seminar that included a question asking permission to contact them directly. No one ever said no. And that, as they say, was that.

This kept my prospect pipe overflowing for six years. I'm convinced that it was because I began to build the connection through an information conduit. It wasn't about selling to women. It was about educating them on what they needed in order to be financially independent. And the whole connection began with a sandwich at "their place."

Informal "Focus Groups" (aka Chat Rooms). Every couple of months, I invited 10 to 12 women to my boardroom and facilitated discussions about their worldview and personal experiences with money. The experience was, to put it simply, profound, not only for me as a service provider but also for the women themselves. The events grew so popular that I'd get calls from complete strangers asking if they could participate in the next "focus group." Frankly, focus group is a misnomer. These women were friends who hadn't met each other yet. Sometimes I changed the venue to a restaurant. I stopped organizing these 12 years ago when I left to write a book, but last I heard, they're still going strong—in women's homes. Of course, this method can be applied to just about any issue or topic—you need to find something for everyone to sink their teeth into that's appropriate for your particular business.

A variation on these meetings is to combine the discussion with a networking event for women entrepreneurs. To introduce the concept, the first one should be held at your location, then rotate the hosting responsibilities among different entrepreneurs at their locations, so they can showcase their business. Invite no more than 12 clients, prospects, referrals, and friends. The meeting should be between 6:30 and 9 p.m., which allows for a half-hour of networking and two hours of meaty discussion time. The host can take five minutes of commercial time to talk about her business, with a tour, if appropriate. Then you can get into the business at hand. Have a facilitator or do it yourself if you're comfortable. Always provide some kind of gift or honorarium for everyone and be sure to get everyone's business card and company information. End the session by getting a volunteer to host the next event.

Another idea is to partner with a local service or retailer to find out what entrepreneurs love or hate about their product (cell phones, for example). Ask them to invite some prospects and ensure you both get the database information.

One company, in an industry you might not think of as a natural for public events, has experienced tremendous growth thanks to seminar marketing.

Talking Out Loud: Good For Her. One day, Carlyle Jansen found herself having to explain sex toys to a group of astonished women at her sister's wedding shower. They were very impressed by the way she talked about sex so comfortably that she decided it would be fun to hold a workshop on sex toys. The feedback was amazing, so Jansen decided to go public. She booked some space at the YMCA (to make it feel safe and "normal"), made some brochures, and relied heavily on word of mouth to advertise. She knew it was going to be hard to market workshops on sex, especially since people are nervous about trusting strangers on that kind of topic. But, like the shower, the workshops went over big and participants wanted more. "We want a place where we feel comfortable purchasing the products you are talking about," they told Jansen, "and we want more workshops." That was the impetus behind opening Good For Her: a cozy, comfortable place where women could feel comfortable exploring, learning about, and discovering their sexuality, and could buy sex toys, books, and woman-positive films.

Jansen realized that the store and workshops could have a mutually beneficial relationship: The store markets the workshops that introduce people to a particular style and approach to sex, and in return the workshops bring customers back. The main focus is on education, allowing customers to be anonymous if they wish.

Good For Her is located in a downtown Toronto neighbourhood that offers privacy and a comfortable atmosphere—stores look like houses and there are several other women-owned and -focused businesses. Instead of blacking out the windows, Jansen installed windowboxes. The books were also put at the front of the store with lots of comfy chairs and the toys are further back. Instead of asking "Can I help you?" sales staff offer tea or water. The store's client profile is 70% female with an even split of straight and gay, the average age being between 28 and 55 years old. To accommodate women who feel uncomfortable, the store also offers women-only hours two days a week. After a positive experience, they usually feel comfortable coming back and spending more time in the store or at a workshop. The women who come into the shop tend to be seeking to educate themselves more about their body. Jansen has observed that women seem quite open to admitting they want to learn—men seem less enthusiastic to learn in workshop settings.

From the original seven workshops, Good For Her now offers 37 different ones over a 10-week season, from learning about topics such as fellatio, online dating, or stripping, to healing shame about sex, to a family dialogue on adolescence, sex, and sexuality, a smut book club, and of course the original Sex Toys 101. Some have sign-language interpretation and there's a wheelchair ramp for accessibility. Before each season is even over, eager learners email and phone in to find out when the next schedule is being released (it has the store's logo prominently figured, and adorns many a refrigerator around town).

Good For Her gets regular requests to lead workshops for shelters, AIDS organizations, and women's groups, and to offer training for staff at sexual education and health centres, for sexual health providers and professionals, as well as for many home parties.

Jansen's philosophy is to value the knowledge of the facilitators on the subject and to recognize that women don't always have the disposable income to attend expensive events. Workshop facilitators are paid the bulk of the admission fee charged, and the store keeps only enough to pay for printing, mailing, and other related costs. There's a sliding scale for customers who cannot afford the whole fee. So the workshops don't necessarily generate revenue, but are a powerful marketing tool that pays for itself. In fact, marketing for the store itself also happens through stories, because people may feel more comfortable telling their friends about a workshop on birth control options or spiritual sex than about the latest vibrator they purchased. The increased number of workshops as well as Good For You's online store has helped with sales growth. They comprise approximately 25% of sales. Plus Carlyle says, "I am having fun and enjoying my work—especially the product research side of it."

Creating Gender Intelligent Information Online

Consumer power is about being informed and the Internet is fuelling that power. Women control most of the purchasing done in the household, and increasing numbers are going online to research those purchases. In fact, the Internet ranks as a favourite source of information for women—who now represent half the shoppers on the Internet.[10] But you need to have some understanding of the women who will come to your website. Older women are generally slower at adopting new technology, but once they do they jump in with a passion. Young women, tweens through to 20-somethings, are the e-generation, totally at home with technology and mass media. When you focus in on the young adult women who grew up with keyboards and mice, you'll see that email, cell phones, and PDAs are all being reinvented to meet their specific needs. These days a huge percentage of young people use their cell phones all of the time, without even installing a land line—behaviour not yet embraced by the older generations. "While they may be heading into purchasing bigger ticket and more sophisticated products," says Andrea Learned, co-founder of ReachWomen, "they should still be approached as the savvy, online-fluent, multi-tasking, peer-driven generation that flocked to instant messaging and downloading music using Napster."

Furthermore, ReachWomen has found that these young adult women distrust the established brands they've watched their parents buy. Traditional marketing messages delivered in the same way won't necessarily work with them, as they tend to be less brand-driven and prefer to individualize and re-create. If you want to reach the women of this generation, Learned says, practise thinking like they do and forget much of what you know about their baby boomer parents.

According to NetSmart Research, by 2005 women will make up 60% of the online population.[11] Lisa Johnson, ReachWomen's other co-founder, says that "women look for technology that makes a difference to their lives, can become a productivity tool, and helps them fulfill the multiple tasks of their daily lives." And when women find such a useful tool, they are less likely to change if their needs are satisfied. "One product to do eight things versus eight products each doing something will be what appeals to women and brings them on board fast," says Johnson. Learned suggests women view technology like a household appliance, while men usually see it as a gizmo, gadget, or toy. She estimates that 80% of women's use of technology is to increase productivity and communication, with the remaining 20% for entertainment; men are split about 50/50.

Cynthia Ross Pedersen (aka the Web Goddess) is a web pioneer, strategist, and the President of Adeo Communications Corporation. She says, "To design websites that work well for women is to design sites that work well for everyone." Nielsen NetRatings found that "women are more efficient in their web usage. They generally know what they want out of their surfing sessions and leave once they achieve their goal. Although women are coming online in record numbers, they are still spending less time there and looking at fewer sites." This is opposite to bricks and mortar shopping, where men are in and out and women like to browse and compare.

Joining the women you seek to reach, wherever they are already gathering, and in the ways they are already interacting about their consumer purchases, should be a central focus of your online approach.

Learned and Johnson suggest that websites that welcome women make information available in four ways[12]:

> Information about the product or service;
> Information to help women evaluate their individual situations;
> Information that helps them comparison shop; and
> Information that supports conversations with sales representatives.

Women gravitate towards the kind of sites that provide a variety of ways to interact, such as an 800 number for 24-hour customer service, prompt email customer service, or a more sophisticated programming for answering questions or placing orders with automatic responders. One thing the experts all clearly agree on: Companies need to figure out "how she buys" more than "what she buys" when they develop their sites.

With the help of the experts at ReachWomen, Pedersen, Ryerson University,[13] and my own experience gleaned from marathon online shopping, I've come up with some must-haves for bringing women consumers to your website. Over and over again.

> *Provide a seamless, tailored experience.* Build profiles, customize messages and offers, and allow the customers to use their profile to tell you what they want. Pedersen suggests that for most websites, less than 20% of the content should be generic to all users.

> *Provide relevant content in understandable language.* Women are looking for trusted filters of information to help them weed through the volume of information available. Use a combination of unique elements, whether in merchandise, services, information, or related links to support what you are selling. And remember, there's no need to impress women with big words and technical jargon.

  For women consumers in particular, relevant, contextual marketing can be very effective. *Chatelaine*'s "Throw Like a Girl" virtual marketing campaign was designed to generate awareness and traffic and build the magazine's email database. Women could sign up at Chatelaine.com and send virtual snowballs by emails. The person on the receiving end got "hit" with a snowball: a snowball graphic that went "splat," followed by a subtle chatelaine.com logo and an invitation to retaliate. There was also a contest to encourage people to visit the site and sign up. In fact, it doubled the traffic on the website and doubled Chatelaine's database.

> *Organize your content effectively.* Develop learning centres that provide information to help women consumers make more educated buying decisions. Come up with a way to present a sample to help them decide. Include summary documents or top-10 lists where appropriate. Women appreciate the opportunity to choose how to interact with a brand before they poke around in other areas, and they'll return for more.

> *Post your corporate soul.* Pedersen declares: "Putting more information about who your company is and what it stands for enriches the corporate profile to the online reader. It's how your online customer

gains an understanding of your organization. That information is often noticeable by its absence. We know in the automotive industry, for instance, that women—more than men—focus on environmental and safety-related information, and judge accordingly. They also evaluate your sense of corporate and employee responsibility, watching how you handle various situations and what contributions you make to society." Learned agrees: "Women notice things in the periphery, such as which social causes your brand supports, if there are women on your board, and whether or not your content is written in a way that speaks to them in their language. The online realm offers much more ability to check these peripheral issues out with ease, so brands must tend to them." Include information about your company's ethics policy, community links, flex-time options, or onsite child care. Pick social causes that reflect your women customers' concerns.

> *Don't waste time.* Women simply don't have any to waste. Research has shown that "the shorter the click path from the home page to the actual transaction, the more likely the customer will buy."[14] Stick to the "eight second, three click rule": If it takes more than three clicks or eight seconds to download a page, forget it. If there is a download or survey, indicate how long it will take and set expectations in advance. Organize searches according to how customers purchase a product (by gender and age, or by department, brand, gender, or use—depending on the industry).

> *Understand women's consumer behaviour.* Women tend to recycle patterns that were successful in the past, so pay attention to what is already working. Also remember women's proclivity for negative trend effects. One or two bad experiences on your site and they'll flee. Maximize retention by becoming the destination site—use loyalty programs and online interactions with expert advisors and chat rooms for like-minded individuals. Share knowledge and allow self-discovery. Maintain some level of friendly human interaction ("live" or via email) with customers through all phases of the purchasing cycle, giving them a sense of access to inside information. Make sure the site makes it easy for women to refer, with pass-along devices such as printer-friendly formats and "email a friend" functionality. Include testimonials, expert reviews, awards, and seals of approval.

> *Be safe.* Research shows women are more concerned than men about online security and privacy. A study from Ryerson[15] found that more than one-third of all the sites fail in this critical component of e-tailing and one-third need improvement to meet the minimum standard.

THE MILLION DOLLAR QUESTION: CAN YOU CREATE RELATIONSHIPS ONLINE?

No.

A car company can use a website to educate women consumers, but if it tries to use it as a mechanism to create relationships with women, it's doomed. The key to success in reaching women—online or otherwise—lies in the general, overall relationship you already have. Doug Airey of Saturn says, "Information has changed the buying and selling experience. But a relationship is built face to face. Websites provide information and a way to maintain a relationship, but you can't establish a relationship there. Don't even try."

Al Sellery, President of Grocery Gateway, an online grocery delivery service, confirms this. "You do not create relationships online," he says. "The online experience is an enabler, an order interface with customers. For us, the relationship starts when the doorbell rings or at the call centre."

Clearly, the interpersonal connection still needs a real, live person, especially in industries with a troubled history with women. It's still about how you, as a service or product provider, make the customer feel.

Jim Barnes, author of *Secrets of Customer Relationship Management*, says, "The implications of customer migration from the offline relationship to an online one can be frightening—encouraging customers to go online leads to declining loyalty and declining referrals and, ultimately, declining profits. Retailers must depend less on price, access to inventory, speed of shipping, and other functional elements as the means of differentiation. There will always be a new kid on the block who is faster, cheaper, or has a greater selection. Retailers must give online customers emotive reasons to stay with them. That means understanding their needs and demonstrating that understanding by providing flexibility and personalization of the online experience."

According to Barnes, there is little improvement in how close the customer feels to companies after beginning to deal with them on the Internet. Customer satisfaction is the same both online and off, but those who buy offline have a stronger relationship than those online. This closeness translates into referrals and future loyalty, with more offline customers likely to recommend the retailer to others and many more likely to remain a customer over the long haul.

The question remains whether you can actually create customer intimacy, and that relationship that women crave, with technology. Learned and Johnson suggest that few succeed unless they have a bricks and mortar offer as well. Pedersen, on the other hand, disagrees: "Absolutely, you can have an online relationship. The power of the Web is its ability to nurture that relationship." The one thing everyone agrees on, however, is that the real challenge is the ability to integrate everything online that contributes to this customer experience.

Around the World: Journeywoman. Of course, it is possible to have a flourishing online community that takes off from a bricks and mortar base —or, in this case, a paper base. Evelyn Hannon started out with a 24-page hard-copy newsletter that today has grown into Journeywoman, the premier travel resource for women on the Internet. She trusted her own good sense, which told her that as an older woman who loved to travel and who knew little about the Internet, she was her own target market. So she built an online community based on trust and reliability by listening to her instincts.

Journeywoman is designed to deliver lots of information with as little fuss as possible. There are no fees, no passwords, and no filling out of forms. Hannon offers many links, because she believed "the more I gave, the more readers would return and spread the word about the website to their friends and family." Advertising and sponsorship are supplemental and are never the main focus, and in fact are selected by Journeywoman rather than the other way around. Says Hannon, "We—readers and advertisers—all work together to inspire women to travel safely and well."

Hannon knew that women simply wanted pure information. And they wanted that information as quickly and easily as possible. So she stuck to several guidelines: Keep the text large so that women from 18 to 80 would find it easy to read on-screen. Create a nurturing and welcoming atmosphere. Use funky female-focused line drawings—no photographs—so the site loads quickly. Make the navigation simple. And don't fool readers by continuously directing them to areas where they have to buy things. "We'd keep all our services free," she says. "My motto became 'Build it and they will come—and they will tell others who will come.'"

From the first day it launched, the Journeywoman website has had a tremendous response. "Mothers are taught that communication with a new infant is crucial for the child's well-being," Hannon says. "The same seemed true for the site—communicate, communicate, communicate with any reader who chooses to email a message. Every single note that came in was answered as quickly as possible and our interactive community began to thrive. Within four years we had welcomed our millionth reader and 42,000 females worldwide were reading our free electronic newsletter." And all this based on women's natural tendency to spread the word if they love something—with no financial backers. Hannon never advertised Journeywoman.

Journeywoman continues to have a full disclosure policy. Its corporate soul shines through: The site is associated with women- and travel-friendly products; there are no advertorials for any sponsors; all the research is done in-house, without sponsorship. In a unique program called Adopt-A-Page, advertisers post their banners permanently on pages of interest to their target market, so readers and advertisers are joined in a way that is inoffensive and beneficial to both sides. Banner advertising also supports other women's work, and there is complimentary advertising for women's charitable causes, as well as for books and videos self-published by women readers.

There's also the Journeywoman Network of Classified Advertisers—since these businesses offer support with their advertising dollars, the site supports them by publishing letters from readers who have used their products. Similarly, if readers complain about a product in the classified section, that ad is examined and pulled if it is deemed unworthy.

Journeywoman has attracted attention around the world. Hannon was named one of the 100 most innovative thinkers of this new century by *Time Magazine,* and the website has been profiled in *People.* "These honours I share fully and completely with my female readers," says

Hannon. "I never, ever could have accomplished this dream without the help of women around the world who feed me travel tips and spread the word about the benefits of belonging to our network of travelling women."

Royal Bank, Carlyle Jansen, and Evelyn Hannon "got" that understanding gender-based nuances in communication, which includes information dissemination, can move women and men from Venus and Mars and put us all squarely where we belong, on Earth. Whether online, with advertising or marketing collateral such as brochures, with one woman face to face or with a group of women in a seminar, being gender intelligent about communication is one of the most important sales skills you can acquire.

We've effectively established that women and men are different from each other. But the next natural progression should not be that all women are the same. There are as many differences within this group—women— as there are between women and men. In the world of marketing, this can be the stuff of sleepless nights.

Multidimensional marketing for multidimensional women

Today, marketing to women consumers is a lot like marketing to mercury—it moves, morphs, expands, and contracts. In the 1950s, selling to women as homemakers was a pretty safe bet. The Avon lady could ring the doorbell and someone would actually be home. Today, considering women to be a homogeneous group could be construed as ruinous. What we mean is women are not only different from each other but also, as individuals, different at different times of their lives, not to mention different at certain points within a single day. Yet, to segment is to lose the essential nature of women's multifaceted lives. Frankly, it's here that my migraine usually starts.

Yes, segmentation is nothing more than a grouping process. Yes, everyone does it. Yes, you can segment the "women's market" based on shopper loyalty, product purchasing, or different biological, demographic, psychographic, sociological, cultural, and ethnic realities. Yes, designing marketing programs to address the needs of groups is more complex than mass marketing but far easier than trying to market to individuals. Yes, creating or repackaging products, services, and marketing efforts to the specific needs of particular groups of customers will enhance customer loyalty. Yes, women couldn't give a hoot about being included in some products or having someone else included in "their" products. Yes, segmentation is legitimate in some products and services and not in others. Yes, regardless, these companies still have a role in meeting the needs of women consumers. Yes, segmentation can also be nothing more than being inclusive. And yes, segmentation is nothing more complicated than connecting with women consumers. Yes, unquestionably, there is an overwhelming business case for specific or inclusive gender-based marketing.

So why does the "how" part of this give people such a headache? I spoke with 12 experts on this topic and got 12 different answers. It depends entirely on whether you sell toilet paper or life insurance. It depends on how you sell it, how much you sell it for, and what women's consumer experiences have been like with you and your product; it depends on whether their mothers used it or shopped at your store and whether they're experiencing kids' "pester" factor. It depends on what the social trends are (healthy versus skinny) and what the societal roles and norms are of the moment. It depends on whether you have women in management, in product development, in all customer points of contact, on your board of directors, and in your advertising.

For people who like tidy little boxes, this is the stuff that drives them screaming into the night.

The very nature of what most women's lives are like makes marketing to them complex indeed. As far as I'm concerned, the word "woman" is synonymous with "multidimensional," which is usually defined or quantified by "three or more." Let's use me as an example, shall we? I shift from being a small-town Main Street woman one minute to a Bay Street woman the next; I go from being a mother playing with my seven-year-old to being a business owner negotiating contracts with large multinational corporations. I read Atwood, Steinem, and *Outdoor Magazine*. I feed myself and my family healthy, whole foods, but am the first in line for chocolate at the movie theatre, resolved to eat better tomorrow. Tomorrow comes and I don't get dressed until noon when I go out for an eight-kilometre run. I don't think I'm very unusual in this context.

Liz Torlee rails against what she calls "arbitrary, mass segmentation designed to shoe-horn products into creatively named different segments." She explains, "Everybody today plays a dozen or more roles—mother, wife, lover, caregiver, A-type business woman, couch potato, community activist, recluse, fitness freak, indulger, disciplinarian etc., etc.—because our complex, chaotic lives now demand this. You choose products according to the role you are playing. If you're being a busy businessperson, you don't want any human contact from a bank, you want a machine to give you money and not question the fact that you might be overdrawn. But if you're facing a serious decision about your family's future, you want someone at the bank who thinks you're the most important person in the world to sit down with you. Different roles, different needs, different marketing angles. Figuring out the male or female 'voice' is not enough—especially because in certain roles, the feelings of men and women will be the same."

Marketers need to figure out the role women are playing, the occasion, and the resulting frame of mind. As Torlee points out, "the process of reaching women is more complex than most marketers realize. Marketers must be aware of the gender difference, but it cannot stop there. They must also understand how that difference influences the particular role the woman is playing when she thinks about or interacts with their product. What values are coming into play, what needs must be satisfied, what mood is the person in, what frame of mind, what are the anxieties that have surfaced, what biases are getting in the way? Far too many marketers buy into the concept that if you know who someone is and you know all the demographics and those precious, useless "psychographics," you know how to market products to that person. Marketing to a 'labelled box' is lazy marketing."

Debbie Gordon of Mediacs adds, "It's hard to find universal truths about women. Of course, we can generalize, but any kind of generalization is short shrift to the individual and just a convenient way for us marketers to package the masses. The one brand that I worked on that approached universality was toilet paper. But then how do you explain the 95% penetration number? What are the other 5% of households using? Even then, we discovered the woman who used one particular top brand was different from the woman who used another popular one, who was different from the woman who used the store's own green brand, and so on. The market, women, was segmented principally by income and attitudes. One brand's users believed their toilet paper—the feel, the weight, the thickness, the logo—was more indulgent and made more of a luxury statement. The women who chose another brand were driven by familial considerations—concerned about softness touted in ads, but in the context of the family's comfort. One has to ask whether the advertising defines the brand or vice versa. In 'adland,' we call this executional equity, when the brand takes on the characteristics or converges with the images put forth in the advertising; the brands were either kitteny, cottony, or puppy soft. Whatever, it fuelled an expectation among women that helped segment the market and better define the target."

Those ellusive universal truths that Gordon talks about not only apply to women's income levels and attitudes, but geographic influences/culture as well. For example, Lise Watier, founder of the Canadian cosmetic company that bears her name, has found that women in Quebec have distinctly different perceptions of themselves and the world. They tend to have a more positive self-image. The women have a different sense of humour than women in other regions. Madame Watier noted a huge difference in what sold in francophone and anglophone Canada. Certain colours couldn't be given away in Quebec, yet couldn't keep stocked in Toronto. Francophone women were much quicker to adopt "spa services" and professional face care products than anglophone women. Investor's Group's research also showed pronounced regional differences in women's investing and saving patterns. Is it possible that there may actually be some unifying regional cultural influences that affect how women consumers behave? The research says absolutely yes. And if we allow for that, might we also allow that there actually exists a kind of "gender-based" culture that influences consumer behaviour? I think so.

Yet, in spite of this very real diversity in the human population, how do you explain the explosion of companies eyeing the retirement market because of the anticipated boom around the corner, or the gay market because of its affluence, or the ethnic market because of Canada being such a desired address for the rest of the world? Or the number of companies profiled in this book that segment women specifically with great success?

Perhaps the question should be whether it's possible to reach 51% of the population that, by its very nature, is a microcosm of society itself and still respect its members' individuality and changing roles?

Take heart. The answer is yes, it's possible.

Even though no two women share the same biological DNA, certain characteristics of women's consumer DNA are more universal than others. This is because much of women's consumer behaviour is taught. In other words, it's a function of socialization and societal values. If you remember, girls are given more purposeful consumer training than boys are. And, of course, there are some biological proclivities thrown into the mix—such as being child bearers and having longer life spans. Social factors play a part, such as being the primary caregivers and having grown up as objects of the gaze. Plus there are consumer realities, such as the fact that women do most of the purchasing, perceive they aren't taken seriously, prefer an information-based sales cycle, frequently pay more than men for many of the same products or services, and have a multidimensional or holistic orientation to their consumer behaviour.

But here's the good news. There are two fundamentals that allow women consumers to be grouped together as an identifiable marketing group. If budget or product precludes you from segmenting or doing frame-of-mind marketing, reaching women can be made immeasurably easier if what you create, produce, or market incorporates these two principles:

> Make her life simpler: Be an ally by offering creative ways to make a woman's life simpler and you'll have a friend (not to mention her friends) for life.
> Support her multidimensional life: Create and position your product or service with an environmental, familial, or personal health benefit, whether that be physical, mental, spiritual, or financial, and you'll resonate with women.

This is not to suggest that if you incorporate both of these elements, you'll propel all women en masse directly to your cash register. But you will connect with a significantly higher number across the full spectrum. Use these as the foundation of any marketing strategy, whether that strategy be mass, frame of mind, or values based; life event; the mommy market, women entrepreneurs, 50-something women, tweens, or piano-playing women. They resonate with women, because they are multidimensional at their innermost core.

The Truth about Time

Saving time is a myth. There are and always will be only 24 hours in a day and everyone gets the same 24 hours. No one will believe you if you tell them you are going to save them time. Saving time only means more time to do something else. However, what you can do is make a woman's complex, multidimensional life simpler. "Multidimensional?" you ask. Here's what I mean.

Mom and Dad were watching TV when Mom said, "I'm tired, and it's getting late. I think I'll go to bed."

She went to the kitchen to make sandwiches for the next day's lunches, rinsed out the popcorn bowls, took meat out of the freezer for supper the following evening, checked the cereal box levels, filled the sugar container, put spoons and bowls on the table, and started the coffee pot for brewing the next morning. She went to the laundry room to put some wet clothes in the dryer, put a load of clothes into the wash, ironed a shirt, and secured a loose button. She picked up the game pieces left on the table and put the telephone book back into the drawer. She watered the plants, emptied a wastebasket, and hung up a towel to dry.

On her way to the bedroom, she stopped by the desk and wrote a note to the teacher, counted out some cash for the field trip, and pulled a textbook out from hiding under the chair. She signed a birthday card for a friend, addressed and stamped the envelope, and wrote a quick list for the grocery store. She put both near her purse. Then she cleaned her face, put on moisturizer, brushed and flossed her teeth, and trimmed her nails.

Dad called, "I thought you were going to bed."

"I'm on my way," she said. She put some water in the dog's dish and put the cat outside, then made sure the doors were locked. She looked in on each of the kids and turned out a bedside lamp, hung up a shirt, threw some dirty socks in the hamper, and had a brief conversation with the one up still doing homework. In her own room, she set the alarm, laid out clothing for the next day, straightened up the shoe rack. She added three things to her list of things to do for tomorrow.

About that time, the hubby turned off the TV and announced to no one in particular, "I'm going to bed."

And he did.

Whatever women's occupations are, they're usually CEO at home. Let's look again at the traditional middle-class married mother profile (remember my mother's job description?). It starts with being Chief Research Officer in charge of getting the goods on any number of family projects, from where to spend summer holidays to what piano to buy. She's the Chief Negotiating Officer with landscapers, roofing contractors, and children (the hardest, by far). She's the Chief Acquisitions Officer responsible for the procurement and preparation of food, clothing, and gifts of any kind. She's the Chief Education Officer in charge of which school the kids go to as well as skiing, music, and swimming lessons, and the Chief Spiritual Officer in charge of the family's soul life. She's the Chief Social Secretary, managing the family's entire social life, and the Chief Medical Officer in charge of dentist and doctor's appointments and administering to the sick. And she's the Chief Financial Officer, paying bills, managing investments, and contributing to the family coffers.

Living multidimensionally is such a lovely way of saying she does way too much. Helen Fisher, author of *The First Sex: The Natural Talents of Women and How They Are Changing the World*, says the corpus callosum, which connects the two sides of the brain, is larger in women than it is in men. "Hence," she says, "the two sides of the brain are better interconnected in women. This means that women can absorb and analyze all sorts of information from the environment simultaneously. This makes women more adept at multitasking, while men tend to do better at tackling one thing at a time."

This really hit me one day while writing this book. In the span of what felt like five minutes on the phone, I made a play date for Kate, booked an interview with the CEO of the country's largest bank, found out when the next parents' association meeting was at Kate's school, scheduled a dentist appointment for the following week, calmed a frazzled sibling, and booked a keynote speech in Vancouver. Am I unusual? Absolutely not. But I am tired. And so are most other women I know. Today, women are required to carry additional responsibilities that most of their mothers didn't. Consider the following Canadian statistics.

> In 1999, 74% of women aged 25 to 44 and 71% aged 45 to 54 worked outside the home.

> In 1999, 7 in 10 employed women with at least 1 child under the age of 16 at home were employed full time.

> In 1997, more than 4 million women (33%) aged 15 or older participated in formal volunteer activities (29% for men).

> In 1996, almost 1 million women aged 25 to 54 (15%) provided both unpaid child care and care or assistance to a senior (9% of men).

Women comprise almost half of the paid labour force yet remain the dominant constituency in the unpaid labour force. Said another way: Two full-time jobs. Statistics Canada reveals that every day Canadian women in the paid labour force perform two hours more of child and home care—over and above their jobs—than their male counterparts. The 1999 United Nations Human Development Report states that women around the world perform the equivalent of US$3 trillion of unpaid work each year.[1]

According to Statistics Canada, the increased complexity of women's role has led to higher levels of time stress, particularly for married parents aged 25 to 44 who are employed full time. Compared with their counterparts without children living at home, married mothers with full-time jobs are twice as likely to be severely time stressed (38% versus 20%). In contrast, there was no difference in the incidence of severe time stress for employed married men with or without children.

So, the results of a study done by W Network are not surprising. Women suffer from "Superwoman Syndrome."

SUPERWOMAN SYNDROME[2]

	Strongly Agree	Somewhat Agree
There are times when I can't meet everyone's expectations	18%	52%
I am expected to be superwoman	26%	42%
I am overwhelmed by the amount of responsibility I carry	8%	25%
Many times I have to cancel my commitments	4%	14%

Superwoman Complex Based on Age

Percentage agree with the statement "I am expected to be superwoman"

35%	16-19
47%	20-29
48%	30-39
45%	40-49
40%	50-64
20%	65+

Women Are Busy.
And This Is News?

Double duty is having a pronounced effect on women's health. Chloe Bird, a researcher from Brown University, studied the impact of the amount of household labour performed and its division within the household on the levels of depression among men and women.[3] She concluded that men's lower contributions explain part of the gender difference in depression— the inequity in the division of labour had more impact on distress than did the amount—and that employment status moderated the effect. She states, "Among those who describe themselves as 'keeping house,' depression was lowest for those who performed 80 percent of housework. In contrast, for those employed full time, the minimum level of depression occurs at 45.8 percent of the household labor. Men report performing 42.3 percent of the housework in their homes compared to 68.1 percent reported by women. Thus, on average women are performing household labor beyond the point of maximum psychological benefit, whereas men are not."

Other research reveals this double duty is also responsible for increases in heart disease among women. Researchers at Laval University found that the combination of high-stress work and child-rearing responsibilities is driving women's blood pressure to persistently high levels, putting them at much greater risk of stroke and heart disease. "It's not the superwoman who's at risk; it's the superwoman in chains," said Alain Milot, a professor of internal medicine at Laval. He found that job strain was characterized by a combination of heavy demands and little decision-making power, while stress at home came principally from having a higher proportion of childcare responsibilities relative to one's partner.

When we say women are busy, as these studies reveal, it is not a trite statement.

Advertising and Marketing "Busy"—A Double-Edged Sword

Doing double duty has profound consumer ramifications. A study by Deloitte and Touche found that time pressures greatly influence how women look for a financial advisor.[4] They look for advisors to handle their accounts so as to maximize time, for example by consolidating accounts, tracking finances, and hiring specialists to handle complicated processes for them. The study said these are busy, time-pressured people who appreciate proactive steps taken by financial service providers to help them manage money efficiently. This is a distinct market of people who value one-on-one contact and immediate resolution of problems and are willing to pay slightly more for quality and superior service.

Putting out the message that your product or service aims to make it easier to find time in the day to get everything done is easy for a bank or a car company. They can tout streamlined credit applications or extended hours of operation. It's trickier in areas that affect women emotionally, such as the food business.

Look at your local grocery store. Most major chains now feature take-out dinners that rival grandma's home-cooked feasts. Chicken, rice salads, ribs, pizza, cabbage rolls. It used to just stock sliced meat and cheese. Now you can serve a five-course dinner from your supermarket's deli. And that's not even considering the frozen entrées or the pre-packaged dinner aisle. The grocery industry has made a fortune because they understand that women are time pressed and will pay more for anything that promises a faster way. It doesn't matter if it's cheaper to make it yourself. Look at drink boxes, sauces, rice, soups, hors d'oeuvres, and those scary pre-packaged lunches, all introduced for our convenience. Of course, the products are rarely positioned or advertised as such because women don't want to feel they are compromising on food preparation. Consequently, advertising focuses on taste. Here's the double-edged sword: Often the message women receive is "shortcut," all the while feeling guilty about trading off taste and nutrition for time. This is a slippery slope for marketers.

Advertisers have to work extra hard to make sure a product doesn't look like a compromise on taste or nutrition. Mom has chosen the convenience food over make-it-from-scratch because she's admitted, at least to herself, that she's pressed for time, but leading with this benefit isn't the way to her purse. According to the Food and Consumer Product Manufacturers of Canada, one-third of Canadian consumers make their weekday evening meal using convenience foods; two-thirds make dinner from scratch, either completely or almost completely. And it found that there's a higher correlation between satisfaction with those prepared from scratch versus evening meals with convenience foods. Clearly, the most meaningful approach to this consumer is to make her feel good about what she's feeding her family, the taste experience, and the nurturing and bonding experience food can provide. If there isn't some kind of emotional payback, and some way to assuage the guilt associated with convenience foods, she might as well cook from scratch. Clearly, it's more emotionally fulfilling. So while women are desperate for meal-prep shortcuts, other high-end emotional benefits often connect better.

In the baby food market, how can a brand be positioned so it recognizes that the future of someone's child is at stake? Chances are Mom thinks dinner in a jar isn't as good as the real thing. (I spent endless hours pulverizing sweet potatoes and green beans and pouring them into ice-cube trays.) But ultimately you want to make Mom feel good about the brand and reassure her that this product, and the company behind it, is a proxy for her and is willing to treat her child as though it's their own. Every so often there's a huge outcry when some baby food or formula is found to be less nutritious than expected. These debacles always underscore the risks associated with convenience foods, which require relying on others.

Convenience, in itself, rarely works. Better to wrap the product up in some images and lead with an emotive benefit. The household cleaning category, for example, has evolved from companies pushing functional benefits, ease, convenience, and cleaning power to companies pushing emotional rewards such as freedom to enjoy life and not obsess about laundry.

Allan Kazmer says the best advertising respects the role the brand plays in the consumer's life. Don't inflate its significance and try to touch people's emotions. In other words, don't manipulate. Authenticate.

The first step is to do anything and everything you can to make it easier for women to manage their time. The answers to the questions listed in Women's Key Consumer Standards: Making Women's Lives Simpler will give you a clue how to do that in your own context.

WOMEN'S KEY CONSUMER STANDARDS: MAKING WOMEN'S LIVES SIMPLER

Think: How does this make life simpler?

Can you make house calls? (Women will often pay extra for this convenience.)

How can you resolve service issues quickly and make sure it only takes one call?

Can you combine, complement, and reuse information, products, and services using only one form instead of several, only one request to enter mailing information, only one lineup?

Have you determined what is really necessary—are all those forms, rules, and lineups even required?

How can you eliminate unnecessary steps, confusing instructions, and delays and errors?

Are e-tailing and extended hours of operation a possibility?

Do you provide choices for services, delivery, and packaging so women have control over how, when, where, how much, and by whom?

Is "helping to manage time" a key message in advertising and marketing material?

Do It When You Want: Grocery Gateway. Grocery Gateway offers a new take on an old idea, *time shifting* rather than time savings. Al Sellery, President and CEO, is adamant they are not in the grocery business. "We are a service company. We recognize that people's lives are busy and the process of shopping for groceries is a necessity. But running to the grocery store on the way home from work, squeezing it in while running kids to baseball, or spending Saturday mornings in the cash line-up is not most people's idea of a good time."

John Mozas, Vice-President of Marketing, says there is an emotional attachment to choosing and providing food for your family. It's part of the desire to care and nurture, but most people dislike the process. You know the drill, finding a time to shop that isn't so busy, shopping with kids in tow, lugging bags and boxes home. So Grocery Gateway targets those annoyances.

Customers can place an order 24 hours a day—after everyone is in bed, before you head off to the office, during a quick break at work. Most people place their orders in the evening. They describe the process as "serene" compared to shopping at a grocery store. "This is what time shifting means: doing the task on your own terms, within your own timeline." It has proven to be immensely popular with time-starved grocery shoppers.

"Our market is women, quite naturally," says Sellery. "What we needed to do was understand the service needs of our customers." So Grocery Gateway designed its service along the following principles.

> Women need flexibility in terms of when they shop, and in terms of shortening the process. The website can store personal shopping lists, and delivery is scheduled within a 90-minute window.

> Women prefer a relationship orientation, so Grocery Gateway hires and trains people who are good at customer service. Drivers work the same delivery area so they get to know their customers. They will also call ahead of a delivery to confirm. Drivers are recognizable by their uniform and take off their shoes when bringing groceries inside.

> Women don't want to trade convenience for less choice or inferior products, so Grocery Gateway offers exclusive items and known name brands.

> Women are concerned about safety, so they can pay at the door by credit card or cheque rather than only online. There is a no-haggle money-back policy.

It's clear from Grocery Gateway's advertising that they understand the multidimensional aspects of women's lives. Their ads feature tag lines such as "You work hard to put food on your table. Let us bring it to your door" and "Everyone promises to make your life easier. We deliver" and even "When was the last time a nice young man showed up at your door with chocolates, a bottle of wine and a 40 lb. bag of kitty litter?" The final proof was in a newspaper insert that listed all the things an average mother does

Wonder where your day went?

Let's review shall we?
You worked.
You drove to soccer practice.
Paid the bills, squeezed in a couple of loads of laundry.
Called your mother, went to a school play.
Gassed up the minivan and put out the recycling.

You pressed a shirt, sewed a button back on.
Made dinner and packed lunches.
You looked for milk money and fed the dog.
Watched your favorite shows, read another chapter.
Kissed someone goodnight, and turned out the light.

Then wondered where your day went.

We're Grocery Gateway.
A dedicated team of helpful people in trucks.
We bring the things you need right to your doorstep,
so you don't have to go get them yourself.

We won't rest as long as there's one uncalled mother,
one unwatched television program,
one unkissed forehead.
In other words,
all the better things you have to do.

We're not trying to save the world.
We just want to do its weekly grocery shopping.

grocerygateway.com

You grocery shop online. We deliver. Now this is progress.

It's clear from this Grocery Gateway ad that they understand the multidimensional aspects of women's lives. (Reprinted by permission.)

in a day, and then described the company as "A dedicated team of helpful people in trucks" who aren't trying to save the world but just "want to do its weekly grocery shopping."

Meeting women where they are in their lives, communicating an understanding of their time challenges, and demonstrating a way to ease the pressure go a long way in building equity in your business relationship. This works with big corporations and one-person shops. It just takes a little resourcefulness, as illustrated by my favourite vet. Bruce McLeod, travelling veterinarian who makes house calls for anything from shots to euthanasia, says 80% of his clients are women, and almost all his business comes from word of mouth. "It's women who look after the animals," he says. "Many of my clients either work at home or are at home raising the kids. Either way, they have a pretty heavy workload. I simply try to ease their time-strained lives a little."

CONNECT IN WAYS THAT MAKE SENSE: MARKETING MULTIDIMENSIONALLY

In Chapter Three, we talked about how women's ability to integrate a myriad of facts is especially evident in their role as consumers. Women tend to approach purchasing decisions from a broader perspective than do their male colleagues, collecting information and options and connecting them together. They're often able to consider more points of view and see several ways to reach solutions to their problems. Helen Fisher, author of *The First Sex*, says, "Psychologists report that women more regularly think contextually; they take a more 'holistic' view of the issue at hand. That is, they integrate more details of the world around them."[5]

In order to support the complexity and multiplicity of all the roles women deal with, it helps to really consider how it all connects. Donna Clark, Publisher of *Chatelaine,* says, "When we were developing a recent ad campaign for Chatelaine.com, we struggled between being too rational (get recipes, get fitness tips, get summaries of the latest articles, etc.) and too emotional and gushy (we are here to support you, understand you). *Chatelaine* is all about 'connecting' women to ideas, services, each other. Gender intelligent advertising respects and reflects women's multi-dimensional lives. Too much of what's out there is the old packaged goods "problem/solution" ads, as if we all live our lives trying to fix problems. The breakthrough came after some insightful research that played up the theme of validation. Women like to identify with others and know their feelings, thoughts, and needs are not unusual. We decided to connect to the idea that our website is like having access to your best friends 24/7—the one who has all the great recipes, who's experienced the same health challenges, and so on—not as a replacement for your friends, just on-line access to all the positives (rational and emotional) when you want it."

The easiest way is to try to understand not necessarily who women are, but rather who they are in relation to what you are trying to sell. Of course, not all products warrant a holistic or multidimensional approach. Women also want products that will do one thing very well. Torlee says, "If we're selling a toilet bowl cleaner, we don't have to imply that it will put their bathroom renovation plans in clearer perspective or help them get in touch with their inner selves. Women want to know it will clean their damn toilet."

There's no top-10 list for becoming a holistic company. Like everything else, it depends on who you are, what you sell, and so on. The only way to illustrate the principle of multidimensional marketing is to look at a wide variety of companies that understand what multidimensional really means. There are endless permutations of what this might look like, and we'll concentrate on just a few.

Connecting Financially to Women Through Corporate, Planet, Physical, and Social Health: Real Assets Management Inc.

Women's definition of health extends beyond their own physical selves. They look outward to the world they live in, and they look for ways to leverage their most precious commodity—time—to make statements about who they are and what they stand for. They want to influence economic, environmental, family, and social issues important to them, by wielding the power of their dollars.

If American statistics are any guide, 60% of socially conscious investors are women—well-educated, affluent, and looking to make decisions based on their core values. As Michael Jantzi, of Michael Jantzi Research Associates Inc., says, "They look behind the product before they buy. They're interested in putting their money to work in ways that are consistent with their personal values."[6]

Deb Abbey is the Chief Executive Officer and Portfolio Manager of Real Assets Investment Management Inc., a Vancouver-based money management firm that focuses exclusively on socially responsible investing. She's also co-author of *The 50 Best Ethical Stocks for Canadians: High Value Investing*, and if she has her way, ethical management will be the standard for the future.

What does ethical investing mean? It means avoiding companies that profit from tobacco, gambling, or alcohol in favour of companies that provide environmentally or socially superior products or services.

Eighty percent of Abbey's clients are women, not because she targets women, but because her accessible approach and ethical focus attract them. In fact, according to the *Ethical Investor* women make up the largest proportion of ethical investors.[7] "I have an educational focus," she says. "I help investors build their own level of expertise rather than holding myself out as the expert. This service orientation sets me somewhat apart in my industry and definitely appeals to women."

And the women who are attracted to this kind of investing tend to be educated boomers who are values-based in their decision-making. "Many younger women are not yet in a position to be investing but they have clearly communicated to us that when they are, they will do it in a socially conscious way," says Abbey. "I'm heartened by the number of younger women who have a depth of conviction about these issues." It make sense. In the 1950s and 1960s, values in the workplace were based on civil liberties. Today's young women already have these liberties as an option, so they're free to focus on ethical issues.

Though a stock or bond is unaware of the chromosomal makeup of its owner, it would appear the chromosomal makeup of the owner may influence whether or not it even gets purchased. These are investors who want to use their money to make the world a better place.

Connect to Women's Physical and Family Health: Nestlé and Lean Cuisine. Nestlé works hard to stay close to its consumers, most of whom are women. Ed Marra, President and CEO of Nestlé Canada, believes it pays to have a balanced team with diversity of experience, age, and gender. "This creates an internal culture focused on communication and where employees know our strategies and have opportunities to ask questions and make suggestions." The senior management team is diverse and has women running major aspects of the business.

When Nestlé looked into women's feelings about preparing meals, they found a lot of complicated feelings were involved—guilt if dinner required only microwaving, pressure to produce something quickly, decreased satisfaction from cooking. In a woman's world, food isn't just food. It is a way she connects with her own body and personal health and is also a means of sustaining her family, for which she holds a sense of responsibility. A woman's values about health, nutrition, body image, and being a partner and parent are inseparable from her relationship with the product.

Nestlé learned about women's definition of healthy: It involves paying attention to mind and spirit as well as body. The company found that women's attitudes towards health also change rapidly.

Lean Cuisine's marketing manager Michele Brown says, "Women's approach to healthy eating has changed over the years as their roles have changed. More and more, what they are looking for is balance—balance for managing their time and in the food choices they make. When it comes to food, it's not so much about dieting as it is about healthy living, which includes eating well, getting enough sleep, and exercise, as well as spending time with people they enjoy." Consequently, Lean Cuisine has moved away from a diet message to emphasize the benefits of how the product fits into a healthy choice lifestyle.

Brown says, "We've also learned that in addition to our single-serve business, there are times when women want the same easy, healthy options for two people. We've expanded the same healthy eating concept into a multi-serve format."

This emphasis on healthy choices is also what's behind the Lean Cuisine website, which reflects the way women use information to educate themselves. There's a section on weight maintenance that has information on meal planning and nutrition analysis, and a section on taking care of yourself, with recipes and health advice and even a link to the Susan G. Komen Breast Cancer Foundation. Nestlé's website also has a women-friendly design, and includes product and service information for new parents, with a toll-free consumer line (that management sits down and listens to every Monday).

Nestlé recognized that priorities and focus shift, says Brown, and the company needed to talk to women in a way that was relevant to the stage of life they're in. While age doesn't define this rigidly, it does provide some loose parameters. Nestlé altered its multidimensional marketing message to connect with their main market, the 40-plus woman. But the fundamentals remained the same regardless of their age: Women want balanced lives and to be connected to their body, family, friends, and community, both locally and globally.

Connect to Women in Their Role as Mothers. While it cannot be disputed that single mothers, a growing consumer group, have a significantly higher degree of financial challenge in their lives, many mothers today have money. Also, many women are having kids later in life so they can get their careers off the ground. Look at the statistics at the beginning of this chapter. Seven out of ten Canadian mothers work outside of the home.

However, when I talk about marketing to working mothers, I mean both the paid and unpaid. Mothers who work unpaid at home raising families share in financial decisions with their partners. As my neighbour once told me, "I have an equal say in family financial decisions and the dominant influence in consumer decisions. Get to me and you get access to my whole family's income."

Understanding mothers goes well beyond marketing products and services, though. Customer service figures very prominently. I remember the first time I met with my personal banker, Carol. At the last minute, babysitting arrangements fell through, so I called her to say I'd have a three-year-old in tow. When we arrived, Carol greeted Kate with a big smile and a colouring book and crayons. I asked her if she kept an emergency stash of kid stuff. I was taken aback when she told me she dashed out and picked them up at a convenience store. I'd only called 10 minutes earlier. Considerable equity was built that day.

Whether you're a one-person shop or a multinational company, the principle behind building relationships with women is the same as it is when you try to simplify their lives. Either you do it yourself or you empower your staff to do it. That can be as simple as allowing staff to make customer service decisions up to a specified dollar value. The concept behind connecting to your customer emanates from the internal culture within the organization. And that needs to involve recognizing that women are often doing more than one thing at a time.

Busy mothers constitute an enormous market. The potential to connect with the "mommy market" lies in the ability to understand how your product or service is experienced by today's mother. You need to determine how to enhance, modify, repackage, or reinvent the experience around your product offering.

Matinees with Babies? Movies 4 Mommies. One afternoon, Robyn Green decided to be decadent and went to a Monday matinee at a local theatre. Somewhere in the darkened theatre, a baby started crying. She was annoyed, having anticipated a few hours of escapism. The thought flitted through her mind that it would be nice if moms could see their own movie with their babies. The following week when she went to another matinee, there was another young mother with a baby, this time only a few seats away. The thought returned.

Instead of watching the movie this time, she found herself envisioning a place where mothers with infants could enjoy a movie and it wouldn't matter if the baby cried. There would be stroller parking and change tables, and sponsors to turn the movie into an event with relevant speakers before the show to talk about baby-focused subjects.

The concept kept haunting her, even though she had no children of her own. She began to stop women in coffee shops, women on the street, in grocery stores, in parks to ask them what they thought of the idea. "I kept track of the responses," Green says. "Out of approximately 200 moms, I received only one negative reply."

So on June 18, 2001, Movies 4 Mommies was born.

This I had to see with my own eyes. Judy and I set off one afternoon to see *The Minority Report* with Tom Cruise. We walked in and surveyed the sight: a change table just outside the screening room, and a long lineup of strollers. The movie was screened without Dolby sound to protect babies' ears. No one cast a disapproving look if a baby cried. In fact, several women were concerned that Judy and I—who had no baby with us—might not know what we were in for. But many of the babies were sound asleep in pretty short order, in spite of Cruise as the leading man. I remember wistfully thinking it would have been nice to have something like this when Kate was little.

Green lines up baby-friendly sponsors to help defray screening costs, such as a photography studio, which set up a booth to advertise child portraits, and a food emporium, which offered generous bowls of fruit to the audience. Mothers—and fathers—have embraced the concept from the start, and it has spread from one theatre to several across Canada.

What Happens if You Connect Everything?: Mount Saint Vincent University. Obviously, the extent to which companies need to modify and reinvent themselves varies greatly. Creating a new experience around a movie is one thing. Most companies can think of a few low-cost modifications to connect better to women—that low-hanging fruit that's not far from reach. But what happens when you go beyond creating an experience around your core product and invent your entire business through a women's lens? If your offering is fundamental to women's lives—if your business has anything to do with food or nutrition, health, the home, or education—this is something to consider.

Mount Saint Vincent University demonstrates multidimensionality in the fullest sense of the word. It illustrates the principles of holism that touch on education, simplifying life, inclusivity, and self-esteem, and serves as a model of support for women's multidimensional lives.

Mount Saint Vincent's primary commitment is to the education of women, of which I was one. Founded in 1873 by the Sisters of Charity of Saint Vincent de Paul, it opened to the community the following year, and although it has been open to men since the 1960s, the student population remains consistent at about 83% women and 17% men. The university's internal culture represents the community and demonstrates the values of a woman-centred culture. Here, 60% of the faculty are women. "You can see women fulfilling a variety of roles at every level," says President Sheila Brown. "Our head groundskeeper is a woman, as are members of our security and engineering staffs."

"Our goal is to make university education available in ways that suit women," she says. "Part-time studies suit women well, as many are balancing family, study, and work all at the same time. Unlike other universities, the profile of our students is a little bit different. Many women come to us later than the average university applicant and have some life and work experience behind them. When admission requirements aren't met by these mature students, we assess related and relevant experience to the study program they are applying to. Women bring different credentials such as work in the community and volunteer sector that must be considered."

Like many universities, Mount Saint Vincent offers distance education delivered via Internet, TV broadcast, or a combination. "When students seeking higher education cannot leave home or work," says Brown, "this is an ideal alternative."

"In terms of course content," she continues, "we see our role as making sure that women's voices are heard across the curriculum. We reflect the contribution of women across the disciplines, for example women and politics, women and science, gender perspectives in a variety of fields, cross-cultural perspectives of women, and so on. Male students take these courses as well. It reflects their personal and career goals, gives them a greater appreciation of the contributions women have made."

Brown has observed that one of the differences in women's and men's learning styles is that women in some cases reflect longer on an instructor's question before responding, while men have their hands up sooner. "In the classroom itself, we look for faculty who understand how to create a positive learning environment. For us, this means content, language of the lectures and handouts that are inclusive—so everyone, women and men, learn in a positive manner and their learning and communication needs are met."

The university, like most universities across Canada, provides support services and policies that reflect and respect the lives of women—services that may not be found in most workplaces. There's a drop-in play centre for students with children and a licensed daycare facility for students, staff, faculty, and community. There are counselling services with staff trained and sensitive to the health and personal issues that concern women, as well as men. There are also policies to promote non-sexist, inclusive language. As Brown says, "Language is a powerful cultural symbol." There are also sexual harassment and fair treatment policies, which help to ensure that all faculty, employees, and students can live, work, and study in a positive environment.

The university honours the role of the family. Its collective agreements reflect the fact that women's lives are different. For example, Brown says, "We have a clause in our faculty agreement that allows a faculty member who takes parental leave to defer for one year their consideration for reappointment or tenure." The timing of Senate meetings is usually around 7:30 in the evenings so faculty have time to be with their families. "We also recognize that women's work lives may have interruptions due to family," she says. "This should not impede someone's career path."

This is what we mean when we talk about women's multidimensional lives. It is about connecting all the parts of women's lives together in an authentic way by marketing truth based on a product that is real. Deb Abbey connected with women by integrating financial health with corporate, social, and environmental health. Nestlé hit on physical health. Smoothwater Outfitters did this by reaching out to mothers through a familial, environmental, and deeply spiritual connection. Saturn and Toyota inadvertently did this by creating a more authentic sales process. And Mount Saint Vincent University did it on all levels.

Companies and organizations that position the benefits of what they provide through a lens that includes different contexts for the family, education, and personal and planet health can't help but resonate with women. Doing so helps companies reconcile what they provide and how they offer it with its authenticity. But how do we know that those are truths that will resonate for women? Take a look at Women's Key Consumer Standards: A Women's Multidimensional Lens.

WOMEN'S KEY CONSUMER STANDARDS: A WOMEN'S MULTIDIMENSIONAL LENS

Is what you are selling a "real" or a pumped-up image?

Does it authentically reflect a woman's world? The people in her life? Her family?

Does it provide support for a woman's many roles or can it serve only one need?

Does your customer service support a relationship-orientation process?

Does it support women's role as primary caregivers?

Does it support women's role as parents, whether single or not?

Does it satisfy women's demand for information?

Does it help women share information?

Does it offer a win/win outcome, ethical solution, or "do good"?

Do the benefits have an impact on issues important to women, namely social, family, health, financial, and environmental issues?

Reap the Rewards from Multidimensional Marketing

You can see by the results from the companies profiled in this chapter that connecting to women multidimensionally works. One of the biggest reasons for this is that if women find a company they believe is authentic, they tell everybody. Women give statistically higher numbers of referrals and generate far greater word of mouth than their male counterparts. Here are the facts:

> Because women build relationships, they like to compare experiences, which helps to forge those relationships.
> As many as 60% of women rely on suggestions from trusted family and friends when investigating a new product.[8]
> Women share both positive and negative experiences.
> More women than men state that word of mouth is extremely or very influential (42% versus 33%). More women than men state that the influence of word of mouth is increasing (35% versus 25%).[9]

Martha Barletta says that "because women customers return more loyalty and referrals to the companies they patronize, every woman convert represents more business in the long run than her male counterpart." This makes the persuasive argument that an incremental marketing dollar applied to reaching women consumers offers a substantial return. As Barletta says, "the simple act of talking to each other, sharing experiences and observations, is one of the fundamental bonding mechanisms of the female gender culture. Whereas men who find themselves in a conversational situation tend to exchange remarks on impersonal topics such as news, work, and sports statistics, women reach out to one another by trading personal stories and highlights from their daily life." The initial buzz about a product or company may attract both women and men, but it's much more likely to be passed along to others by women. Barletta says, "The more women you reach with your message, the more you multiply the impact of your media budget. Tap into the power of women's referral network by recognizing that a woman is always looking out for information relevant to everyone in her daily circle. Throughout the day, she seeks to reinforce relationships by offering ideas to help with whatever aspect of life comes up in the conversation."

Think about how women's referral network can apply to your own industry or company and figure out ways to incorporate this into your marketing strategy. Look among mothers to see how effective a referral network can be. If one person has done the research on a school or product or program or doctor, that information is shared with everyone in order to save others time.

The best referral programs start at the grass roots. For example, Grocery Gateway attributes its high numbers of referrals to its positive brand awareness, which gives the company credibility. Recognizing the power of word of mouth, they often offer "random acts of kindness" to reward customers for repeat business—a pair of theatre tickets might find its way into an order, for example. They also reward referrals in a way that appeals to women's social conscience: For each referral they contribute a dollar's worth of food to a local food bank.

Even asking your own clients—over lunch, for example—for referrals can be effective. You've won them over, so you can be comfortable giving them the opportunity to reaffirm their good judgement. Women consumers not only want to see you do well, but they also want their friends and colleagues to benefit from whom they know as well.

Even if they don't pan out, it's important to reward referrals. It could be as simple as sending a thank-you letter, or it could be a referral back to them—the best kind of thank-you. For multiple referrals, you can invite them to one of your networking events. The value of the reward should match the frequency, not necessarily the dollar amount. But remember, if the person being referred isn't working out, move on quickly.

David Chilton, author of *The Wealthy Barber* and part of the Looneyspoons team, sums it up nicely. "I've learned that there is nothing you can do in marketing that can achieve the same level of success as garnering word of mouth from women consumers. If women like you, your product, and what you stand for, they're much more likely to tell all of their friends and then some. Then again, the reverse is also true."

Remember What Women Value

At the end of the day, what is essential to remember in marketing multidimensionally is that it cannot be done in a vacuum. It is of great value to know that more women feel such and such about the environment than men do. But it's also important to know how a market segments in relationship to the product in question. How do you create something with gender intelligence that expresses an authentic reality to a group as diverse as women—a group that can be segmented six ways to Sunday? There's no set formula. Connecting to women, or to anyone for that matter, starts with a full audit of your consumers' lives and all the possible interaction points they have with your product. Marrying these insights with the features and benefits of your product generates the insights that help position your brand in its market and in the mind of your consumer.

When you're looking at women's multidimensional consumer needs, turn the mirror around. Women's—everyone's—desire to see something true goes way beyond a cleaner that works and a company with extended hours. It incorporates who your company is. That means finding your corporate soul.

5

Wear your soul on your sleeve

Whether you're a large corporation or a home-based business, demonstrating your corporate soul is one of the strongest hooks for brand differentiation among women. As we've seen, women make up the largest percentage of ethical investors and perform the majority of volunteering done in this country.[1] Fifty-seven percent of women will change a brand to support the environment.[2] Women tend to be society's custodians of social order and values.[3] The numbers strongly suggest that women make more value-based buying decisions than men. Our study was also clear. Seventy-five percent of Canadian women want to see corporate soul—a company that cares about the community and its employees. If you want their business, they say, you'd better be a good corporate citizen.[4]

At its heart, corporate soul is based on a model of authentic marketing, human resources, and business practices that is used by a healthy number of Canadian companies and supported by the social or ethical investing industry. In fact, companies with ethical business practices that give back to their employees and are veritable stalwarts of the community tend to enjoy high levels of customer satisfaction. Showing people that you aren't simply money-grabbing monoliths, especially in industries where the products and services are simply commodities (a car is a car is a car, after all), has become a point of competitive distinction.

But wait—what's that noise?

That would be the sound of Enron, Arthur Andersen, and WorldCom imploding from unethical accounting practices. It's the sound of defensive dodging from CEOs for questionable disclosure about executive salaries and stock options exceeding anyone's wildest imagination. It's the sound of protestors howling about corporate labour practices and human rights violations around the world. It's the sound of thousands of wildlife species perishing because of slipshod safety and environmental standards. It's the sound of alarmed parents watching their children be transformed into high-worth marketing categories. It's the indignation of women who continue to be invisible consumers at the hands of companies.

Consumer and investor confidence levels in the ethics of corporate North America have been rocked to the core. What once was a means of conducting business authentically is dangerously close to becoming an anachronism.

The whole notion of marketing corporate soul is a slippery slope indeed. One false move and a hard-earned, carefully executed image becomes hamster dust. More than once during the research on companies for this book, we were forced to look long and hard at the meaning of this term. Companies we thought were enlightened in terms of understanding women consumers have been hammered for serious infractions, from labour practices to highly questionable promotion of products in developing countries. We agonized whether to include them. Ethical investment companies rebuke companies that deal in alcohol, yet the Liquor Control Board of Ontario broke new ground in reaching women consumers. Women continue to be furious at their treatment by car companies and financial institutions, yet Saturn, Toyota, RBC Royal Bank, and BMO Financial Group have set new benchmarks for doing business with women. The church has been pummelled for the residential school debacle, yet the United Church of Canada has done remarkable work on gender-inclusive language. When it comes to meeting the multidimensional needs of women and portraying them respectfully and intelligently, Nestlé ranked near the top and yet faced a boycott of its infant formula products. And in most cases, the competitors' stories weren't much better. So many churches were involved in residential schools. Sportswear manufacturers, clothing designers, and pretty much everybody manufactures in export-processing zones, and car companies and financial institutions, well, they regularly annoy everyone. What's an author to do? This was going to be a short book.

In choosing companies, we talked extensively with everyone from the president through to the frontline staff. We learned a lot. Many are better than others and some are better than they used to be.

We decided to include some companies that do good work with women consumers, but that have ended up in trouble in other areas of their business. But we do so mindful of the controversies.

Let's take two particular companies, The Body Shop and Nike. In the U.S., The Body Shop has problems with disgruntled franchisees and media reports questioning their trade and environmental practices; these weren't in the same league as Nike's, but they are real issues nonetheless and there are lessons to be learned from both. The Body Shop, having had corporate soul at its very heart from the first day it opened its doors, encountered what may be called bumps in the road, but they're certainly not tantamount to having to reinvent themselves completely. Nike, on the other hand, came to this place of corporate soul after a global thrashing so severe that it shook the company to its very core. Nike has since embarked on a tough journey in an attempt to try to reinvent itself into what The Body Shop has been all along—a values-based company that works hard to match its inside to its outside.

The Marketing Consequences of Soul Searching

Considering that women rank corporate soul as one of the most important criteria in choosing whom to do business with, one can wisely surmise that women's market share and brand equity suffer when trouble hits. There is a difference in "overall effect" with employees and general perceptions of consumers alike. Nike has had to work hard to turn the Queen Mary of public perception around, but The Body Shop is better equipped to deal with periodic headwinds. Though critics are often quick to point out that the brand is "dated" and "tired," one area is tough to question—the company's soul.

FROM THE START: THE BODY SHOP

Margot Franssen has been president and partner of The Body Shop Canada since its inception in 1979. With 125 corporate and franchised shops across the country, a head office staff of more than 130 people, and sales surpassing $135 million, Margot and her partners—husband, Quig Tingley, and sister, Betty-Ann Franssen—have created a company heralded for its authentic business practices. Though currently looking for new owners, Franssen and her organization have always been committed to promoting positive self-esteem and "profits with principles," often with a healthy sense of humour. As Franssen says with a smile, "If you are selling a frivolous product, you need substance in your company. Every woman knows this is true. Cosmetics can be positioned as 'making you beautiful to get a guy' or as 'toys for big girls.'"

Franssen doesn't joke about the issues of values and corporate soul. "The reality is that women know that money has the power to drive change, so they buy with a different point of view," she says. "They're aware of what is truth and what is not truth. True values are not about marketing. A values program only makes sense if it is driven by people, not by a marketing or finance department. If you market well internally, you never have to market externally. The people inside the organization demonstrate company values in their work. It's about being authentic and transparent. Authenticity is equity on estrogen."

"The power of the individual is the only way to bring about positive change," says Rifka Khalilieh, Values Facilitator. (Yes, it's a real title for a real job.) "If you think you're too small to be effective, you've never been in bed with a mosquito." The Body Shop asks its employees to be active. Each of the Canadian shops is encouraged to donate an average of 14 hours of paid employee time per month to local, community-based organizations. "Volunteer opportunities allow people to express their value objectives," says Khalilieh.

Campaigning for social and environmental causes is also integral to the company. "We're responsible for driving social change, not merely responding to it," says Franssen. "But social marketing is very different from marketing a social cause. Social marketing is run by accountants and marketing departments. It vanishes when the business dries up. Companies that are trying to embrace a new found social vision are often confused about its meaning. They create a values story around their production and sales activities, instead of living their values by organizing their sales and production activities to create added value to human life."

The company has a special commitment to women's issues—90% of its staff and customers are women. Eight years ago a study revealed that 51% of all women in Canada have experienced some form of violence. The Body Shop decided to take up this huge issue. "We didn't want to write a cheque and disappear," explains Khalilieh. "We know how to communicate to our customers but we're not experts on violence against women so we partnered with organizations that deliver prevention and recovery programs, such as Amnesty International, the YMCA, and the Canadian Women's Foundation. Our role was to provide relevant and concise information about the issue and create the opportunity for more information and for people to take action."

But The Body Shop's commitment to women's well-being starts with the products it sells and the way it sells them. Despite the fact that they sell cosmetics and skincare products, the company tries to distance itself from the rest of the cosmetic and fashion industry, which makes millions of dollars from creating and feeding insecurities. "We operate in an industry that creates fear and need," says Franssen. "It creates an artificial definition of beauty and sets physical standards for weight and size. We have some sense of guilt about that. So in response to that we created the Ruby Poster." Ruby was a plus-sized doll lying naked on a bed of leaves, under which was printed a message that clearly made the point that most women are not built like supermodels.

This campaign drew some backlash from people who thought The Body Shop was promoting obesity and disparaging skinny women. But Khalilieh says, "We believe self-esteem and beauty come through the celebration of diversity." Accordingly, the models who appear in their ads

There are
3 billion women
who don't look
like supermodels
and only 8 who do.

ACTIVATE SELF ESTEEM | SUPPORT COMMUNITY TRADE | PROTECT OUR PLANET | AGAINST ANIMAL TESTING | DEFEND HUMAN RIGHTS

know your mind love your body

THE BODY SHOP®

www.thebodyshop.ca

This ad challenges conventions continually put forth by the skin care and cosmetics industries. (Reprinted by permission.)

include women and men of colour and plus-sized women, and they do not airbrush the images. For Mother's Day, they created a poster with images of women of all ages. One of my favourites is a poster of founder Anita Roddick's face that explains the source of each of the lines around her eyes. One is from smiling at her grandchild. "We want a sense of reality in all our visuals," Khalilieh says. "Wrinkles, scars, bits, and bumps are okay."

The bottom line, says Franssen, is that "our customers are not just walking wallets. They are our partners. If our community is healthy, our business is healthy. If our community is healthy, our economy is healthy. To sustain a healthy community, you must put back, rather than just take."

The Body Shop is an excellent model for other companies when it comes to wearing your corporate soul on your sleeve. However, the lesson here is if you hold yourself out as a values champion, you will bear unbelievable scrutiny. A good example is Mountain Equipment Co-op, one of the strongest values-based companies in Canada (more on them in the next chapter). Everyone we talked to there told us that they get nervous when they are held out in this light. Patrick Stratton, Vice-President of Product, said, "The fact we keep our head down and avoid the spotlight may be simply a 'Canadian' thing. But frankly, when you start championing yourself publicly this way, people start gunning for you. We keep our nose pretty clean."

AFTER THE FACT: NIKE

I have to admit that including Nike scared us silly. Nike's public relations nightmare over labour practices is never-ending. Reading Naomi Klein's *No Logo* made me want to run out and set fire to all of the world's swooshes. How does Nike reconcile the overwhelming issues it has about corporate responsibility and its desire to reach women? If, as Nike claims, women join a brand, what exactly is it they are joining? It wasn't until Barbara, Judy, and I had lunch with Anne Gillespie, a buyer with Mountain Equipment Co-op—one of Canada's most highly regarded companies because of its ethical and environmental practices—that we began to think there was more to Nike's story than the one of the one-eyed evil corporate giant. She told us, "The company that impresses me the most in terms of ethical accountability and practices is Nike. They're one of the world leaders in improving the standards for socially responsible business." Our reply was the sound of three forks dropping.

Nike is the industry leader in the sporting goods market, generating $9 billion in sales globally and employing directly and indirectly close to a million people worldwide. Consequently, the company accepts the fact that it is a lightning rod for public scrutiny. Pat Zeedick, President of Nike

Canada, says, "We know that women know about our previous labour practices. They don't feel comfortable if the company they're doing business with doesn't display corporate responsibility. Today, we have built our business on the three pillars of inspiration, innovation, and social responsibility, but not always without serious struggle and conflict."

Nike had to deliver not just to the outside world but also to its staff, because ultimately they're the ones with the energy, creativity, and skills to create and sell the products. In 1997, when Maria Eitel was Vice-President and senior advisor for corporate responsibility, Nike was being roundly criticized as one of the worst examples of corporate social responsibility with respect to its labour practices. When asked if the vitriol damaged the brand and affected sales, Eitel responds, "It hurt our business because it hurt our people. Individual employees at Nike began to wonder what kind of company they were working for and what message was being sent about the people who worked there. That was the biggest damage for the company, and that is where we had to spend a lot of energy."

Zeedick says that it will take time for people to comprehend the changes that Nike has implemented, which are ongoing. "The question that is always paramount," she says, "is how are we going to be a leader in the area of corporate responsibility? If we tout all the things we've done, people will be skeptical. So we fund organizations such as the Canadian Centre for Business Ethics and Corporate Policy and we share our business practices with others through the Retail Council of Canada. We're also involved in local community sponsorships to provide kids with access to physical activities and to protect the environment." In its partner factories around the world, for example, it has set standards for working conditions and implemented benefits programs for the workers. However, critics continue to charge that not nearly enough is being done.

As for Nike's approach to women consumers, the top five priorities each year include the women's market, and Nike Canada now has a senior "Women's Champion" who is also the Director of Apparel. Nike's organizational structure is based on team strength and areas of priority, and a communication process that touches all aspects of the organization domestically and globally—sales, marketing, research and development, distribution, everything.

Part of integrating women into the company-wide marketing strategy was an internally focused campaign, complete with videos, to help everyone in the company understand the market. (I reviewed this material and it was simply brilliant. Authentic and very emotive.) Zeedick says, "Integrating internally what we market externally helps translate the right message into all facets of the organization."

Nike's marketing worldview of women is based on its belief that women don't want to be targeted or singled out. "This part of the market wants to be spoken to 'like a girlfriend,'" says Zeedick. The result was a highly emotive series of commercials portraying women as real, human, diverse, mature, struggling, accomplished, with different ages and body types, alone and together. The ads talk about stress relief, relaxation, feeling good, and accomplishment—"Not for some guy, not to beat men," she points out, "but to beat themselves. It's about strength of character as well as physical strength and the spirit of being who you are, not what people expect."

In fact, Nike has produced some spectacular, award-winning ads that challenge many social conventions and assumptions. They describe the intense struggle in working towards a personal goal, with ads that featured women, some famous for sports (Silken Laumann, Cassie Campbell, Marilyn Bell) and some from other realms (Roberta Bondar, suffragettes), and their tremendous achievements.

Another series of ads tackled the perceptions that women can't play sports or should look a certain way. One featured Canada's highly successful national women's hockey program and shattered the usual clichés why women and playing hockey don't go together. Images of girls and women playing hockey at different levels of intensity are shown while a litany of reasons why women can't play hockey are recited in the background. The players are having too much fun even to hear the reasons why they shouldn't be playing.

Another was the tremendously successful "Perfect Ass" spot, with its powerful message that perfection is an illusion. An attractive woman describes the perfect female body (size 5), the perfect waist (24 inches), the perfect breasts (can fill a champagne cup), and the end proclaimed the perfect ass "is anyone who believed that crap." The company was flooded with letters from girls and women who applauded the company for the positive message it conveyed.

Another of my favourites is the "Like I Care" spot with elite athlete Alison Sydor. It emphasized sport for sport's sake: Sydor, hair matted with sweat, clothes sprinkled with mud, is shown racing over various terrains, accompanied by her voiceover that reveals ambivalence about the attributes of a perfect woman. At the end, she looks into the camera with a smirk and asks, "Do I look like I care?"

The television campaign was followed up by a number of print ads. The first ran in glossy fashion magazines, and had plastic tabs that extended from the inside pages of the magazine. One said "Sex" and bookmarked an ad featuring a fully clothed jogger and the line "Sex is often less satisfying and almost always over quicker than 10K." Another tab read "Thin Is In," in the shouting headline style of these kinds of magazines, and bookmarked an ad that pictured a woman doing squats at the gym and a tag line that read: "If you are a cell phone or a maxi-pad."

Have they arrived? Nike themselves are the first to say no. Educating staff is one matter. Talking to women another. Getting through to women consumers and getting them to buy are something else entirely. Nike has not been able to put women's wear on the same shelf as men's and have it sell, even though the women's market represents 24% of sales in Canada. "Getting access to women has become a global issue as this market has developed," says Michelle Noble, Manager of Public Relations. "Our experience is that we need to connect with women in a different way," says Noble. "Our current retail distributors are athletic shops and their target market is male. Women don't necessarily feel comfortable going into these stores and if they do, they don't stay long. The key for us is to go where women shop. We need to create a retail environment that is comfortable for women, has product and information that meets their needs, and is not staffed by young males."

Jim Rennie, publisher and editor of a variety of sports-related journals, agrees. "Women represent the majority of participants in several outdoor activities and influence the purchasing decision of most sporting goods. And yet women's merchandise represents only 22% of industry wide sales, which hasn't changed much over the past decade." Why can't companies increase sales of women's merchandise even to one-quarter of overall sales? He says the answer is retail environments developed specifically for men. "Today, female-friendly environmental designs offer a competitive advantage, while tomorrow they will be needed for most retailers to stay in business."[5]

The caption on this Nike ad reads: "10K is often more satisfying and almost always lasts longer than sex. Not that sex is half bad. It's just that running is so great. Great for your body. For your insides. For de-stressing. Some swear it's even great for keeping you young. And when your running gear is working as hard as you are, it's even better. The Nike Dri-FIT Filament Tight and Long Sleeve Base Layer Crew wick sweat away from your skin, keeping you dry. The Therma-FIT Chamois Vest is shaped for your curves, adding insulation without bulk. And the lightweight Air Coverage Max is designed specifically for your female foot and the way you run. Footwear and apparel that fit. On a body that's fit. Now that's what a gal calls gratifying." (Reprinted by permission.)

So, in 2002, Nike Canada opened its first store dedicated to Canadian women. The store is located in Vancouver's high-end fashion district and features wood and soft lighting to offer women a spa-like feeling. Product displays give women many ideas about how to put together outfits. The changing rooms are large, inviting, and well lit. The all-women sales staff knows the product and can provide wardrobe advice. "This is a recent concept and is still developing," admits Zeedick.

We have seen many companies caught between an old business model and a new one. The old way was how many used to do business, without a great deal of consciousness about socioeconomic or environmental impacts at the local level. The new way involves a growing global consumer concern about the working conditions and salaries of the people involved in making the product, how much toxic waste goes into the air, water, and ground while the product is being produced straight through to when it is finally sold. It also involves understanding the powerful nature of the woman consumer—what you make, how you make it, where you sell it, and how you advertise it all count for something. Next to fixing the monumental problems that have been created, reconciling the old-model consumer view with new internal initiatives is potentially the greatest marketing challenge Nike faces. Zeedick concludes, "We're still working on it. We haven't figured it all out yet."

GOTTA HAVE SOUL

When it comes to efforts to learn about women consumers, Nike Canada and The Body Shop rank high. Their product development and subsequent marketing machines show gender intelligence, built on listening to what women say they want. We wondered whether we needed to narrow our definition of corporate soul to gender-related criteria, but that would exclude macro-level issues that women care about. An in-depth treatment of labour practices and environmental issues may be best left to those with that specific expertise, but good corporate behaviour is one of the criteria women use in choosing whom they do business with. Women consumers don't narrow down their view of corporate soul when assessing a company.

Pat Zeedick and Margot Franssen both agree that the impact of corporate soul, which includes ethical business practices, affects women consumers more deeply than men. Ed Mara, CEO of Nestlé Canada, told us he sees it becoming increasingly important in the post-Enron world for both men and women, especially among young people.

But authentic corporate soul is not just about labour practices and being good to the environment. To do it right, one needs to create, transform, and nurture an internal culture where all employees at every point of contact with customers not only understand and believe, but actually live and breathe what marketing is saying. It creates a place where women—everyone—are fully integrated into the company hierarchy, from the mailroom to the executive suites. The extent to which an internal culture respects, listens to, and responds to employees mirrors the company's ability to do the same for its external audience. Authentic corporate soul takes a responsible position on how it relates to women and portrays them in advertising. It doesn't pander to sexist, demeaning, or old-fashioned social conventions, nor does it promote the irresponsible message that women can have it all. And it recognizes that women consumers drive public opinion. Women carry considerable weight because of the size and influence of their family position and pocketbooks. Women can make or break a company, and they can turn it around 180 degrees.

But What Kind of Soul?

There are endless permutations of corporate soul, but let's concentrate on three types:

> Corporate soul by chequebook,
> Corporate soul through advertising, and
> Corporate soul—inside and out.

THE CHEQUEBOOK VARIETY

It's simple, right? All you have to do is donate to charities, recycle, and sponsor a girls' hockey team. And watch the women line up at your cash register.

You'd be wrong.

Yes, sponsorships and charitable donations—chequebook charity—are mandatory for establishing corporate soul and brand. But just shelling out money does not make the motivation authentic. It's the same principle as advertising. Let's say your company gets on women's radar because it sponsors a women's golf event; you'd better be sure there is a direct connection with the image you are portraying and the experience women end up having. Let's look at sports sponsorship as a specific example.

According to Pierre Major, an agent who represents Danièle Sauvageau, coach of Canada's gold-medal women's hockey team, if your company is unknown to women consumers, then going after big-name athletes or events is a good tactic. Major told us that many companies use women athletes to connect with a market they haven't historically served. Many brands are turning to what he calls "the locomotive of consumer spending." "Women athletes represent a new and booming market," he says. "They aren't pigeonholed into representing only traditional brands like shampoo and cosmetics. Women athletes are extremely credible in representing things like finance, health, and nutrition, much more so than their male counterparts."

The other area Major feels is a strong point for sponsorships is the ability of athletes to reach employees. "When Danièle Sauvageau represents their brand, employees take great pride in being part of that."

The trend must be improving. Laura Robinson, author of *Black Tights*, says, "More enlightened corporations are getting involved in mixed or women's sports and are not caught up in the male sports heroic ideology." Women have had enough of being ignored. "For generations," she says, "girls used to be thankful to get use of the boys' facilities—a gym, hockey rink, or soccer field—but now they feel it is my road, my gym, my rink, and my field."

There are several benefits to sponsoring women athletes and sports. The first is that, for many, the presence of male athletes has reached a point of saturation. The second is that men watch women's sports, too, so sponsors get double exposure. In fact, the women's sports channel WTSN says they actually have more men watching than women.

Sponsorship of sports for girls also does a few other things: It reaches their parents and establishes loyalty. It also sets up role models admired for their skill rather than the way they look. This will have a long-term effect on the way women athletes are perceived—Robinson complains that women athletes are still measured more by their sex appeal than their abilities, pointing to the focus on clothing and looks in golf and tennis. She is involved in a program at Chippewa of Nawash First Nation Cape Kroker Elementary School aimed at healthy lifestyle diabetes prevention (a major concern with First Nations people). She sees firsthand the impact on young girls when they are handed out cycling helmets. "I know the girls remember the company that supplied them."

Set the Standard: Mr Muffler. Mr Muffler is a Quebec-based corporation with two corporate and 73 franchise locations. The chain has been top in its field in Quebec since 1956. Daniel Malandruccolo, Vice President, says that although the company was started by Claude Despatie, it was his widow, Clara Despatie, "who made an empire of Mr Muffler, running the business until 1975." The chain has been monitoring its share of women consumers since 1996 and is constantly looking for ways to be women friendly. "We recognize that women are often the ones bringing in the cars and we want to ensure the premises, the service, and the image of Mr Muffler are welcoming." We've already seen how they have trained their staff to communicate effectively with women.

But this training is only good if they have customers to practise on. This is what makes Mr Muffler noteworthy. They have embarked on a two-year program to revamp their premises: adjusting the lighting, changing the logo and colour scheme, improving restrooms and waiting areas, even installing high-speed Internet service for customer use. They've changed the prizes in customer contests, too, focusing on family-friendly trips and rewards. They offer car clinics for women highlighting information about tune-ups, what to keep in your trunk, and tire safety. But the most visible commitment has been the hiring of Danièle Sauvageau as their spokesperson. Mr Muffler sponsored the website that chronicled the 2002 Olympic performance of Canada's women's hockey team. They have life-size point-of-sale displays in every store for the Sauvageau credit card. Part of the revenues go to charity and the national women's hockey team.

Why Sauvageau? Malandruccolo is clear. "It's a good fit for us in so many ways. She has a profile with women and in Quebec; she is a positive image for both women and men of what women can do."

Sponsorships aren't enough in themselves, but they go a considerable distance in helping women connect to your brand, especially if a role model like Laumann or Sauvageau is involved. "Women are definitely the best source of referrals for us," says Charlebois. "If she is happy with the service, she will tell others. Women don't shop like men; they build trust and a relationship and are very loyal customers." The result of Mr Muffler's keen gender intelligence and deep corporate soul is a market share increase from about 35% when they started to a 50/50 split today. And Malandruccolo says, "We aren't done yet."

GRASSROOTS SPONSORSHIP

One of my favourite forms of showing corporate soul is grassroots sponsorships—sponsoring local charities like women's shelters that have limited or no access to government funding. Being seen in the community rather than simply at the Canadian Open or some other monster event really touches women where they live. When I see my bank as the sponsor for a women's shelter in my town I take note. Grassroots sponsorship is a great way for the big to connect with the small—the individual in the community. And when you consider that women do most of the volunteering in the country, it's a good way to reach them.

Not all companies have the resources to sponsor a national event or engage a known sports figure as their spokesperson. The magic of corporate soul is that it works equally well for entrepreneurs trying to get established in the local community. I remember taking my daughter, Kate, to the local library for a story-telling event. Sitting in the room were six five-year-olds sporting soccer uniforms with "Dr. Lynn Granson" on their backs. Here was a local physician, new in town, who decided to get her practice known by sponsoring a local soccer team. Brilliant.

SHOW CORPORATE SOUL THROUGH YOUR ADVERTISING

So how is gender intelligent advertising different from the garden-variety type? I have heard many in the ad business say Clairol Herbal Essence Shampoo, with its orgasm-producing results, actually has phenomenal brand equity. Everyone knows its name and the commercials. The fact that this campaign actually made it to air—let alone stayed on air for as annoyingly long as it has—really does speak volumes. In that sense, yes, it's successful. But let's briefly visit the real world. Every woman I know sits in stunned amazement at watching one of their own in a gas station or airplane washroom have an orgasm brought on by the pleasure of washing her hair. Advertising specialist Mary Koven explains, "The real downside is that for every bottle of Clairol Herbal Essence sold, there is a woman who not only zaps that commercial, but also hard-wires her brain to never, ever buy this product. The company runs the risk of double jeopardy because a lot of women may never buy another Clairol product of any kind. These commercials have the dubious distinction of being the first commercials I zap every time I see them. Every time."

Marketers argue that sales have skyrocketed since the inception of the campaign. However, if you could get the same results or better using a more authentic approach that portrays women as having collective intellects somewhat higher than shoelaces, wouldn't you use it? Ad man Benjamin Vendramin says, "It's amazing that there is still advertising that claims 'If you use our product you too can have beautiful hair, face, or body.' When we researched for Salon Selectives a few years ago, we learned that women don't believe that the beautiful, flowing, silky, shiny, bouncy hair demo seen in most haircare commercials is even attainable."

If you want other examples of gender intelligent advertising, look again at the stuff put out by The Body Shop and Nike. I can guarantee you when I look at these ads, the message they portray is one I want my daughter to see and hear.

This leads to another critical aspect to this whole notion of gender intelligent advertising: If you knew that women would pass brand loyalty on to their daughters, wouldn't that be incentive enough to use it? Our consumer behaviour comes from one of two places: imprinting, or word of mouth, and the media. Mothers can be very influential in matters of toothpaste, soap, laundry detergent, credit cards—the less fashion-sensitive categories. If mom is put off, you've put off future generations of consumers.

Do we really want to see a guilty, frazzled mother sitting on a beach talking to her office on a cell phone with her happy children cavorting around her? Both Liz Torlee and Debbie Gordon argue that this particular ad appeals because it acknowledges women's multidimensional, time-stressed lives, and it may well have been a milestone from that point of view. Torlee doesn't defend the ad but says the fact that it did strike a chord can't be ignored. As she explains, "I doubt the women who liked it are misguided, silly, behind the times or dorks. Advertising does not have to reflect reality—it is often fantasy. Why does a man buy a Porsche? Because of the German engineering? I don't think so. It's because of the fantasy, the unreality, and escape of the world it opens to him."

I, however, was disturbed by the success of this particular campaign. I maintain that ad implies you can have it all—kids, beach, and the office—and you don't have to compromise on any of it. Is there a woman among us who lives this reality? (Don't get me wrong. I think women can have it all, just not all at the same time.) But Torlee is right on one thing: Some of the best advertising is in fantasyland. If I had my druthers, I'd be screaming down the highway in the Porsche and my husband would be the one picking sand out of his cell phone.

This "you-can-have-it-all" brand of feminism or advertising is dangerous. It's not difficult to see a connection when you look at studies that show women are suffering from increasing levels of heart disease and depression directly attributed to the phenomenon known as "superwoman syndrome." However, there is another side to consider. I can guarantee you that you will not build authentic brand equity this way. Whatever rise in sales you enjoy from this kind of advertising will, at best, be a blip on the radar compared to what you can achieve if you implement gender intelligence. Gender intelligent advertising can give you customer loyalty that endures well beyond the next new commercial. It will create a relationship with longevity with consumers who see your product or service as aligned with their lives, as opposed to a short-lived desire to try something new or faddish.

Gender Intelligent Advertising: Zig. Advertising that connects with women needs to understand that it's not about making women feel "different" or "less than" or "better than" what they are now—it has to take them seriously. And when we say seriously, we are not talking about sombre, grave, humourless advertising campaigns. Nothing could be further from the truth. Look at what Zig produces.

I can spot a Zig ad from a mile away with one eye closed. I've met with two of the company's three principals, Lorraine Tao and Elspeth Lynn, many times to try to pin down their ability to produce material that resonates with women. Our conversations usually go like this:

Me: How do you do it?

Them: (*shrug*)

Me: Come on, guys. Tell me how you can consistently create inspiring 60-second ads with so much humour and realism that women don't hit the mute button?

Them: Don't know. We just do it.

Me: There's no formula? No tricks? Come on, spill.

Them: Don't know. Honest. We just do it.

I've come to the earth-shattering conclusion that they just do it. Zig named their agency after a dictum from Helmut Krone, one of the most powerful and influential art directors in the world: "Zig when they zag." Along with their partner, Andy McAuley, Zig's innovative and clever work has earned them *Marketing Magazine*'s "Agency of the Year" award for 2002. Even today, only one woman is the owner of a large Canadian marketing agency, so Zig remains an exception. It simply screams gender intelligence, although initially, Lynn and Tao didn't view their new company as having a "women's specialty." They thought that promoting themselves as a "chick shop" would cut them off from other types of business. But as their reputation and successes grew, they realized they had inadvertently stumbled onto something that was bigger than the both of them. They were simply too good at it.

"What advertising generally doesn't have is humanity," says Lynn. "But even though it's only advertising, if you can touch someone emotionally, it's an amazing thing. We take a humanistic approach to advertising. We believe in being very insightful to our target, so not all consumers are going to understand it all the time. When women are our target, we are women speaking to women as women. Women are about feeling a connection with a product."

Tao adds, "For decades, women have been spoken to in the voice of men. Creative departments have always been made up of men, so naturally—through no fault of their own—they tend to create advertising from a distinctly male perspective. This is changing, but they still represent the majority."

First there was their successful Kellogg's Special K ad, which they worked on while with another agency. For decades, Special K had been positioned as a diet cereal, which, for the men who created the ad campaigns, meant dieting to look good for them. So the cereal's advertising evolved from "Can't pinch an inch" to women trying to look good for their husbands—a history of setting unrealistic standards for women to live up to. "The men would have no idea how deeply these notions offended women and how damaging they were to women's psyches," says Tao. "The problem was, the campaign was selling cereal. Women in focus groups found the campaign insulting, yet sales showed that they were buying the diet cereal regardless. In our view, that was because women were stuck between a rock and a hard place. They had grown up with 'the beauty myth,' so their body image issues were too deeply ingrained to stop them from responding to advertising that insulted them. We couldn't bring ourselves to continue the campaign. We managed to convince skeptics to change direction strategically and shift the focus from 'looking good for others' to 'looking good on your own terms.' In the new campaign, we decided to confront body image issues head on and in the process, become a champion of change." Their ad was a brilliant example of gender role reversal and showed a bunch of very manly men sitting around complaining about "having their mothers' thighs" and asking, "Do I look fat?"

"To our immense relief," she continues, "the response was staggering. Letters of support from women across Canada poured in. Sales went up 16% from baseline share. The press went nuts. By the way, we notice when there are male creatives behind the latest installments in the campaign, the female insights seem to be lacking and the emphasis goes back to losing weight."

Then came the "Fruit of the Loom" ads, with thongs and bikini briefs hanging on a clothesline, followed by comfortable cotton underwear. The tag lines said things like "Tell him to wear the lace and garters for a change" and "What supermodels wear on their day off," always ending with "Really, really comfortable underwear." Most ads for women's underwear are either women dancing around their bedrooms in their underwear, catalogues of busty models in lingerie, or models lying seductively on billboards—they appeal to men but have no connection to women. "We felt there was a huge opportunity to speak directly and insightfully to women," says Tao.

A Zig classic.
(Reprinted by permission.)

"We chose not to show a woman in any of the ads," she continues. "It allowed us to avoid perpetuating the 'perfect body' stereotype that using a model would have forced us to do."

Sales increased by 200% immediately after the campaign broke. Stores had to scramble to get more products on the shelves. The campaign was picked up in the U.S. and Mexico and expanded to include the entire line of underwear and clothing. Calls and letters of praise poured in from women consumers all over North America.

Then came another groundbreaking commercial, this time for Vaseline Intensive Care, which they created while at another agency. It featured a woman's leg being caressed under the family dinner table by a younger man. The tag was "How beautiful feels." Because the woman was older than the usual women in skincare commercials, the focus was on feeling beautiful rather than looking beautiful. Lynn and Tao, with their unerring intuition, understood what's important to women, how they felt about themselves, their personality quirks and deficiencies, their obsessions and interests, which is why one-size-fits-all marketing and advertising don't work.

According to Debbie Gordon, "the best advertising zeroes in on an insight that generally stems from some deep-rooted knowledge about your target group and, yes, that means excluding a large chunk of the buying public. In Tao and Lynn's Vaseline campaign, they recognized that beauty is traditionally defined one dimensionally, in terms of women's looks. Their insight was that beauty is as much a feeling as it is a look, and we can feel beautiful at any age."

Tao and Lynn's insight has served them well time and time again. There was the provocative and hilarious commercial that took a sensitive subject—breast cancer screening—and, using respectful but flat-out irreverent humour, impelled women to reach inside their shirts to examine their breasts. "Cam's Breast Exam" garnered attention in all major Toronto newspapers and newscasts at the time of its launch for the different approach it took.

W Meets Zig. When WTN decided to rebrand itself as W Network, general manager Wendy Montgomery wanted to promote it as "a destination station for women, one they tune to first because they believe that they are likely to find the type of programs they want to watch. In addition we wanted the service to be inclusive, a place where both men and women felt comfortable watching TV together. And we wanted to recognize, of course, that women are a diverse group and may want to watch programs that are made by and about men too." Most of the work needed to be about how the network was perceived, especially by buyers in ad agencies, so W turned to Zig purely on the basis of their reputation for "getting women." Lynn and Tao started with a wildly funny but thought-provoking campaign on the theme of "Imagine TV without Women." W has seen 19% growth in weekly reach for women between 18 and 49 since its relaunch.

Then Zig set about generating a buzz around the relaunch within the agency world. In order to demonstrate W's understanding of women, Zig went into the offices of each ad agency and decorated one stall in both the women's and men's washrooms with feminine touches like fresh towels, hand lotion, cozy bathroom mats, framed photos, magazines, three-ply

An example of W Network's rebranding, created by Zig. (Reprinted by permission.)

toilet paper, and potpourri. At the back of the stall was a framed card that read in large type "W was here" and then, in smaller type, "No network understands life from a female point of view better than W Network. We've got everything from popular dramas and blockbuster movies to documentaries and lifestyle programming. If your target is women, your network is W."

The results? Zig and W received a slew of spontaneous calls from media planners and buyers praising the idea. "Now this is insightful," was one response. "It's the kind of thing we always talk about doing but never do." The idea created so much talk that it was written up in *Marketing Magazine* and *Strategy*, two key trade magazines. As Lynn and Tao say, "Mission accomplished."

It's evident that Zig is driven by instinct and core values that have turned it into one of the country's most gender intelligent agencies. Tao,

Lynn, and McAuley so completely understand the gender dynamic that they intentionally created gender-balanced creative teams. They'll put together an all-women, all-men, or mixed-gender creative team, depending on the project. Gender-based hiring is a conscious choice.

Consequently, they produce innovative and award-winning ads and strategies that resonate powerfully with women. They have won more awards than Tom Hanks. They were the cover story for *Report on Business* Magazine. Tao and Lynn are among *Maclean's* "100 People to Watch" and are listed in *Who's Who in Canada*. Zig has been profiled in the *Toronto Star*, the *National Post*, and *The Globe and Mail*. Since they opened their doors in 1999, they've grown from three people to 30. All this, for simply understanding intuitively what richness a diversity of worldviews can bring to the creative process.

Rethink's Chris Staples also has an uncanny ability to avoid stereotypes and create advertisements that women love. His sardonic humour is evident in his "Feel Inadequate for 10% Less" ad (see page 200) that he created for Save-On-Foods. I asked him his secret. "We subscribe to the Seinfeld school of advertising," says Staples. "Our insights generally come from observations like, 'Have you ever noticed when . . .' or 'Isn't it funny when . . .' In fact, we look for Seinfeld-type people who get a kick from looking at human nature. I look at what the brand or category is doing in advertising, then go out and do exactly the opposite."

What he typically finds are clichés, and he avoids them. He uses hair care as an example.

STAPLES RULES: SIX THINGS I WILL NOT DO WITH HAIR

1. I will not show a woman in a bikini on a beach.

2. I will not show hair flip shots.

3. I will not show glam shots.

4. I will not use pseudo-science about silk proteins or close-ups of hair shafts.

5. I will not use ridiculous jingles.

6. I will not use women in the ads.

Huh? No women?

Both Staples and Zig's Tao and Lynn maintain that the best advertising doesn't use women because it invariably falls into the trap of using models who rarely represent most of the women in the target audience. All our experts agree that advertising to women is about learning the truth, and the truth isn't about the product—it's about the person using it.

That means understanding this doesn't include a lengthy discourse about babies instead of market volatility or engine torque. A good example is a spot created by Benjamin Vendramin for Nissan Canada, made even more interesting by being an example of a company wanting to get a product perceived as for men into the hands of women. "In research it kept coming out that women loved SUVs because they feel more in charge and safer on the road," he says. "It was also a fact that more women were buying SUVs instead of minivans, but Nissan didn't want to make the Pathfinder into the SUV for chicks. How do we get the story of its powerful new engine across, plus target men without alienating women?" They had to find the truth about how women felt about driving SUVs. The spot opens on a Pathfinder chasing a lion through Africa—very masculine. The SUV stops on top of a hill, letting the lion get away. The driver's side door opens and an antelope gracefully and confidently steps out from behind the wheel to stand heroically in front of the vehicle and watch the lion run off. The voice-over says "Power changes everything." "The idea enabled us to dramatically demonstrate the engine's superiority and at the same time imply that a gentler creature, a woman, is now in charge."

While this spot demonstrates corporate soul, Alan Kazmer's advice for creating real gender intelligent advertising is to use women's voices for half of the voice-overs, especially in ads created to reach them. Sadly, in the Nissan spot, a male voice-over was used, which worked against it. Vendramin was obliged to use Nissan's brand "voice," which has been used for every vehicle Nissan advertises.

Corporate Soul Includes Everyone. Gender intelligent advertising means understanding that what appeals to men doesn't necessarily appeal to women, but it also means understanding how to create marketing messages that can appeal to both. One simply has to look at Scotiabank's advertising. These ads may not target women specifically, but they work diligently to include women in their advertising in an authentic way. Rick

Feel inadequate for 10% less.

Or informed. Entertained. Even inspired.

It's easy. Because we stock almost 400 magazine titles at Save-On-Foods. On topics ranging from computers to fitness and glamour.

Plus they're all 10% off the cover price. Every single day. And that includes our wide selection of paperback books and greeting cards.

In fact, we offer lower prices throughout our store. And we back them up with the Save-On-Foods Guarantee. If you find a lower advertised price on any item we carry, at any Safeway or IGA store in Fort McMurray, we'll beat that price by 10 percent.

Come to think of it, with such a huge selection of magazines at 10% off everyday, only our competition should feel inadequate.

SAVE-ON-FOODS
Believe it.

Another shining example of poking fun at convention. (Reprinted by permission.)

White, Scotiabank's Vice-President of Brand and Marketing Management, credits a gender-balanced team that looks for issues that bring together women and men as the central premise for their ads. The ads that get created are based on universal concerns with lots of wonderful humour, often at the bank's expense. Witness the "Polaroid" campaign, with a guy flipping several pictures of people his new employee needs to deal with at the bank. Or the one where the guy gets up and leaves in disgust after his banker (a woman) tells him he was approved for a small business loan because he fully expected to be turned down. He's halfway out the door before he realizes she actually said yes. But my real favourite is an ad with a scene that I can envision playing out in homes right across Canada. It begins with a woman sitting at her computer looking at her online bank account. She's calling to her husband, who is only a disembodied voice and a pair of feet sitting in an easy chair in another room. You're left with the impression he doesn't know she's online scrutinizing the money he spent the day before. She begins by asking about his visit with his mother.

He replies, "We went out."

"Where'd you go?" she inquires, already knowing the answer written on the screen in front of her.

"We went out for lunch."

"What did she have?"

"Sea bass. And I bought her flowers too."

The wife sees the purchase on her computer, and is quite touched by the gesture. "I love you, hon," she calls to the feet.

His response: "Yeah? And I bought a new DVD player with cash I borrowed from my mom that won't show up on your screen."

According to White, one of the tricks is simply to reverse the genders of the actors in all of the ads, to be sure it resonates both ways. Scotiabank's use of playful and self-deprecating humour, real-life situations, and familiar issues makes them a leader in gender-inclusive advertising. This particular campaign cleaned up in the financial services category, winning gold medals in the ad industry's award competitions.

Kazmer agrees with White. "Find universal points of view and sell to the heart," he says. "The heart then seduces the mind. But first you need to go through a social checklist to weed out insensitivity." When he finished an ad, Kazmer always asked, "I wonder whom I have inadvertently offended, hurt, overlooked, or misrepresented? Then I would go out and see if I could find out. Usually that meant taking it home to my wife, Karen."

MATCHING YOUR INSIDE WITH YOUR OUTSIDE

I wish I could tell you the top 10 things you need to know in order to connect with women, but there are only two.

> There are no rules.
> Your outside message needs to match your inside.

According to Jim Barnes, author of *Secrets of Customer Relationship Management*, customer relationships are a genuine emotional connection between two people. "Relationships are not functional," Barnes says. "A brand is more than a name or a logo in the same way that a relationship is more than an interaction. A brand is more than a corporate identification or name of the firm. It's not design or packaging; it's an emotional connection between a company and its customers and the public. It's not what we sell; it's who we are, what we stand for, and what we mean to people."

As he works with clients around the world, Barnes notices that those involved in customer relationship management are predominantly women. "Marketing is evolving away from the old toolkit with the four Ps"—product, place, price, promotion—"that we used to 'do' to people," he says. "Today, marketing is the job of everyone in the organization. Every employee has the potential to influence customer satisfaction directly or indirectly. It's not a department, it's a state of mind. Today, the four Ps are product, processes, people, and performance. Staff impact or interpersonal interaction can make or break the relationship."

Ann Coombs weighs in. She is the President of Coombs Consulting Ltd., a firm that studies consumer trends and facilitates corporate change management programs. She is also author of *The Living Workplace: Soul, Spirit, and Success in the 21st Century*, which describes a "living workplace" where consistency, authenticity, and respect form the foundation of business relationships. Coombs talks about a fundamental re-examination of our intent, and replaces competition with collaboration.

"Are we communicating our heartfelt intent to honour the wholeness and spirituality of individuals, or are we trying to manipulate? People know when they are being manipulated. When women are dealing with broken marriages, menopause, and their children fighting drugs in the schoolyard, what messages are we sending them? Are they messages of concern, support, and caring, or are they all about having another 'thing' to anesthetize us? Where is the honesty and truth in the communication? Intent is carrying authority with dignity. It is about authenticity, about saying in a real way that we honour the importance of women in the working and consumer marketplace."

So, the first step is to convert your internal corporate and sales culture into a gender intelligent one. We've talked about this before (in Chapter Three)—there are a million different ways to do this. But how do you let the world know you're genuinely trying to change? And if you let them know what great sponsorships, donations, and initiatives you have undertaken, will your adversaries criticize you for blowing your own horn or—much worse—for trying to make a buck out of misfortune? Tough call . . .

Matching your inside to your outside requires a gender/diversity analysis of your current culture and a determination of where it needs to go. How do your employees view the company's efforts? What gets noticed and rewarded? Everyone always says their people are their greatest asset, but do your people feel that way? And don't make the mistake of thinking a few lunch-and-learns and some guidelines about harassment will cut it. Such programs are absolute necessities, but they are the low-hanging fruit—too easy to pick and not enough to provide any competitive leverage. Corporate soul has to live and breathe in every corner and crevice of the company.

We asked Bobbie Gaunt, former CEO of Ford Canada, for her take on creating a women-friendly company with internal policies aligned with its external marketing messages. She has an unparalleled understanding of the challenges involved in opening up the worldview of a notoriously old-boy company.

"It begins with the CEO and the leadership team, and the company's board of directors in the case of publicly held companies," says Gaunt. "They must have a clear, articulated, visible, involved commitment to respecting and promoting diversity inside the company, in the marketplace, and in the community at large, and it must be derived from a solid business case. This is where much time is wasted and where commitments waver. Whether we like it or not, publicly held corporations must provide shareholder value, which they do by adding value to the bottom line. Having a solid business case to support one's commitment to diversity not only provides focus, but also reassures all important constituencies that a commitment to diversity is consistent with both the soft and hard values.

"There are at least four indicators that immediately signal to the diverse marketplace whether a company 'gets it,'" she says. "They're family-friendly work policies and working environment, intelligently designed products appropriate for the target market, respectful and relevant communications practices, and retail and service processes that assure your customer that you're caring and thoughtful." Sounds somewhat familiar.

How to Create a Gender Intelligent Inside

One might assume that all companies do pretty much the same thing to address internal gender imbalances. When you look at statistics on women in senior management, many companies are at Statistics Canada's measure of 21%, or lower. Their human resources gender awareness training programs are similar; the sponsorship and donation money—all similar. So why do some companies stand out and others struggle to make progress? Something called authenticity. Companies that forge a genuine relationship with people build a foundation of respect and trust that takes them through the difficult times and lets them soar in better times.

To match your company's inside with your outside and build real corporate soul, you need to know what areas to cast through the gender lens. Here are the Women's Key Consumer Standards for creating corporate soul.

WOMEN'S KEY CONSUMER STANDARDS: CREATING CORPORATE SOUL

Strategy	Have you done a complete audit of your company processes using a gender lens?
	Determine your authenticity account. Does it need shoring up?
	Is your brand experience consistent at every possible point throughout the organization?
	Is there a means to "measure" what women value in the consumer relationship and integrate it into company processes?
	Are there financial and organizational resources available to hire and keep women employees for the long run?
	Are the events and organizations you sponsor relevant? Do they make a difference in women's lives?
	Do your advertising and marketing materials realistically portray women?
Management	Can management articulate what the company brand means to women and can they communicate this effectively to employees?
	Can management quantify the potential of women consumers in terms of volume, market share, and profit opportunities?
	Is management performance "measured" and rewarded based on customer satisfaction, sales, and market share, as well as employee satisfaction and leadership practices?
Employees	Do staff understand and support the corporate strategy behind better meeting the needs of women consumers?
	Are your customer touch points equipped to handle or reflect gender differences in communication and consumer behaviour?
	Do you measure and reward employee behaviour that positively influences customer relationships and that is consistent with your company's goals of a gender-balanced workplace and customer base?
	Is there a means for taking action against non-compliant behaviour?
	Do you solicit and act on ideas and opinions from all stakeholders—customers and employees—alike?
	Does your sales force mirror the market you serve?

Some might say this list isn't tactical, and they're right. Developing genuine corporate soul looks like and feels like different things to different companies. So much depends on your history, current status, and future goals. Each element requires challenging values and beliefs and requires a willingness to risk the status quo that might seem to be working very well.

But the world has changed. Consumers and employees expect more from corporations and the bar is being raised. Companies that respond with authenticity will be rewarded with multiple paybacks, innovative ideas, higher productivity, talent that comes and sticks around, community recognition, customer satisfaction, and—yes, indeed—shareholder value.

These diverse and complex issues play out differently for each company so companies need to make it their own way. That's what makes it authentic. It's the struggle and the journey that puts the soul in corporate soul.

6

More than the sum of its parts

Whether it means a separate or distinct marketing strategy or several tweaks to the status quo, one thing is certain: Reaching women is clearly more than the sum of its parts. What you get back is proportional and then some to what you put out through gender intelligent connections. This means connecting authentically through your marketing communications, brochures, advertising, and direct mail. It means connecting face to face in your distribution and contact channels as well as electronically or by telephone, with a gender intelligent sales and service force. It means connecting globally, ethically, environmentally, and through diversity. It means connecting by being intelligent about gender differences. It means connecting by taking an educational and informative approach. It means connecting by making life simpler. It means connecting by contributing to the relationship in every interaction.

In short, it means stitching gender intelligence into every part of the company fabric.

Only then can you reach your end goal of a sustained, loyal, and mutually beneficial business relationship. Is there any company that manages to do all of this? Well, no. No one gets it right every single time. Frankly, if there are 5 million companies in Canada, there are also 5 million ways to build relationships with women consumers. But all the companies we've included in this book have had some measure of success at reaching women. The last two companies we're going to consider stand out in terms of their ability to integrate and speak to all the touchstones of gender intelligence, but, more importantly, because they are so utterly different from each other, they demonstrate the full range of possibilities.

One comes from the ivory towers of the financial district of Toronto's Bay Street and brings with it all that this entails—the quintessential middle-aged white male game of finance. Even in an industry with a challenged history with women like this one, the right combination of strategy, budget, and heart where and when you need it can create authentic relationships with women consumers. RBC Royal Bank, although not without its warts, has made a long-term commitment to transforming itself into a culture that supports, among other things, women employees and women clients. We asked president and CEO Gordon Nixon if RBC Royal Bank targets women, and he said, "Absolutely."

The other example comes from the other side of the country and other end of the spectrum. An upstart entrepreneurial venture that grew out of the no-holds-barred, male-dominated outdoor adventure scene in Vancouver, Mountain Equipment Co-op is one of the most gender intelligent companies we've seen to date. It came out of the gates, for the most part, committed to serving its constituency in a values-driven way. Gender intelligence has always been intrinsic and instinctive. We asked CEO Peter Robinson if MEC targets women, and he said, "Nope."

Two very different companies, two very different approaches. Yet both exemplify the principles in this book and successfully offer women an authentic consumer experience. And both are reaping the rewards of their efforts.

Learning to Look Through a Gender Intelligent Lens

RBC Royal Bank serves a mere 12 million clients. This works out to one in three Canadians and one in three women-led businesses. It includes more than half a million businesses through more than 1,300 service delivery units in Canada alone, not counting automated banking units and the rest of the world. The bank is the largest small business lender in Canada, with $20 billion in authorized loans to roughly half a million small business clients. The bank employs 60,000 people, of whom 73% are women. Almost a third of its Canadian executives are women.

How did the RBC Royal Bank, in that exclusively male culture of high finance, come to change the way it interacts with the society it serves?

It all began with Mary.

In the 1960s, Royal Bank devised a marketing strategy based on a character named Mary. As Duncan McDowall describes in *Quick to the Frontier: Canada's Royal Bank*, Mary signalled the beginning of the consumer-oriented approach to banking. The embodiment of personable banking service in a friendly, attractive, efficient, girl-next-door, dream teller, she became one of the best-known advertising personalities in Canada. But the growing concern over the place of women in Canadian society eventually exposed her as a prime example of sexual stereotyping in advertising. In 1976, Laura Sabia, head of the newly established Status of Women Council, bought a single Royal Bank share, attended the annual meeting, and demanded when the bank would take "that idiot advertisement" off the air. Mary retired soon after.

A few years later, CEO Roland Frazee launched the Task Force of Women in Management. One of the first things the bank recognized was that changing attitudes and education were essential to break up the old boys' network. A sociologist was hired to sensitize Royal Bank's senior management to gender issues, and all the materials in training courses were reworked to remove stereotyping.

The bank's initial approach was to look inward first, which is paramount to the success of any gender-based initiative. But it also realized that just having gender-aware executives and management wouldn't necessarily translate into an improved face-to-face customer experience. By the 1990s, under the expert guidance of Charlie Coffey and Anne Sutherland, the predominantly male sales force in business banking were receiving training on gender-based communication skills. "Women need to be understood and respected by the business community," says Betty Wood, National Marketing Manager, Women Entrepreneurs. "When we embarked on this journey, women told us that they were not being taken seriously as businesspeople—especially by the banks. Handing out pink cheque books just wouldn't cut it."

Nixon says women are a top priority for the bank. Yet the companies that are most successful at creating authentic and sustainable change are the ones that transcend strategy, often led by champions committed to the "cause." It wasn't just the strategy, the profitable business case, or the sponsorship dollars that were responsible for the bank's initial success in this market. It was Charlie Coffey as front man leading his team, pure and simple. Yes, a banker to be sure, but one with a passion for improving the experience of women entrepreneurs with his bank.

Under Coffey's watch and with a talented and committed team, the bank created advisory councils of women entrepreneurs. Women told the bank to put dollars into providing education and support, break down barriers, and help build networks. And the bank set out to do just that—touching on all four principles of reaching women consumers while they were at it.

Reliable, real research is the only way to tell whether women's claims of inferior service and discriminatory practices were real or perceived, and it's virtually indispensable when it comes to developing gender intelligence. The bank analyzes market research, customer satisfaction surveys, and consumer feedback by gender. In fact, nothing hits the street that doesn't get tested in the marketplace and with women first.

Research has shown that women are likely to use their personal savings and credit cards to finance their businesses, rather than using loans. Women also perceive business financing as hard to get and business banking as intimidating. Financial support for start-up and expansion can be a significant hurdle for many new businesses.

RBC Royal Bank's response? When the applicant doesn't fit the usual criteria, the bank works with partners such as the Canadian Youth

Business Foundation and Alberta Women's Enterprise Initiative Association. The bank has found technological solutions that speed the processing and reduce the opportunity for bias, gender or otherwise. Each application goes through a scoring model and, because the model doesn't take gender into account, there is less opportunity for gender bias. (Today, all banks use this credit scoring model.) The bank offers a mortgage product that allows four months' payments to be skipped for special circumstances such as maternity leave. And when the accounts are joint, so are the mailing addresses.

Wood told us that women want practical information about business plans, income and expense statements, cash flow, profit margins, and so on, and aren't afraid to ask for it. "As bankers," she says, "we've learned that women entrepreneurs are generally a determined bunch and they'll learn it with or without us. If we can make it easier for them to find more useful information faster, that's good relationship-building for us." All banks have truckloads of information available for the taking, but RBC Royal Bank has tailored some of it to meet the needs of women entrepreneurs. Getting through with intelligent communication is also the rationale behind the bank's focus on education specifically for women entrepreneurs, which made possible a wide variety of seminar offerings and a newsletter, twice a year, filled with inspirational stories and client profiles, useful news, offers, and discounts.

Another successful initiative is the bank's website for women entrepreneurs, a comprehensive, one-stop source of information, association and events listings, publications, resources, and news. This enabled the bank to reach well beyond its existing customer base to create a virtual network that offers women an online community that spans the country.

RBC Royal Bank has also been working on ways to recognize the multiple dimensions and complexities of all of its customers, women in particular. It came up with a multi-layered matrix of segments according to age and life-cycle stages, financial characteristics, and business activities. The matrix includes life events that have financial implications, such as buying a car, going to college, getting married, having a baby, and buying a house, as well as business events, such as starting up, growing, and retiring and planning for succession. While segmentation and markets are commonplace, the additional lens of life events creates the opportunity to build life-long relationships with customers and their families. Thanks to this matrix, Anne Lockie, Executive Vice-President, says, "every time we look at our client base, we understand the interconnection of the family. Our strategy is an evolving pathway and the emerging theme is to understand individuals within the context of their lives, which certainly includes gender, among other things."

So how do women benefit from this multidimensional approach? Certain personal life events may be driven more or less by women, so the bank can tailor its services appropriately. For example, the bank struck a partnership with *Wedding Bells* magazine, because women do most of the organizing involved in weddings. Also, when a couple is planning to buy a home, the focus of the information is different. Women are more likely to do the research and are more interested in some of the more non-financial information such as location of schools and what community facilities are available, so the bank responds accordingly.

The bank has set up a national network of more than 100 account managers called "Women's Champions" who share a passion for better serving the needs of women entrepreneurs. They understand that women look to banks for more than traditional financing. They provide strategic input and advice and are tied into women's business organizations within their communities.

The bank also creates strong bonds with its women clients by celebrating their accomplishments. It hosts numerous events at the executive dining facilities at its Toronto headquarters, including book launches, small business networking, and community events. It features women clients in ads and marketing materials. Wood says, "These activities are a way for us to reciprocate and give something back to our clients by promoting their businesses—and women appreciate that." Not only does the bank celebrate its clients' accomplishments, it also supports them by choosing to do business with them as well, where possible.

In fact, look at any major sponsorship opportunity that involves women in business and you will likely see a RBC Royal Bank connection. The bank believes that these networking events are an important way to develop contacts and relationships that yield profitable business. Examples include support for the Canadian Association of Women Executives and Entrepreneurs, which offers regular meetings and professional development opportunities to women, and Step Ahead, a mentoring program that matches women who want to take their businesses to the next level with successful women entrepreneurs whose companies have gone through a growth cycle. The bank has been the lead sponsor of a number of trade initiatives that have opened the exporting door for many women entrepreneurs, such as two Women's Trade Missions to the United States and the 1999 Canada/USA Businesswomen's Trade Summit. They also sponsor the Uniquely Canada Creative Arts Show, an annual fair for micro gift producers, 60% of whom are women.

RBC Royal Bank continues to garner international recognition and awards as a world leader in supporting women entrepreneurs. In 2001, Wood went to Paris to address the Organisation for Economic Co-operation and Development's conference on women in small and medium-sized enterprises. As a result of sharing its best practices, the bank was instrumental in launching the Global Banking Alliance for Women, a group of five international banks that have programs dedicated to actively supporting women in business through training, mentoring, sponsorships, and access to networks and markets. These banks have been actively sharing marketing information in order to accelerate domestic programs and initiatives for women. Eventually the plan is to engage other banks around the world to contribute and learn from best practice models.

For six years in a row, RBC Royal Bank was named the top corporation in corporate social responsibility in *The Globe and Mail*'s annual list of Canada's Most Respected Corporations. This category includes charitable giving, employee volunteerism, sponsorships, community involvement, corporate governance, and ethical business practices. The bank contributes generously through an employee donation plan that awards a cash donation to charities to which employees give their time, and it supports in-kind donations for local community involvement initiatives.

The bank's corporate soul is evident in another category in the *Globe*'s annual poll—people management—for four consecutive years, thanks to its leading-edge human resource programs. For example, almost one-third of the bank's employees have some form of flexible work situation, such as modified work weeks, job sharing, and work-at-home arrangements, making it easier for women to juggle their various responsibilities. It also offers such innovative programs as community service leave and phased retirement, and more than 90% of employees take part in a share-ownership plan.

The heights reached by the women's market initiative are complemented by the ongoing work "on the inside." Elisabetta Bigsby, Senior Executive Vice-President, Human Resources and Public Affairs, says the RBC brand—"building relationships, delivering value"—means that everything the bank does is intended to provide for client needs, not simply in a transactional way but in a way that develops long-term relationships. Bigsby says, "The brand becomes the embodiment of the values, and employees are the key to client satisfaction."

In 2001, RBC Royal Bank took the unusual step of combining responsibility for the external brand and internal employee franchise into one role. "By doing so we are not talking across silos," says Bigsby, who heads up this initiative. "I talk to myself. Corporate values and vision are more than half of how an employee feels about her or his role, and that directly affects how that employee delivers to the customer. Every successful brand has an employee brand and a customer brand, but the two are interlinked. Your brand lives through employees delivering to the customer."

While there are many things that support RBC Royal Bank's approach to women customers, one of the values that builds a solid foundation to ensure that gender remains on the radar is diversity. "Our definition of diversity welcomes a different point of view," says Bigsby. "The origin of that point of view doesn't matter—we reflect our external community and thus all views are important. Gender is now ingrained in everything we do." President and CEO Gordon Nixon chairs the bank's diversity committee and says, "The substantial and ongoing attention to diversity has made sure employee programs and marketing programs are consistent with our diversity values."

Does it pay off to live your corporate soul? In that *Globe and Mail* poll, RBC Royal Bank Group was also named the top corporation in terms of financial performance. Even the bean counters are happy.

Meeting the needs of women consumers may be fully integrated into how the bank does business. But, as Nixon says, "the last frontier remains the investment business. Companies may hire one and a half women for every man, but they still can't retain them. Recruiting doesn't solve the issue, certainly not with a male-centric model like the investment business. Even though it's draconian, you still need to incorporate hiring women into the business plan, and the working environment and culture need to support the policy, otherwise, it's not going to happen."

Coffey adds, "The impact and influence of women on the prosperity of Canada is not lost on me. Yes, it was self-interest that led us to go after this market, but at the same time, I saw many other agendas at play. The big one was the critical and strategic importance of the contributions women make to advancing a civil society. When I think about it, there was a common thread all along the way. The thousands of women I've met over the years have given me insight into the strong connection between the economic and social agendas of this country, and our work in the women's market has led the bank to a much better understanding that Canada's prosperity is a strong link between these two agendas."

Nixon concludes, "The women's market initiatives have evolved from needing a champion to being a priority market for the bank. Champions create awareness of the issue but the really successful ones, like Charlie Coffey, inculcate permanent change so the organization doesn't need them anymore. We now want to take an integrative approach, at least where a foundation of work is already done. I'd love to say it would be a natural way of how to do business, but the reality is that women will remain a key segment of our business. Frankly, change doesn't happen by accident and we still need to focus. But we are on the right track. Even if the bank's next CEO was a woman, the bank wouldn't change its focus."

Starting Out with a Gender Intelligent Perspective

We now move from the Toronto-centric world of the country's largest financial institution to the glorious mountains of Vancouver. Here we find a hip retail company with a combination of adrenaline and values that has created a gender intelligent sales experience that beautifully meets the needs of both women and men. And they say they don't market to women. We respectfully disagree.

Mountain Equipment Co-op's raison d'être is to provide outdoor gear affordable enough that there's still money left over to go out and play. This socially and environmentally responsible retail cooperative is the best example we found of a company that lives its values from the inside out and, in so doing, demonstrates all four principles of connecting with women consumers. Peter Robinson, CEO, says, "There is no one reason for MEC having the heart that it does. This company is 31 years old. The initial structure of being a not-for-profit cooperative was created by the founders, who were a group of students who simply wanted to get quality gear and access to the outdoors, hiking, and the mountains." Today, Mountain Equipment Co-op has seven stores across Canada and currently enjoys close to 50% market share of the outdoor industry. "None of this was consciously planned," Robinson says. "We never could have predicted that we would have 1.6 million members from coast to coast." The gender breakdown of those members is 50/50.

The very fact that Robinson was hired for the CEO position speaks to the culture of the company. He had no retail or conventional marketing background when he assumed the leadership role of MEC two and a half years ago. What he did have was an extraordinary social conscience. His CV includes jobs as diverse as park ranger to head of a Crown corporation that developed subsidized housing. He worked with the Red Cross, which has taken him to various disaster relief projects in places such as Rwanda. His appointment at MEC brought him back full circle to his original work—he meshes his passion for the outdoors and stewardship of the environment with his management and leadership experience. "It is my firm belief that the values Mountain Equipment Co-op stands for couldn't have been sustained without the cooperative structure," he says. "It's not profit driven; it's values driven. It's about delivering good quality at a good price in a service-based environment. We still must be financially robust, but the bottom line is very different." The company operates on a 3% surplus revenue format and gains about 7% revenue growth annually, which is reinvested in the business.

Robinson says the company is successful for a variety of reasons. "I would have to say our primary strength is our staff," he says. "We provide people with vigorous training and skills and reinforce activity training with the seven principles of a cooperative structure so that all of our staff can talk about it and what it means. This then gets translated into the culture.

The values don't come from the top down; they are integral and permeate throughout the organization. Everyone has a keen awareness of our values and the system thus becomes self-fulfilling. Like is attracted to like."

Hiring practices focus on getting the right people who believe in working to live, not living to work. "We believe that the way we treat our employees will positively affect how our members are treated," says Toronto assistant manager Sean McSweeney. "We show respect for others in our words and actions. We act in the spirit of community and cooperation. We respect and protect our natural environment. We strive for personal growth, continual learning, and adventure."

At the store level, this is reflected in management style. "Our role is to support individual needs while also ensuring the viability of the business and maintaining the store community," says McSweeney. There are no policies or practices in place that specifically focus on women and family needs; instead, the emphasis is on different individual needs within a diverse working community. "Our work culture means that we have a large number of women who work for us but not always in the traditional areas," he says. "We judge people based on their skills and values, not on traditional assumptions about what roles people play. For example, the team leader for women's clothing is a man, the team leader for climbing is a woman, my administrative assistant is a man, and the Chief Information Officer is a woman."

Mountain Equipment Co-op strongly encourages the use of parental leave with no repercussions to the individual's career path. "In fact, we look at it as an opportunity for the individual to come back re-energized," McSweeney says. This also creates opportunities for replacement staff to gain job experience they may not otherwise have access to. Retail hours offer a lot of flexibility with respect to scheduling and time off, which provides support for staff with family and daycare issues, or other demands on their time, such as night school or training for a marathon. McSweeney says, "Many of our staff, both men and women, work flexible hours in order to balance work and family. We also job share, even at a senior management level. We have staff who tele-commute at head office. We strive to help individuals achieve a balance between work and life. MEC will authorize a leave of absence for as long as three months so that employees can trek through the Himalayas." McSweeney himself just returned from several months of parental leave.

Hiring is based on integrity and values, and many of MEC's initiatives come from employees who have special interests. There are also built-in checks and balances for diversity and functionality. MEC always hires on merit, a policy that consistently works because there are no barriers to gender and diversity. It promotes from within unless an internal candidate can't be found or there is a special need in a high specialty area. "We are not a hierarchical system," Robinson says. "We have a diverse board of directors whose role is to ensure that our policies reinforce the unique nature of our business. Within our organization we hold a real respect for debate. The downside is that it can take a long time to make decisions, but the upside is that we take the time to have those debates and to check whether our actions and decisions are in line with our values."

McSweeney says, "Our corporate culture is a 'ground up' learning culture based on sharing information. Understanding what the member wants is a major part of it. We have weekly team meetings at which six or eight members of each section discuss issues such as member feedback on service and products, or how to improve processes. We conduct surveys with members. We use information-based selling. For us, this means added value learning about products and their application."

All this has a huge effect on how Mountain Equipment Co-op approaches the needs of women consumers. Its approach is evident in everything it does, from the design of a store to staffing. It includes things like the money-back guarantee and the fact that MEC does something no one else in that industry does—it stocks all spare parts for the equipment it sells. That's certainly a huge benefit to that time-starved, rock-climbing mother of two, or her mountain-biking sister stuck for long hours in the boardroom.

According to MEC, older women are more active than older men. Women shoppers want more information, ask more questions, and ask for more attention than men do. Women want a facilitated experience. Women and children typically shop together, so the two departments are situated side by side, with women's change rooms next to the family washroom. In the Toronto store, there's a play area in between these two sections so kids can play safely within view of their mothers. When it comes to merchandise, MEC requires the same functionality and performance in children's gear as in the adults', and the kids' colour selection—hallelujah—is not gender specific.

McSweeney notes, "Men know they are and always have been a size 36. Many pick out their pant size and a large shirt without even trying them on. It's just the simple truth that women come in more sizes and shapes than men. There is also more variation in sizing from manufacturer to manufacturer. Therefore, women need to try on more clothing in order to get the fit they are looking for." These differences are reflected in the way MEC services its members. "As a result," says McSweeney, "we have a higher ratio of staff servicing the women's apparel section."

Until eight years ago, MEC sold only unisex clothing and had hit the ceiling with respect to market share. Around that time the industry started to focus on women consumers with gender-specific clothing. MEC saw the market as a new growth opportunity and began to produce its own line of women's clothing. In 1994, the ratio of men to women members was 70 to 30. Since 1999, it has grown to an even split. How did these numbers evolve so significantly? According to McSweeney, "When developing or buying a product, we start by thinking about who is using the products and how things are going to be used. This is a shift from the traditional profit-driven or design-driven thinking. From this point of view, women have different considerations, especially where fit is concerned. This applies to clothing, fitted equipment such as harnesses, and technical footwear. We also realized things like the weight of equipment, like boats, were also an issue."

Anne Gillespie, activewear buyer, says, "Many lines still take the men's design and just shrink it for women or label it unisex with a S, M, L, or XL sizing, which doesn't fit most women properly. But when we offered something tailored to one gender or the other"—she calls it gendering an item—"the response was overwhelming. We saw sales on gendered fleece increase by 50% and sales on gendered organic t-shirts for women jump by 100%. After those results, we gendered all clothing and even gear where it made sense."

Patrick Stratton, Vice-President of Merchandise, says that often "marketing to women" can be nothing more than a trend. "We researched the idea of a woman-sized sleeping bag," he explains. "However, the staff's reaction was 'This is just marketing hype.' Many of the features touted as beneficial for women were appropriate for anyone sleeping in a bag (such as extra insulation in the foot area), which we'd already incorporated into our designs." This was an instance where classifying something according to S, M, and L actually suited everyone.

Gillespie notes, "All of our buyers, women and men, are very conscious of women and their role in the market. They know that a women's product must be authentic. Function will always be first. Fashion is not a bad thing but we will never design out functionality. Women are going to get the same quality, durability, and performance as men, with the difference being in sizing, shape, and design." When Mountain Equipment Co-op implemented this policy, it introduced change first through sizing, then it moved on to colour, and now it focuses on styling features. Today, MEC has many products with different designs for both women and men.

Some of the enhancements made for women are attractive to men. When MEC introduced different sizes of backpacks to accommodate women, they found that in fact they were able to accommodate different sizes of any body. Women have narrower feet and heels and so required a different shoe design, which resulted in a greater range of footwear options, which benefited men who needed a narrower fit. Narrow, smaller sunglasses were offered for kids, and then women adopted them because sunglasses had previously only been available for "white men with large heads," according to Gillespie. A woman-specific harness was designed with a wider area of padding around the waist, a design feature now incorporated into the design of the men's equivalent. A cycling seat designed for women with a cutout in the centre (as she says, "to avoid crushing the little man in the canoe") has since moved into the men's market. In fact, men's cutaway seats now make up 42% of all bicycle seat sales, with gel seats (a modified version of the cutaway) making up another 10%. The brake placement on bikes was moved closer to the handlebars, which, originally designed to help women cyclists, suited men with smaller hands.

There remain many products that are "gendered," such as lifejackets and skis (which require different flex patterns because of women's lighter weight), but the principle of "women-friendly equals everybody-friendly" really flourishes here.

Until 2002, Mountain Equipment Co-op didn't have a dedicated communications and marketing department. As Robinson says, "Word of mouth has been an excellent way of building our business." The catalogue and website support ongoing communication with members after the initial relationship has been established. Through the website, members can shop, trade used gear, and receive bulletins and newsletters. The stores themselves are located in downtown areas, rather than in malls, and are accessible by public transit. In essence, MEC sets down roots and becomes a permanent part of the communities it serves. This, more than anything else, sustains and strengthens the relationships the company has with its members.

But what keeps members coming back is the alignment of members' values with the delivery of products and services that meet their needs. Today, the organization has competitors that use conventional marketing and sales strategies, and consumers are conditioned to this.

MEC is responding. "We need to adapt to a changing economic environment," Robinson says, "and we need to do it in such a way that we retain existing members as well as attract new ones, and stay true to our values. We do that by being open and transparent about how we manufacture and where products come from. We tell stories about how our stores are connected to their local communities and how they act as a catalyst for such initiatives as river clean-ups, and assisting groups buying endangered land. Our role is to create awareness and make this information available to the marketplace." This may be tough for MEC to do, but in the end, as in the beginning, solid values form the foundation of its business.

Mountain Equipment Co-op has many social and environmental practices in place to ensure that it gives back to the community and causes that align with the company's values. Members expect MEC to make ethical decisions on their behalf. As a percentage of gross sales, the company is one of the largest funders of environmental causes in Canada. Roughly $700,000 or close to half a percent of gross sales is donated annually. Mountain Equipment Co-op's Endowment Fund for the Environment is a registered charitable foundation that accepts tax-deductible donations directly from co-op members as well as the public. This fund has grown to more than $1 million with the substantial interest going to support Canadian environmental projects.

The environmental fund also supports wilderness-oriented, Canadian-based projects. Since 1987, it has contributed more than $4 million to wilderness preservation and conservation endeavours. In addition, each store has a Social and Environmental Responsibility Coordinator who manages a local environment fund of $10,000 not connected to the store's revenue, which goes towards programs such as the Green Thumbs/ Growing Things kids' program at Toronto's Riverdale Farm, Women with Wrenches to teach women about bike repair and maintenance, and the Everdale Environmental Learning Centre. There are also community funds varying according to the revenue of the store, that have supported programs such as Paddle to a Cure for the Canadian Breast Cancer Society, Project Canoe, a Trails Youth Initiative, and Friends for Life bike rally.

The coordinator also handles all store and community events, including talking to schools about everything from business ethics to winter camping, informing local media of community involvement, as well as coordinating donations and gifting. Those donations may be as small as a daypack or as large as several thousand dollars for a touring theatre group that teaches kids about the environment. At the store level, this is probably the most active way to connect with members in order to build relationships outside of regular service transactions.

Ethical product sourcing is a corporate mandate. Forty-five percent of Mountain Equipment Co-op's products are Canadian, with the rest coming from Europe, the U.S., China, and Asia. Currently 90% of the clothing is branded, meaning MEC contracts out its own designs to factories, which must meet strict approval standards. MEC uses its own supplier team evaluation program to screen sources and recently began using third-party audit teams as well. Production plants are inspected and a 50-page questionnaire evaluates health and payment records of employees, conditions of the factory, and the local community.

MEC's Toronto store is in a state-of-the-art green commercial building and the new Montreal, Ottawa, and Winnipeg stores are joining the ranks of the greenest commercial buildings in North America. MEC assesses the impact of buildings and products to have the least possible effect on the environment. The stores sponsor seasonal gear swaps so members can trade or sell used equipment and clothing (in addition to the feature on the website). Gillespie says, "We recognize that this means we may not sell something, but recycling is a strong part of our values."

Robinson believes that if someone tried to replicate Mountain Equipment Co-op from scratch today, it wouldn't work. "We were there first," he says. "We were allowed to develop culturally without the intense pressure of a competitive market environment. I believe a co-operative business can succeed in a young and emerging industry—it's a format that works well if you're at the front of the wave. But now we have many competitors emulating us. Going forward, we cannot afford to be complacent."

Gillespie believes that women are dramatically changing her industry. "It's my belief that women are the strongest drivers behind organic cotton, sustainable product, and social responsibility agendas all over the world. In terms of outdoor activities and sports, women are achieving all kinds of firsts in cycling, paddling, and bouldering that have traditionally been male dominated. Seeing women being women in sports is defining a new kind of femininity."

When MEC surveyed its members about why they were attracted to the company, 20% said they came simply because of MEC's values. In this category, 60% were women. It would appear Mountain Equipment Co-op's intuitive approach to retailing naturally resonates with what women value in a retail experience.

Where Does All This Get Us?

Now that we've seen the full range of possibilities for putting the needs of women consumers on the radar, with examples from the realms of not-for-profits, small entrepreneurs, big corporate multinationals, and education, where did the women's marketing initiatives get them? Simply put, satisfied customers and increased market share.

> *The Globe and Mail* readership among women in major markets moved from 39% to 46%.
> W saw a 19% growth in weekly reach among women aged 18 to 49.
> Toronto's Holiday Inn on King saw a 400% rise in occupancy rates among women business travellers.
> Aero experienced a 42% increase in sales, moving from eighth to second in the highly competitive chocolate bar industry.

> RBC Royal Bank gained a 12-point market share lead in small and medium-sized enterprises in the women's market.
> Toyota Canada customers rated overall performance of Access salespersons almost double that at a national level, and market share increased half a point in one region—an amount equal to $175 million.
> RONA witnessed an annual growth rate of 39%.
> Evelyn Hannon, founder of Journeywoman.com, was named by *Time* Magazine as one of the "100 Most Innovative Thinkers of this New Century."
> Lean Cuisine's "real women" TV campaign resulted in a 10% unit sales increase against a category that was flat at 0%.
> Mountain Equipment Co-op watched its member profile move from a 70/30 male-to-female split to an even 50/50.

And there's so much more. I've been able to fill this book with success stories about people and companies that have picked up that gender lens and seen a whole new world through it. I wish this book were three times as long. The issues are complex and systemic, but as you've seen there are plenty of ways to tackle them. The successful companies have moved beyond balance sheets and profit statements and are taking Canadian women consumers seriously. In effect, they have recognized the 80% minority as a majority. In return, they've been amply rewarded with women's loyalty.

The world will open up to you when you weave a gender worldview into every aspect of what your company does. You'll increase satisfaction levels not only among the country's most powerful consumer group— women—but also among your employees, men, suppliers, the gay and lesbian population, Aboriginal people, environmentalists, parents, children . . . the list is very, very long.

Remember the tortoise and the hare. There's still plenty of time to get into the race.

Endnotes

Introduction

1. "Reaching Canada's 80% Minority," The Thomas Yaccato Group and Thompson Lightstone, August 2002.
2. Statistics Canada, 1996 Census reported in "Single Women Lead Charge in House Buying," *The Globe and Mail*, March 12, 1999; Re/max Promotions Inc., "Real Estate Buyers Focus Groups," Angus Reid Inc., 1998; National Foundation of Women Business Owners (now Center for Women's Business Research), News Release, December 1, 1999; Tom Peters, *The Circle of Innovation*, Vintage Books, 1999; "2000 Zagat NYC Restaurant Survey: Still A Man's World," 2000; Faith Popcorn, *EVEolution: The Eight Truths of Marketing to Women*, Hyperion, 2000; "WOW! Facts 2002," Business Women's Network, Diversity Best Practices, and iVillage.

Chapter 1

1. 1991 and 1996 Census of Canada, Industry Canada.
2. AdEdge Report on Marketing to Women, Television Bureau of Canada, 2001.
3. Paula England and Teresa Gardner, "Sex Differentiation in Magazine Advertisements: A Content Analysis Using Log-Linear Modeling," *Current Issues and Research in Advertising*, volume 6, number 1, 1983.
4. Gary Warren Melton and Gilbert Fowler, Jr., "Female Roles in Radio Advertising," *Journalism Quarterly*, volume 64, number 1, 1987.
5. Jane Simmons, "Gender Differences of Nonverbal Power Cues in Television Commercials," *Proceedings of the 1986 Convention of the American Academy of Advertising*, edited by Ernest Larkin.
6. Marjorie Caballero and William Pride, "Selected Effects of Salesperson Sex and Attractiveness in Direct Mail Advertisements," *Journal of Marketing*, volume 48 (Winter), 1984.
7. William Kilbourne, "An Exploratory Study of Sex Roles in Advertising and Women's Perceptions of Managerial Attributes in Women," *Advances in Consumer Research*, volume 11, 1983.
8. "Work Life Compendium 2001: 150 Canadian Statistics on Work, Family, and Well-Being," Centre for Families, Work, and Well-Being, University of Guelph and Human Resources Development Canada, 2001.
9. "Aiming to Please Women, Business Travel Industry Introduces More Services for Female Customers," *USA Today*, June 10, 1999.

Chapter 2

1. Dr. Linda Duxbury, *Men and Women Working as Partners: A Reality Check of Canadian Organizations*, Centre for Research and Education on Women and Work, Carleton University, Ottawa, 1996.
2. Statistics Canada, "Annual Demographic Statistics," 2001, catalogue no. 91-213-XPB; "Age, Sex, and Marital Status," 1992, catalogue no. 93-310-XPB.
3. Joan Meyers-Levy, "Mixed Messages," *Capital Ideas*, volume 1, number 3, 1998.
4. Meyers-Levy, 1998.
5. Meyers-Levy, 1998.
6. Meyers-Levy, 1998.
7. Roger Masters and Stephen Carlotti, "Gender Differences in Responses to Political Leaders," in *Social Stratification and Socioeconomic Inequality*, edited by Lee Ellis, Praeger, Boulder CO, 1994.
8. "Hearts and Minds: A Study of Canadian Women," WTN, 1999.
9. Philip Kotler, Gary Armstrong, and Peggy H. Cunningham, *Principles of Marketing*, 4th Canadian edition, Prentice-Hall, Scarborough, 1999.
10. Kotler, Armstrong, and Cunningham, 1999.
11. Gail Vaz-Oxlade, *Women of Independent Means: A Woman's Guide to Full Financial Security*, Stoddart, Toronto, 1999.
12. My dad.
13. Renate Schubert, Martin Brown, Matthias Gysler, and Hans Wolfgang Brachinger, "Financial Decision Making: Are Women Really More Risk Averse?" *American Economic Review*, volume 89, number 2, 1999.
14. "Women Debunk Risk-Taking Myth," *The Globe and Mail*, June 7, 1999.
15. "I Am Woman, Watch My Stocks Soar," *The Globe and Mail*, April 17, 1999.
16. "Men's and Women's Investment Practices," *Canadian Investment Review*, summer 1997.
17. California Assembly Committee on Consumer Protection, 1994.
18. Frances Cerra Whittelsey and Marcia Carroll, *Women Pay More (and How to Put a Stop to It)*, New Press, New York, 1995 (originally published by Center for Study of Responsive Law, 1993 and 1995).
19. Aaron Freeman, *The Human Rights Law Implications of Gender-Based Pricing*, 1998.
20. "Why Do Female Consumers Pay More Than Men Do?" *The Toronto Star*, January 3, 1992.
21. Assembly Bill No. 1100, *An Act to Add Section 51.6 to the Civil Code, Relating to Civil Rights* [approved by Governor, October 13, 1995].

Chapter 3

1. Erin Strout, "Tough Customers," *Sales and Marketing Management*, January 2000.
2. Heather Dryburg, "Changing Our Ways: Why and How Canadians Use the Internet," 2000 General Social Survey Data, Statistics Canada, 2000.
3. Dryburg, 2000.
4. AdEdge Report on Marketing to Women, Television Bureau of Canada, 2001.
5. Julia Scott and Steve Harvey, "Men's and Women's Investment Habits," *Canadian Investment Review*, issue 10, 1997.

6. "Just Language: A Guide to Inclusive Language in The United Church of Canada," United Church of Canada <www.united-church.ca/ucc/justlanguage.htm> (November 2002).

7. Deborah Tannen, *Talking from 9 to 5—Women and Men in the Workplace: Language, Sex, and Power*, Avon Books, New York, 1995.

8. Centre for Women's Business Research (formerly the National Foundation for Women Business Owners), Washington DC, 1996.

9. Study on advertising, brochures, and seminars, research commissioned by Marketing Dimensions and conducted by PMG Consulting, March 1999.

10. Dryburg, 2000.

11. "What Makes Women Click?" NewSmart Research, 1998.

12. Lisa Johnson, "Becoming A Part of 'Her'," *RW Listens*, July 2002.

13. Shirley Dawe and Wendy Evans, with M. Denney, "Top of the Class: Ranking and Best Practices of Over 170 Web Sites," Ryerson University's Centre for the Study of Commercial Activity, 2000.

14. *Inside Retailing*, Special Report (Lake West Group Ltd.), Lebhar-Friedman Inc., New York.

15. Dawe and Evans, 2000.

Chapter 4

1. United Nations Development Programme, *Human Development Report*, Oxford University Press, New York, 1999.

2. "Hearts and Minds, A Study of Canadian Women," WTN, 1999.

3. Chloe E. Bird, "Gender, Household Labor, and Psychological Distress: The Impact of the Amount and Division of Housework," *Journal of Health and Social Behaviour*, volume 40, 1999.

4. Deloitte and Touche, "She Said: A Study of Affluent Women and Personal Finances," 1998.

5. Helen Fisher, *The First Sex: The Natural Talents of Women and How They Are Changing the World*, Random House, New York, 1999.

6. Michael Jantzi, "A Market Backgrounder," Michael Jantzi Reseach Associates Inc., 2001.

7. "Are Ethical Investors Different from Conventional Investors?" *Ethical Investor*, 2001.

8. Yankelovich Monitor, as reported in *About Women & Marketing*, October 1998.

9. AdEdge Report on Marketing to Women, Television Bureau of Canada, 2001.

Chapter 5

1. "Women in Canada 2000: A Gender-Based Statistical Report," National Survey on Giving, Volunteering and Participating, Statistics Canada, 2000.

2. AdEdge Report on Marketing to Women, Television Bureau of Canada, 2001.

3. AdEdge Report, 2001.

4. "Canada's 80% Minority," The Thomas Yaccato Group and Thompson Lightstone, 2002.

5. Jim Rennie's Sports Letter, January 3, 2000.

Index

A

Abbey, Deb, 165

Access Toyota Canada, 129–131

accompanied shops, 85

Addis, Richard, 71

Addition-Elle, 69–70

Adeo Communications Corporation, 141

advertising

    Canadian advertising experts' view, 19–23

    corporate soul, 190–202

    dumbing down men, trend of, 17, 20

    and eating disorders, 18

    gender inequality, reinforcement of, 22–23

    and gender-role identity, 65–66

    having-it-all campaigns, 191–192

    humanist approach to, 193

    inclusivity, 200–202

    minorities, portrayal of, 21

    mothers, 191

    multidimensional needs of women, 158–163

    no women in ads, 199–200

    object of the gaze, 17

    portrayal of women, 17–19

    role portrayal, 19

    sex differentiation studies, 18–19

    stereotyping, little change in, 18–19

    voice-overs, 200

    women in, 20–21

    Zig, 192–200

Aero chocolate bar, 97–99

ageism, 21

Air Canada, 15, 49–50, 51, 52, 53–54

airbag design, 25–26

Airey, Doug, 33, 144

airline industry

    Air Canada, 53–54

    babies on, 47–48

    business class lounges, 47

    Frequent Female Air Travellers study (Air Canada), 49–50, 51, 52

    non-gender intelligent communication skills, 50–51

    seats, design of, 24

    women and business class travel market, 49–50

Airport Architects Canada, 95

Alan Davis Salon, 105

Alberta Women's Enterprise Initiative Association, 211

AQUEOUS Advisory Group Inc., 90

Arthur Andersen, 176

Assembly Committee on Consumer Protection (U.S.), 101

auto industry
  airbag design, 25–26
  car dealers, and gender-based
    pricing, 102–103
  car finance products, 108–110
  distance to pedals, 24
  Ford Windstar, 99–100
  Saturn, 33–34
  Toyota Canada, 129–131
  women's customer satisfaction
    levels, 77–78
auto repairs, and gender-based
    pricing, 103
Automobile Protection Agency, 25
Automobile Protection Association
    (APA), 103

B

baby food market, 159
Barletta, Martha, 58, 172–173
Barnes, Jim, 67, 144–145, 202
Barron, Jennifer, 129, 131
Bermingham, Jen, 82, 85, 87
Bernier, Claude, 41–42
Betty Crocker, 18
Bigsby, Elisabetta, 214
biology, and gender identification, 62
Biondi, Matt, 72
Bird, Chloe, 157
BMO Financial Group, 34, 37–39
body language, 124–126
The Body Shop, 177, 178–181, 191
The Body Shop Canada, 178–181
Bonnick, Jackie, 44
brand equity, 28–29
breast cancer screening, 196
Brown, Michele, 166

Brown, Sheila, 169–171
Browns Shoes, 18
Bugelli, Ernie, 34

C

calculated risk takers *vs.* unwilling
    risk takers, 79
Calvin Klein, 18
Canadian Association of Women
    Executives and Entrepreneurs,
    212–213
Canadian Automotive Association,
    15, 114
Canadian Youth Business Foundation,
    210–211
Cardinal, Nancy, 43, 44
Carlson Wagonlit, 75
Catalyst, 57
Cato Institute, 104
Center for Women's Business
    Research, 15
Charlebois, Luc, 72, 190
"chat rooms," 137–138
Chatelaine, 65, 142, 163
Chilton, David, 93, 95, 173–174
chocolate, 97–99
Clairol Herbal Essence Shampoo,
    190–191
Clark, Donna, 163–164
"Closing the Gap Study," 57
Coffey, Charlie, 118, 210, 215
Cohen, Shaughnessy, 102
Colman, Carol, 91–92
communication
    body language, 124–126
    different rituals for different
      cultures, 123–131

face-to-face sales experience,
improvement of, 119–123

face-to-face sales experience, gender
differences in, 115–116

gender intelligent, 50–51

informal "focus groups," 137–138

information channels, 132–140

keynote networking event, 133–136

online, 140–147

sales force, 113–119

seminars, 132–138

through a gender lens, 115–119

communication styles and rituals

adoption of different styles when
warranted, 127–128

body language, 124–126

vs. character trait, 123–124

devil's advocate, 126–127

different rituals for different
cultures, 123–131

direct eye contact, 125–126

direct style, 127–128

gender differences, understanding,
115–119

miscues, 125–126

negotiation and, 128–131

nodding as listening cue, 124–125

shared rituals, need for, 127

Comper, Tony, 37–39

Conference Board of Canada, 57

consumer discrimination, 5

consumer influence of women, 3, 4

convenience, 159–160

conversational rituals, 123

Coombs, Ann, 202–203

Coombs Consulting Ltd., 202

Cooper, Heather, 44

corporate Canada

gender awareness training, and
women, 113

sales forces, 114

corporate responsibility. *See* corporate
soul

corporate soul

advertising, 190–202

authenticity, 187, 204–206

The Body Shop, 177, 178–181

and brand differentiation among
women, 175

chequebook variety, 187–190

gender intelligence and, 52–53

grassroots sponsorship, 190

impact of, 186–187

inclusive nature of, 200–202

on Internet, 142–143

at keynote events, 133

matching inside with outside,
202–204

Mountain Equipment Co-op, 181,
215–223

Mr Muffler, 189–190

Nike, 177, 178, 181–186

RBC Royal Bank, 213–214

sports sponsorships, 188–189

women's key consumer
standards, 205

Zig, 192–200

cosmetics industry, 64–65

Crazy Plates Meal Plates, 93–94

Crazy Plates (Podleski and Podleski),
93

customer relations, 67

D

Das, Mallika, 63, 66, 68
Davis, Alan, 105
DeHavilland, 24
Deloitte and Touche, 15, 158
Despatie, Clara, 189
DesRosiers, Dennis, 77–78
direct eye contact, 125–126
disability insurance, 104
discriminatory pricing. *See* gender-based pricing
distance education, 170
Dodge La Femme, 27–28
Doherty, Brian, 104
Duxbury, Linda, 57

E

eating disorders, 18
Eitel, Maria, 182
emotions, 66–67
    negative, 74, 123
Enron Corporation, 176
equality, flaws in interpretation of, 27
equity, 28
ethical investing, 164–165
Ethical Investor, 165
ethical product sourcing, 222
ethnographic research, 85
Ettleman, Laura, 95–96
Evian bottled water, 72
executional equity, 152

F

face-to-face sales process, 72
fashion industry
    plus-sized market segment, 69–70
    thinness and, 65

financial services
    advisor training, 116
    BMO Financial Group, 37–39
    communications styles and, 123–124
    correspondence, address of, 13
    credit scoring model, 211
    Ford Credit Canada, 108–110
    gender-based risk behaviour, 79–80, 81–82
    product development, 24–25
    RBC Investments, 80–82
    RBC Royal Bank, 117–119, 209–215
    sales forces in, 116–119
Finesse shampoo, 86–87
Fiorino, Nella, 44
Fisher, Helen, 155, 163
focus groups
    informal, 137–138
    women-only, 13
Food and Consumer Product Manufacturers of Canada, 159
Foot, David, 109
Ford Canada, 83, 203
Ford Credit Canada, 108–110
Ford Motor Company, 18, 73, 78, 99–100
Ford Windstar, 99–100
Frank, Elizabeth, 97–98
Franssen, Margot, 178, 179, 181, 187
Frazee, Roland, 209
Freeman, Aaron, 101
Frensel, Barbara, 7
Fruit of the Loom, 194–195

G

Gaunt, Bobbie, 7, 83, 203–204
Gee, Larry, 43
gender anxiety, 58
gender awareness training, 113,
117–119
gender-based consumer behaviour hit
list, 67–73
gender-based marketing, and sex-
based roles, 63
gender-based pricing
alterations, 102
auto repairs, 103
car dealers and, 102–103
and civil rights, 105
deodorant, 103
dry cleaning, 102
hair salons, 101–102
and the law, 105
legitimate price differences, 104
prevalence of, 101
pricing factors, 104
ridiculous excuses for, 103
sampling of, 101–103
gender bias
in market research, 76
in sales experience, 118
unconscious nature of, 119
gender differences
affiliation-oriented *vs.* achievement-
oriented, 115
in consumers, 64–67
corporate angst about, 58–61
in depression, 157
in face-to-face sales experience,
115–116
and face-to-face sales process, 72

gender-based consumer behaviour
hit list, 67–73
vs. gender identity, 65–66
and generalizations, 61–62
ignoring, in product
development, 25
improved customer service
argument, 59
information processing, 67–71
intelligence about, 50
and market research, 75–78
metaphors, processing of, 71–72
in motivation, 72–73
negative emotions, focus on, 74
in negotiation, 128–131
origins of, 62–63
pink collar argument, 59
and pricing, 100–105
and product development, 88–100
product perception, 82
technology, views and uses of, 141
wide continuum *vs.* cut-and-
dried, 5
women's key consumer standards,
106–108
in worldviews, 55–57
gender identity, 65–66
gender-inclusive language, 120, 121,
122–123
gender inequality
advertising's reinforcement
of, 22–23
equality, flaws in interpretation
of, 27
gender intelligence
acquisition of, 32–33
balance, 39–45

belief system of decision-maker, 79

benefits for a company, 30–31

brand equity and, 28–29

and company bottom line, 30

and corporate soul, 52–53

fundamentals of, 8–10, 46

green field approach, 33–34, 43

holistic nature of, 207–208

looking inward, 34–39

management support of, 30

and marginalization, 60

reasonable, inexpensive changes,
   45–46

separate *vs.* inclusive, 31–32

gender intelligent marketing

benefits of, 223–224

equity and, 28

face-to-face sales experience,
   improvement of, 119–123

market segmentation, more
   than, 29–30

by men, to women, 40

sales force, 113–114

women outside the organization
   and, 60

women's key consumer standards,
   106–108, 160

gender-role attitudes, 65–66

"gender tax." *See* gender-based
   pricing

Gender Tax Repeal Act (California),
   105

General Motors, 33–34

generalizations, 61–62, 151

Gillespie, Anne, 181, 219, 220, 222

Global Banking Alliance for Women,
   213

The Globe and Mail, 71, 213, 214

Good for Her, 138–140

Gordon, Debbie, 7, 22–23, 63, 84,
   151–152, 191-192, 196

"grandmother research," 84

Granet Publishing Inc., 93

grassroots sponsorship, 190

Green, Robyn, 168–169

Grocery Gateway, 144, 160–163, 173

grocery industry, 158–159, 160–163

H

hair salons, and gender-based
   pricing, 101–102

Hannon, Evelyn, 145–147

Harris, Graeme, 80–81, 82

Harrod, Brian, 7, 19–20

health

   and double duty, 157–158

   multidimensional marketing
     and, 165–167

heart disease, 157–158

Holiday Inn, 75–76

home equality, 27, 155

home improvement industry, 41–43

Hooters restaurants, 23

hospitality industry, 26, 75–76

household cleaning products,
   159–160

household labour, 156, 157

I

improved customer service argument,
   59

independent market research
   professionals, 83

industry satisfaction ratings, 15–17

informal "focus groups," 137–138

information channels

   gender intelligent, 132–140

informal "focus groups," 137–138

keynote networking event, 133–136

"lunch and learns," 136–137

online, 140–147

regular, intimate seminars, 136

seminars, 132–138

information processing, 67–71

Institute of Communications and
    Advertising, 61

Internet

corporate responsibility, 142–143

Journeywoman, 145–147

negative trend effects, 143

online communication, 140–147

online relationships, 144–147

privacy, 144

safety, 144

short transaction times, 143

website design, 141–144

young adult women, 140–141

Internet-based surveys, 85

Investor's Group, 152

invisibility in sales transactions, 14

Iny, George, 25, 103

*Is It Her Voice or Her Place that
    Makes a Difference?* (Kolb),
    128–129

J

Jaeger, Judy, 7

Jansen, Carlyle, 138–140, 147

Jantzi, Michael, 164–165

JD power, 129

Johnson, Lisa, 141, 145

Journeywoman, 145–147

Jubinville, Paula, 90

K

Kahlúa Black Russian, 18

Kaléidovision Inc., 60

Kazmer, Allan, 7, 19–20, 160, 200,
    201–202

Kellogg's, 21

Kellogg's Special K, 194

Kerton, Robert, 104

keynote networking event, 133–136

Khalilieh, Rifka, 178, 179–180

Kilbourne, Jean, 21

Klein, Naomi, 181

Kolb, Deborah, 128–129

Koven, Mary, 7, 13, 54, 191

L

Langevin, Daniel, 69, 70

LCBO. *See* Liquor Control Board of
    Ontario (LCBO)

Lean Cuisine, 166

Learned, Andrea, 83–84, 140–141,
    143, 145

Lee, Linda, 73, 78, 99, 100

Lester B. Pearson International
    Airport, 95–96

Lightstone, Ian, 7, 76, 78–79, 85

Liquor Control Board of Ontario
    (LCBO), 35, 43–45

listening cues, 124–125

listening events, 84

The Living Workplace (Coombs), 202

Lockie, Anne, 81–82, 212

Looneyspoons (Podleski and
    Podleski), 92–95

"lunch and learns," 136–137

Lynn, Elspeth, 7, 193, 196, 197,
    198, 200

M

MacDonald, Noni, 24
Magnotta, Rossana, 35–37
Magnotta Wineries, 34, 35–37
Major, Pierre, 188
Malandruccolo, Daniel, 189
Mara, Ed, 187
Maritz annual new car buyer
    survey, 131
Maritz: Thompson Lightstone, 76
market research
    control, transfer of, 84–85
    creative ways to listen, 83–84
    and gender bias, 76
    gender differences and, 75–78
    gender intelligent, 82–87
    getting it right, 76–77
    independent professionals, 83
    information sources, 77
    Internet-based surveys, 85
    interpretation, 77, 78–82, 86–87
    perspective, 87
    problems with, 5–6
    qualitative research, 85
    quantitative research, 85
    right questions, 77–78
    surveys, responses to, 78
market segmentation, 29–30,
    149–150
Marketing Magazine, 197
"marketing to women"
    female detractors of, 59–60
    genesis of term "women's market,"
    61–62
    men and, 112
Marra, Ed, 167
Martin, Anne, 121
Masters, Roger, 73

Maynard, Rona, 65
Maytag, 100
McAuley, Andy, 193, 198
McCoomb, Lloyd, 95
McCrea, Marilyn, 7
McDowall, Duncan, 209
McKee, Charles, 53
McLeod, Bruce, 163
McSweeney, Sean, 217, 219
media literacy, importance of, 22
Mediacs, 22, 151
MediaWatch, 18–19
men, and marketing to women, 112
men's customer service issues, 13
metaphors, processing of, 71–72
Metropolitan Drycleaners
    Association, 102
Meyers-Levy, Joan, 66–67, 67,
    68–69, 72
Michael Jantzi Research Associates
    Inc., 164–165
military metaphors, 123
Milot, Alain, 157–158
minorities, portrayal of, 21
Money Magazine, 116
Montgomery, Wendy, 196
Morissette, Sylvain, 41, 42–43
mothers, 167–169, 191
motivation, gender differences in,
    72–73
Mount Saint Vincent University,
    169–171
Mountain Equipment Co-op, 31, 181,
    208, 215–223
Movies 4 Mommies, 168–169
Mozas, John, 161
Mr Muffler, 72, 189–190

multidimensional living
 advertising, 158–163
 cultural differences, 152
 double duty, and health, 157–158
 and generalizations, 151
 Grocery Gateway, 160–163
 market segmentation and, 149–150
 marketing, 163–172
 principles of marketing, 153
 statistics, 155–156
 "Superwoman Syndrome,"
  156–157
 time, 154–157
 time shifting, 160
 understanding the complexity,
  51–52
 and unpaid labour force, 156
multidimensional marketing
 ethical investing, 164–165
 Lean Cuisine, 166
 mothers, role as, 167–169
 Mount Saint Vincent University,
  169–171
 Movies 4 Mommies, 168–169
 Nestlé, 165–167
 permutations, 164
 physical health, 165–167
 Real Assets Investment
  Management Inc., 165
 referrals, 172–173
 rewards of, 172–174
 women's key consumer standards,
  171–172

N

Nakatani, Yoshio, 129–130
negotiation, gender differences in,
 128–131

Nestlé, 31, 97–99, 165–167
Nestlé Canada, 167, 187
NetSmart Research, 141
Nielsen NetRatings, 141
Nike, 177, 178, 181–186, 191
Nike Canada, 181–182, 186
Nissan Canada, 200
Nixon, Gordon, 208, 210, 214–215
No Logo (Klein), 180
Noble, Michelle, 185
Nurse, Anne, 59

O

Olfert, Kevin, 129, 131
online communication. See Internet
online relationships, 144–147
Ontario Medical Association,
 127–128

P

Pedersen, Cynthia Ross, 141,
 142–143, 145
pink collar argument, 59
plus-sized women, 69–70
Podleski, Greta, 92–95
Podleski, Janet, 92–95
pricing. See gender-based pricing
Procter & Gamble, 31
product development
 examples of gender intelligence in,
  89–90
 financial services, 24–25
 and gender differences, 25, 88–100
 making things different, 99–100
 male-designated products,
  repackaging of, 27–28
 sources for ideas, 88–89
 starting from scratch, 90–96

thinking, shifts in, 97–99
trends in, 89–90
wide product view, 97
and women, 23–26
product perception, 82

Q

Quick to the Frontier: Canada's Royal Bank (McDowall), 209

R

RBC Investments, 80–82
RBC Royal Bank, 114, 117–119, 147, 208, 209–215
"Reaching Canada's 80% Minority," 3
ReachWomen, 83–84, 140–141, 142
Real Assets Investment Management Inc., 165
referrals, 91, 139–140, 172–173
regional differences, 152
Regulation magazine, 104
Rennie, Jim, 185–186
Retail Council of Canada, 45
Rethink, 20, 198
Reuber, Becky, 79
Rideout, Ted, 98
risk behaviour, 79–80, 81–82
Robinson, Laura, 188–189
Robinson, Peter, 208, 216–217, 220–221, 223
Roddick, Anita, 180
RONA, 15, 41–43
Ryerson University, 142, 144

S

Sabia, Laura, 209
safety, 73, 144
sales experience

face-to-face sales experience, improvement of, 119–123
gender bias, 118
inclusive language, 120, 121, 122–123
women consumers, and bad sales experiences, 59
sales force. *See* sales experience
Salon Selectives, 191
Saturn, 33–34, 144
Sauvageau, Danièle, 188, 189
Save-On-Foods, 198
Schleese Saddlery, 97
Scotiabank, 200–201
Secrets of Customer Relationship Management (Barnes), 67, 144, 202
segmentation. *See* market segmentation
selectivity hypothesis, 67
Sellery, Al, 144, 160
seminars
informal "focus groups," 137–138
keynote networking event, 133–136
"lunch and learns," 136–137
regular, intimate seminars, 136
relevance of content, 132–133
women's preferred form of marketing, 132
Shirmax Ltee, 69–70
shop-along grocery research, 85
Shoppers Cosmetics, 64–65
Sinuita, Peter, 108
Skidmore, Owings & Merrill, 95
small businesses. *See* women entrepreneurs
Smoothwater Outfitters & Ecolodge, 91–92

social conditioning, 64

socialization, and gender identification, 63

sports metaphors, 123

sports sponsorships, 188–189

Staples, Chris, 20–21, 86, 198–199

Statistics Canada, 108–109, 156, 204

Status of Women Council, 209

Strategic Navigator, 82

Strategy, 197

Stratton, Patrick, 181, 219–220

"Superwoman Syndrome," 156–157

surveys, responses to, 78

Sutherland, Anne, 118, 210

Swiss Federal Institute of Technology, 79

Sydor, Alison, 185

T

Talking from 9 to 5 (Tannen), 123

Tannen, Deborah, 123

Tao, Lorraine, 7, 193, 196, 197, 198, 200

technology, views of, 141

Television Bureau of Canada, 17

thinness, 21, 65

The Thomas Yaccato Group, 3, 4, 6, 24, 101, 119

Thompson Lightstone & Company, 3, 4, 7

Tim Hortons, 99

time, 154–157, 160

Tingley, Quig, 178

Todd, Linda, 7

Torlee, Liz, 7, 60–61, 74, 151, 164, 191–192

Toyota Canada, 129–131

trend effects, 74, 143

TrendSight Group, 58

Turpin, Lou, 96

U

Uniquely Canada Creative Arts Show, 213

unisex concept, 27, 28

United Church of Canada, 121

United Nations Human Development Report, 156

unpaid labour force, 156

U.S. Office of Human Rights, 102

V

Vaseline Intensive Care, 195–196

Vendramin, Benjamin, 7, 64–65, 191, 200

Vichy, 18

voice-overs, 200

Volvo, 23–24

W

W Network (WTN), 196–200

Wall Street Journal, 104

Wang, Penelope, 80

Watier, Lise, 152

Web Goddess, 141

website design, 141–144

Wedding Bells magazine, 212

White, Rick, 200–201

wine industry, 35–37, 87

women consumers

bad sales experiences, 59

cultural differences, 152

customer service issues, and gender, 13

industry satisfaction ratings, 15–17

mothers, role as, 167–169

negative experiences, effect of, 74
statistics, 111–112
value-based buying decisions, 175
women's key consumer standards.
    See women's key consumer
    standards
women entrepreneurs
    being taken seriously, 124
    government-sponsored maternity
        benefits, denial of, 25
    small businesses, 12
women's key consumer standards
    corporate soul, 205
    gender differences, 106–108
    gender intelligent marketing,
        106–108, 160
    multidimensional marketing,
        171–172

"women's market," as term, 61–62
women's market revolution, 12
Wood, Betty, 210, 213
Working Women Magazine, 80
workplace equality, 27
workplace equity, 29
WorldCom, 176

Y

YM, 65
young adult women, 140–141

Z

Zaget, 15
Zeedick, Pat, 181–182, 183, 186, 187
Zig, 192–200